Jerry Moffatt
Revelati

Jerry Moffatt began climbing while at s̶ ̶ ̶ ̶ ̶ ̶ ̶ ̶ ̶ ̶ ̶ ̶.
During the 1980s he was widely regarded as ᴛʜᴇ best climber in the world,
making groundbreaking ascents in the UK, Europe, the USA and Japan.
He continued to dominate the sport throughout the 1990s before
retiring from professional climbing in 2002. There are few climbers who
can be acknowledged as the best of their generation,
Jerry Moffatt is one of them.

Niall Grimes has contributed articles to a variety of climbing
magazines such as Climb, Climber, High and Summit (UK),
Climbing and Rock & Ice (US), Klettern (Germany) and
The Mountain Log in his native Ireland. Niall is also the guidebook
co-ordinator for the British Mountaineering Council and was responsible
for the Burbage, Millstone and Beyond guidebook, winner of the
Mountain Exposition Award at the *Banff Mountain Book Festival* in 2006.

GRAND PRIZE WINNER –
BANFF MOUNTAIN BOOK FESTIVAL 2009
FINALIST – BOARDMAN TASKER PRIZE 2009

"In terms of pace there's no stopping.
I don't read a lot, but with this book I could barely put it down."
Steve McClure, Climb Magazine

"Revelations beautifully captures the awe-inspiring exploits of
one of the world's greatest ever climbers."
Climb Magazine

"If you are off on holiday and you pack only one book to read –
make it this one. It is a revelation."
UKClimbing.com

"Revelations is a superb book about a superb climber.
Honest, witty and pithy, it explains to us mere mortals exactly what it
takes to be the best climber in the world."
planetFear.com

Jerry Moffatt
Revelations

with Niall Grimes

Vertebrate Publishing, Sheffield
www.v-publishing.co.uk

VERTEBRATE PUBLISHING
Crescent House, 228 Psalter Lane, Sheffield, S11 8UT
www.v-publishing.co.uk

First published in 2009 by Vertebrate Publishing,
an imprint of Vertebrate Graphics Ltd.
Paperback edition first published 2010. Reprinted 2012.

This book is a work of non-fiction based on the life, experiences and
recollections of Jerry Moffatt. In some limited cases the names of people,
places, dates and sequences or the detail of events have been changed solely
to protect the privacy of others. The authors have stated to the publishers
that, except in such minor respects not affecting the substantial accuracy
of the work, the contents of the book are true.

A CIP catalogue record for this book is available from the British Library.

ISBN: 978-1-906148-19-5   ISBN: 978-1-906148-40-9 (ebook)

Every effort has been made to obtain the necessary permissions with
reference to copyright material, both illustrative and quoted. We apologise
for any omissions in this respect and will be pleased to make the appropriate
acknowledgements in any future edition.

Designed and typeset in Adobe Caslon by Vertebrate Graphics Ltd, Sheffield.
www.v-graphics.co.uk

Printed in China by XY Digital.

*For Toby, Wolfgang, Andrew, Noddy
and my other friends whose lives have been
tragically taken away far too soon.*

Contents

Illustrations

Glossary illustrations by Simon Norris, Vertebrate Graphics

Alone

It's the summer of 1983. I'm twenty years old, standing alone by the side of the road. The sun is blazing over the beautiful mountains of Snowdonia in North Wales. The Llanberis Pass snakes down from the slopes of Snowdon itself, flanked on both sides by some of the greatest and most historic cliffs in the country: Dinas Mot, Carreg Wastad, Clogwyn y Grochan, Cyrn Las and above me, the greatest of them all. A towering pyramid of stone dominates the skyline a quarter of a mile up the steep rocky hillside – Dinas Cromlech. Two huge black walls, almost a hundred and fifty feet high, dominate the centre of the crag, forming an open book. This is where the best climbers of the last hundred years have added the greatest climbs.

I look up. It's midweek and the crag is practically deserted. I see only two climbers just starting up a long, easy route on the more broken rock on the left-hand side. I pick up my rucksack, heavy with ropes, climbing hardware, rock boots, chalk bag and harness, and begin the hot slog up to the cliff above.

I know what's coming, but I'm keeping it a secret from myself.

I promised myself I wouldn't do this again. I had decided to take a step back for a bit. Only yesterday I'd fought my way up one of the most famous unclimbed sheets of rock in the country, Master's Wall on Clogwyn Du'r Arddu. I came so close to death that I told myself I wasn't going to do anything dangerous again for a long time. And today, that's why I need to pretend. I just want to lead a few routes, I tell myself. I'll get up there and find someone hanging around who doesn't have a partner and who fancies a climb. We'll team up and climb together for the day, taking turns to lead and second the climbs. It'll be a nice day out.

Almost believing this, I soon arrive hot and sweaty at the base of the corner. It's deserted. Of course it is, but I'm here now and I'm ready. Standing in the centre of the great black corner I look at the familiar climbs that I have worked my way through so far in my climbing life. These climbs, with their increasing difficulty, are markers I've passed while growing stronger and more experienced. I see the line of Cemetery Gates, Joe Brown and Don Whillans' exposed E1 crack climb up the very edge of the right-hand wall. I put on my worn rock shoes and chalk bag, leaving all the heavy ropes and hardware behind and, dressed only in a pair of shorts, climb the long, vertical pitch. It takes less than five minutes. It feels incredible to be climbing in total solitude with such a vast feeling of space and the freedom of having only the climbing to think about. Any thoughts of danger or safety are left a long way below. Near the top I hang out from the rock on two good holds, look down at the space beneath my feet, then to the road a long way beyond and let myself take it all in. What a place to be.

At the top of the crag, I down-climb Ivy Sepulchre. Three years ago, this had been my first ever HVS lead and as I solo down through the crux, memories of my struggle that day flood into my mind. Soon I arrive again at the base of the big corner. On the wall opposite Cemetery Gates, a thin crack climb splits the otherwise featureless face. This is Left Wall. Graded E2, I had led it two years before, fighting metal wedges into the thin cracks, clipping in ropes to catch me in the event of a fall. Today, with only fingertips inside the crack and the ends of my toes smearing on the rock, I cruise to the top with ease. I run down again and on the way, look up to see the other two climbers still about their business on their V Diff. I imagine they are enjoying themselves in the sunshine. On the ground again, I solo Cenotaph Corner, one of Brown's greatest routes, blasting straight up the central corner. I have never done it before and its relatively low grade hides the fact it is a desperate solo. At a hundred feet I have to fight with slippery crux moves, palming my weight against the greasy walls, without any real holds to hang on to. Momentum carries me through.

I am on fire. I am having one of those unforgettable days when everything comes together: the place, the situation, the weather, the climbs, my fitness, my desire and my state of mind. Without a rope or protection to save me if I make a single error, one miscalculation means death. But nothing I do, no matter how hard, feels like a battle today. It feels like destiny.

Memory Lane, the left edge of the left wall, goes by in a blur. Foil, to its left, is harder and steeper than the other climbs. I did it a couple of years before, when it was a good breakthrough into a new grade, my first E3. It has desperate climbing, strenuous and pumpy, but it follows the safety of a good crack that swallows protection. Today, without the protection, it is just as strenuous. At the top of the crack section, a hundred feet above the rocky ground, I reach the crux. It involves a long powerful move off a flake of rock to a good hold high above. I grab the flake, but it is loose. It rattles in my hand. The rock is steep and I must trust all my weight on this one hold to gain the height I need. The force I'm using must surely snap the hold off. I know what will happen if it does.

I can't reverse the moves I have made to get here. I am fully committed. I feel lactic acid pumping through my forearms, the first sign of tiring muscles. I need to do something. I decide to try to knock the loose hold off, and if I can't, then I'll assume it's solid enough. I bang it with the fist of my right hand several times. The smacking makes it budge a little further, but still it doesn't come free. There are no other options. I switch into survival mode, calm and detached. Holding the flake, I run my feet up the steep wall, getting my body as high as possible. I suck in a lungful of air and crank all my weight onto the loose flake. It stays put and I grab the good holds above. Relief and joy fill me as I race up easy climbing to the top of the cliff.

At the top of the crag I decide I've had enough, but once again I find myself in the corner. The hardest route here is Ron Fawcett's recent climb, Lord of the Flies. I led it last year, but it is too close to my physical limit to climb without the assurance of a rope and protection. To its right is Right Wall, Pete Livesey's all-time classic E5, the hardest route in the country in 1974.

Right Wall is steep, with long, hard sections on very small holds. I climb past these sections without the slightest doubt. High on the wall I reach for a very small, brittle-looking flake of rock, like an ice-cream wafer stuck onto the rock. Perhaps after my experience on Foil, I think it moves as I pull on it. Should I trust my weight to this tiny flake? Did it really move? I decide it hasn't. I curl the fingertips of both hands onto this tiny brittle blade of rock, all my weight hanging on it, a hundred and twenty feet up, all alone in the middle of the week on a mountain in Wales.

Then, a feeling comes over me, a feeling of the most incredible euphoria. Nothing else in the world matters except where I am and what I'm doing at that instant. I feel totally in control, happy and fully relaxed. Everything is perfect. Of course the rock will hold, because this really is my destiny. I shall never forget that moment. I confidently pull through on the wafer, get to better, more solid holds above and cruise to the top of the crag. Even though I am only twenty years old, I know this is one of my special days.

Twenty-five years later I can still remember every detail, every feeling I experienced. It seemed like I was on a path. My early childhood was great. I grew up in the country and was very close to my parents and two brothers.

At school, I may have struggled academically, but I enjoyed sport and did well at that. I lived a perfectly normal life. Then, aged fifteen, someone took me rock climbing and nothing was ever the same again.

ONE

First Steps

Miss Pyper had sent me out of class. I had been naughty again and told to stand in the corridor. The sun was slanting through the windows, and I remember there was a wooden chest where we put all the toys we brought to school. From inside the class I heard the other children reciting something. I wanted to be in there too, reciting what they were, but I knew I wouldn't understand it. I rarely did. I looked down at the parquet floor, with its criss-cross wooden tiles, and began to tiptoe up and down the corridor, looking down at my feet at right-angles to each other, trying to avoid standing on the lines between the tiles.

'I wish she wouldn't send me out,' I thought. 'I wish I wasn't naughty. I wish I understood.' But I just didn't.

I grew up just outside the city of Leicester, in a little village called Bushby. It was out in the countryside and we lived in a big converted farmhouse, mum, dad, Simon my elder brother, Toby, my younger brother, and me. Farmland, woods and streams surrounded the village and I loved wandering through it. I went to Duncairn Kindergarten from the age of four to the age of eight. Every Christmas, Easter and summer, the school sent a report to my parents on my progress. I still have these, and they make fascinating reading.

'He is still very much a baby in his approach. A live wire!' reported the first, from Christmas, 1967. Things never seemed to improve much beyond that.

'I still can't report much progress. We must hope that he will soon show some interest in "learning". He is always happy and smiling and is a great favourite with the other children.'

Sometimes there were signs of hope: 'It is at last possible to see progress although he finds it hard to retain what he is taught.'

But my restless energy often got in the way: 'A good term in many ways but his behaviour is often uncontrollable.'

At times my teacher seemed to despair of me: 'Jeremy is now *pathetically* anxious to succeed. His progress is still very uneven. He seems to remember for a time, then one finds that earlier work is forgotten.'

I was popular and I did well in games and art class. Best of all, I had a good time. But my reports showed a worrying lack of progress. Miss Pyper tried hard to get me to learn, but the school's final opinion of me in Easter 1971 didn't offer much hope:

'With all the efforts that have been made to help, it is disappointing that he has not achieved a higher standard. We wish him well and hope that a complete change will have the desired effect.'

After Duncairn I went to a prep school called Stoneygate. This was a traditional, all-boys school. Before I went, I remember my mum dressing me up. I had to wear a grey blazer and shorts, a white shirt and a red tie. I had a pair of black leather shoes, and I was told to rub them until they shone. I was dropped off outside the school and went into a large hall for assembly. The children sat very quietly in rows, and they all seemed very well behaved. I felt intimidated by these boys, especially the older ones, but there was one really exciting thing about this school. My big brother, Simon, was there. Simon is fifteen months older than me, and I really looked up to him. He was good at sports too, but was also really clever, just the way all children want to be.

I enjoyed my time at Stoneygate but it was more academic than my first school and, as I went through my first year, I struggled in all my subjects. I didn't seem to be doing well in any of them. I tried in class, and worked hard when I got home, but still never seemed to understand what the teachers were telling me. At the end of the first year we did exams. I came last in the class. The teachers called my parents in and it was decided that I would do the first year again to see if I could pick it up the second time around. After that year went by I repeated the exams. This time I was extremely relieved to come second to last. Someone had done worse than me. That was a great relief. During the summer that followed, I was at home one day, and heard my mum and dad talking. They called me down and told me that they had had a word with the school.

'The school thinks it would be better if you left,' my mum told me.

I was devastated. I didn't want to leave. That was mine and Simon's school. I wanted to stay there with him.

'We know it's not because you have been naughty, and your dad and I both know you have worked hard and done your best, but we think it would be best if you moved to the local school here.'

Stoneygate was a school for high-achievers, but I was falling so far short of the standard. There was no way I could have carried on. I was sent to the state school in the village, which was just a short walk from where I lived. The village school wasn't as academic and I moved up through the years with all the other boys until I was eleven years old. But I still wasn't doing well in class, constantly wondering what was wrong with me. How come all these other people were learning things and I wasn't? I can remember being in science class, with the teacher chattering away, and just wondering, 'What is this gobbledygook?' I didn't have any idea what he was talking about. I would sit at the back of class, and show off to girls and try to make them laugh.

In those years I failed repeatedly at exams and continually came last in class. I was desperate to do well, but was left with the feeling that there was something wrong with me. I wasn't very old, but I could still see my chances disappearing. I was aware of what it meant to have no exams, and I felt I was shut out of what everyone else had. Years later, when I became a climber, I would think that climbing was all I ever wanted to do. But then I think back to those times and I know that if I could have waved a wand and changed anything, I would have asked to be normal, to have the abilities and opportunities that everyone else had. I didn't want to be shut out of class.

To make up for this I threw myself into sport and games. In classes, it just didn't seem possible to do any better than I was doing. But on the pitch or on race tracks, if I pushed myself really hard, then I could do better. I remember thinking, okay, you people might be smarter than me, but you're not going to beat me in this race, or you're not going to catch me when I have the ball. And they wouldn't.

I was lucky to have very supportive parents. My father was a company secretary and my mother was a nurse, and later on did a lot of work for the terminally ill. They both had good careers, and both had a really top education. My father went to King's College Canterbury and my mother to Cheltenham Ladies' College. At the time these were two of the best schools in the country, so they both really valued education, and wanted me to do well academically too. My mum remembers thinking that I would be the bright child in the family, as I began to communicate and draw at a very early age, but through my years at Duncairn, and then at Stoneygate, their concerns about my progress grew and grew.

During my time at school my parents had tests done on me to find out why I wasn't learning. They knew I wasn't stupid. I was articulate and good with people, and they knew I was working, but still, by the age of eleven, I could only just about read, and my writing was very poor. Numbers were a complete mystery. Near the end of my time at the village school, an expert told my mum that I had dyslexia. This was only starting to be diagnosed in children at the time, and I think it was a relief to my parents finally to have some sort of explanation.

I always felt I had a big chink in my armour because of my poor academic performance. I had a sense there was something wrong with me, of not being normal. Inferior. The diagnosis didn't mean that much to me, and I was still left wondering about myself. Maybe I was simply thick. But I felt I just had a very bad memory for certain things. For academic things. If you asked me how many fingers fitted onto the crux hold of a route I did in 1979, I could tell you. If you wanted to know what size of nut goes into the crack at the top of Profit of Doom on Curbar Edge, I could tell you. I could still tell you every hand and foot movement of a hundred and fifty feet of overhanging limestone in the south of France from 1987. But things like that aren't how people judge intelligence.

Bruce Lee said that knowledge is the ability to remember things, which I think is true. My mum is very well read, and it seems like she has the ability to remember everything she reads. Some people go through school and they remember everything they are taught. They never have to revise and they sail through exams. These are the people who are seen as the smart people. But really, often they are just lucky enough to have a very good memory for what they are being taught. It doesn't necessarily mean they are smarter than people who don't – or can't – remember those things.

Once I was diagnosed with dyslexia, my parents looked into how they could help me. They heard about a school called Eddington, just outside Glastonbury in Somerset, a long way from our home. It was going to be a special school for dyslexics, the first one in the country. They applied for a place for me and I was accepted as the first pupil. That September my mum drove me the two hundred miles to Glastonbury. It was a boarding school, and as she dropped me off and said goodbye, she started to cry. She later told me that she cried all the way home.

But I loved it at Eddington. At the village school there were about thirty of us to a class. In this new school, we were about four or five to a class. We were taught maths and English in a very modern way, so we could finally understand it. It was taken very slowly, and no one ever got left behind. I spent two years there and it was great for my confidence. I loved boarding, and made friends with all the other boys. As it wasn't designed to produce great exam results, we were free to concentrate on sports. The headmaster had once played cricket for Somerset, so we played a lot of that. I did very well at cross-country racing but my main love was rugby. Between the sport, and gaining some confidence academically, Eddington was a very good experience.

After two years there I went to a boarding school in North Wales called St David's College. St David's had a special dyslexia department, and like

Eddington, offered lots of sport. Not many pupils achieved top grades in their exams, but they were getting a good education. I got into cross-country running and ended up doing a lot of it. I beat the school record, and won the county championships against all the other schools in the North Wales area. Although I was good at running, I didn't like it all that much, and once I had won the county championships, I was made to train and run every weekend, which soon became a drag.

I enjoyed rugby much more. I played scrum-half, and quickly got onto the first team, the youngest player ever to do so, at fifteen. The school had a rugby cup for the player who did best overall in each year, and I won that. I loved playing matches and spent lots of weekends playing against various teams from the area. However, one Saturday, we were playing against another local school from Llandudno, John Bright's. I played a really good game, made lots of good plays and tried really hard. Yet we still lost. The other team hadn't played all that well, but the rest of my team had played terribly. It had been an important match and I was bitterly disappointed. I felt a real sense of disappointment with the other players. Despite having done my best, I had been let down. What was the point, I thought. Why play in a team when you don't have any control over whether you win or lose? That one game really disillusioned me with team sports, and I started looking towards more individual activities. Luckily for me, something else had recently come along.

My best friend at St David's was Andrew Henry. The school had a climbing club, and he had been going out to do this a few times.

'Rock climbing's brilliant,' he told me. 'You should do it.'

I told him no, that I didn't much fancy the idea of hill walking, and anyway, I was so busy doing other sports that I didn't have the time. Andrew and some other friends kept going, and would talk about it a lot. It seemed to get them really excited, and when they came back from climbing days, they were buzzing about it for hours. I slowly started fancying a go, but by this stage, Andrew and the others had been doing it for months. I didn't want to go out with them and find that they had become really good and I couldn't do it, so I always turned down their offers to take me out. One Saturday there was to be another climbing trip. It so happened that Andrew and the others couldn't go. This was my chance. I asked the climbing master, Mr Levers, if I could come along, and he said yes.

We met on the Saturday morning, and he loaded the school minibus with coiled ropes, loads of little metal things, red webbing harnesses, yellow helmets and big boots. I climbed in. We were going to a cliff called Craig-y-Forwyn, he told me. After a twenty-minute drive we arrived at a car park. I put on one of the huge pairs of heavy leather boots, was given a harness and rope to carry, and walked up through the trees after Mr Levers. I don't know what I thought rock climbing was. I think I imagined something like a steep hill walk, where you pull on some bits of rock to help you along from time to time. But we turned a corner, and there in front of me was an enormous vertical sheet of white rock. It must have been a hundred feet tall, and looked completely blank and featureless.

'You don't mean we're going to climb up that?'

I couldn't believe it.

'Yes,' he told me. 'Now come over here, I'm going to show you how all this stuff works.'

He was laying the various bits from his rucksack onto the grass beneath the cliff.

'Now, first of all, I'm going to lead a climb. This means I attach the rope to my harness and climb up with it below me. I will put protection into the cracks and clip the rope into the protection using karabiners.'

He held up one of the D-shaped metal rings that had a sprung gate on one side, and let it flick shut a few times. A karabiner. Then he held up a bunch of loops of rope with little square or hexagonal-shaped blobs of metal on the end of them.

'And this is my protection. These are nuts. They are called nuts because years ago Joe Brown and Don Whillans used to use engineering nuts with bits of rope tied through them for protection. Nowadays you can buy them specially made. You slot them into cracks and they are bomb-proof. These bigger ones here are called hexes.'

He held up some bigger versions, great lumps of metal the size of a tea mug. I was looking and listening, but I don't really think I was taking it all in.

'I insert one of these into the rock and clip the karabiner into the end of it then clip my rope into the karabiner. The rope runs freely through these. They are called "running belays". Runners. Got all that?'

What was he saying?

'Good. So I'm going to lead off, and you belay me. This means you pay out the rope just as I need it. If I fall off, it's your job to hold the rope tight using a belay device. Then the protection will stop my fall. You are a belayer, you are standing on a belay, and it's your job to belay me. When I get to the top, I will set up another belay. Then you will second the pitch – we call the distance between two belays a pitch – and remove the runners that I put in. The rope will be at the top for you. We call that a top-rope. If you slip off, you won't fall any distance. Does all this make sense?'

I nodded.

'Right-oh.'

He climbed upwards following a groove crack thing for about sixty feet, and just as he disappeared out of sight, he leaned over and looked at me.

'Safe!' he called.

I looked at him.

'I'm safe. That means you can take me off belay and get ready to second me.'

I looked down at the rope going to my harness, the belay. Mr Levers had given me a metal plate about the size of a biscuit with slots for the rope – the belay device – which would be how I would control the running of the rope to him. The ropes ran through the slots and into a heavy karabiner clipped into my red nylon waist-belt. I had found earlier that it had interrupted the flow of the rope as he climbed upwards, so had disengaged it from the system to stop it confusing me. He looked to be off belay already. I walked towards the cliff face and Mr Levers took in the rope. The slack loops at my feet snaked upwards until it came tight onto my harness. He looked over again.

'Climb when ready,' he called to me.

I was wearing a massive pair of leather boots designed for walking through ice and snow. They weighed a ton and I couldn't feel anything through them. Our school had a policy that wearing these monsters would give you good footwork in the end, so I bashed my way up the climb on top-rope.

It was a cold December day and as the blood began to pump into my cold hands, my fingers began to throb. Climbing is very painful, I thought. I had never heard of hot-aches before. We did a couple more climbs, and these hurt too. On the way home in the school minibus, I asked Mr Levers how he thought I had done.

'You did great,' he told me.

'Really? Were those hard climbs we did, sir?'

'Well,' he said. 'The first climb you did was one of the easiest. That was a Very Difficult, or V Diff. The next one was a bit harder, Severe. And we finished on a Hard Severe.'

'Is that good?'

'Yeah. That's okay.'

'What's after that?'

'Then you have Very Severe, or VS, then Hard VS. Then you're into the Extremes, E1, E2. Desperate stuff. Absolutely desperate.'

'Have you done extreme, sir?'

'No, I haven't. I've done HVS.'

'And what about Andrew and the others?'

'They have done VS.'

VS? I had done Hard Severe, and Very Severe was the next one up. And this was my first time. On the drive home I felt really happy that the others were only one better than me, and that they had been doing it for months now. I might do rock climbing again.

Over the next few months I started going out more often with Andrew and the others. We all really enjoyed it, although we didn't go every weekend. Some Saturdays we would just hang around Llandudno and go to the amusement arcades. We were keen though. We used to look at the magazines and read about great climbers, about Joe Brown, Don Whillans, Ron Fawcett and Pete Livesey and about what people were doing in America. We talked about it a lot, and used the words we read: 'That was epic!' 'What a run-out!' 'Those moves were heinous.'

Over a few months of climbing, as winter turned into spring, and the painful cold gave way to more enjoyable warmth, I became much keener. I couldn't wait for our weekend visits to Forwyn. At school, we found that a previous climbing instructor had climbed a lot on the walls of the school for training. One long vertical wall had little slots between the bricks where you could get your fingers in, and go across, or climb up to the top. We started climbing there too, and gave these 'routes' names and grades. The Dinner Table, HVS. Break Time, Hard Severe. Henry's Horror, Severe. We would visit these walls almost daily, and this satisfied our need to climb when we couldn't get to Forwyn.

At the crag we always seconded or top-roped routes. Some of the boys led sometimes, climbing up first and placing protection, but that risked long falls onto the rope, and sometimes the ground. I couldn't see the point of that. Sometimes we would see climbers climb solo, with no ropes at all, where a fall would mean certain death, and that seemed crazy to me. Slowly, people in the climbing club started saying that you'd only really done a route when you'd led it, and that leading was such a buzz. Hearing this, I wanted to lead. One day at a little crag near Betws-y-Coed, the climbing master said we could lead something. I wanted to lead a Severe, but was only allowed to lead a V Diff. It felt too easy but it was still exciting, and at least I'd done my first lead.

At Forwyn there's a big steep VS crack called The Flue, with a reputation for being tough for the grade. If you led The Flue, you really had climbed Very Severe, and that was a big deal. Not many people did Very Severe. One day, after I had been seconding VS and HVS climbs for a few weeks, and had led some HSs, I asked Mr Levers if I could try The Flue. He said yes, and gave me some of the protection I would need. Nervously I got ready and set off. I forced myself upwards and, at about thirty feet, unclipped a massive hex from my harness, the size of a cow bell. I threw it deep into the crack, clipped in the rope and pressed on. The route followed a steep, wide crack, and the rock all around it was polished. I shoved my hands and arms deep inside, twisting and writhing to make anything stick. Nothing felt positive and I became totally out of breath. I knew that I just had to keep moving up. I got high above the hex, but my arms felt too tired to stop and place any more protection. I fought on, almost falling off every move, and somehow clawed to the top. I hauled myself over onto the grassy summit, wheezing and dry-mouthed, but triumphant. I had done it. I had done The Flue. I was leading Very Severe. That was my first big lead, and I was addicted.

The next step was a trip to the mountains. Snowdonia, and the Llanberis Pass, were about an hour's drive from school, which made it a bit too far to drive to very often, but the day came when Mr Levers said we were going. We were so excited. Andrew and I spent the week looking at the guidebook. The Llanberis Pass was one of the most legendary climbing areas in the country. Joe Brown and Don Whillans had climbed there, doing some of their hardest routes on Dinas Cromlech. Modern climbers like Pete Livesey and Ron Fawcett had done the same.

We thought the weekend would never come, but eventually Saturday arrived. It was a beautiful, sunny day, and on the journey down the Llanberis Pass we craned our necks out the window recognising crags from the pictures we had seen in the magazines. We parked in a lay-by. I looked up, and high above us I saw the unmistakable crown of the Cromlech. It looked amazing, and I could see a few teams of climbers on it already. We had been given packed lunches of hard-boiled eggs, a pork pie, a bag of crisps, and as I sat beside the window eating this I picked out the routes from the guidebook. The Cromlech was a special place.

'Which route are we going to do, sir?' I asked.

'Oh, we're not going up there. It's too crowded, and crowds aren't good. We're going up there.'

He pointed at the other side of the valley. We all shuffled across the bus to look out the opposite window, and there, in the shadows, loomed a dark, sunless slab of brown rock, with grass growing all over its ledges. Dinas Mot. Our hearts sank.

Andrew and I checked the guidebook again and found a route called Lorraine. It was four pitches long, meaning we would need to stop and belay after each of four rope lengths because the route was so long. We finished our lunches and headed into the shadows. As we got closer the crag seemed to rise up in steepness and become bigger and longer. From the car park it had looked like an easy-angled slab. Now, standing underneath, it looked like a real mountain. The rock seemed much less featured, and it looked very steep. We felt such a sense of uncertainty about it all. Could we do this? My mouth felt dry.

Andrew was still climbing better than me at this point, so I would lead the first pitch, which was Hard Severe, and he would lead the next three, which were harder. Even though I had led The Flue, I knew I wasn't ready to lead three pitches of VS. The route followed a layback flake, and we struggled and shuffled our big mountain boots higher and higher, pitch after pitch. This climb was to be one of the most memorable I ever did. There we were, aged sixteen, all alone on this huge sheet of rock in the mountains. It was incredible. As far as we were concerned we were on the hardest route in the world. When we arrived at the easier ground at the end of the fourth pitch, we felt like heroes. We had done it, and we could hardly believe it.

After that I was on a high for days. It was the first time since I began climbing that I had felt like this, where days later I could still feel myself buzzing with excitement. Thirty years later I can still recall the thrill I felt after my day on Lorraine in the Llanberis pass with Andrew Henry on a sunny Saturday in May 1979. It was the first of many such days, and that feeling is the reason I devoted most of my life to climbing.

The climbing club was at Forwyn one day, top-roping some climbs, when one of the boys called from the ground.

'Someone is on MOJO!'

Mojo was one of the big routes at the crag. It was Extremely Severe, E1, and you hardly ever saw people on routes of that grade. We all went over for a look. Mojo climbs up a corner, before traversing out the underside of a huge, ten-foot roof of rock. It looked incredible. We ran around to watch, and there really was someone leading it. He was wearing just a pair of denim shorts and a headband. He had a small bag tied around his waist containing powdered gymnast's chalk, a new thing that some of the top British climbers had started picking up from American climbers. Magazines talked about its use being controversial. The climber was hanging from just one hand on the very lip of the roof and his ropes dangled free below him, blowing in the breeze. We couldn't take our eyes off him. We all said how amazing it looked, and how brilliant the climber must be. Mojo looked incredible.

I said to myself: 'I'm going to do Mojo.'

That was our last climbing day of that term. The following week I returned home to Leicester for the summer. It was a beautiful summer. I had always been into shooting and even wanted to become a gamekeeper when I grew up. In the summer months I went on lots of long walks with our dog, Penny, a beautiful Dalmatian, shooting pigeons or rabbits. I always ate them.

The other thing I did was nail four blocks of wood onto the outside wall of a building beside our house.

By that stage I was starting to become obsessed by climbing. As I couldn't face the thought of a summer without it, I would swing along these blocks, hanging on with my fingers, my Dunlop Green Flash tennis shoes smearing over the brickwork below. Years later I would do the exact same thing, only on ever smaller holds on ever steeper walls, in order to train my arms and fingers. It's called traversing, where you move from side to side rather than upwards. All climbers do it to train, but I wasn't training. This was climbing to me. I was really only doing it for its own sake, and loving every minute of it. I did this most days, sometimes using smaller exposed brick-edges instead of the bigger blocks. By the end of the summer I could go all the way across the wall on just the tiny brick-edges. When my mum could, I would get her to take me to an outcrop near our home called Beacon Hill, which had a few short climbs, or to Slawston Bridge, an abandoned railway bridge where I could do problems like those we did on the wall at school. That was a brilliant summer.

In the new autumn term we went for our first visit of the season to Forwyn. Right away I put a top-rope down Mojo. I tied on, and the climbing teacher belayed me. I shot up it with no trouble. Afterwards Mr Levers tied on, but fell once, and didn't do it. He was really impressed by this, and was really happy for me. He couldn't believe how much I had improved over the summer break. It had all been down to the traverses of the back wall in my garden. That was a great eye-opener.

I had talked about climbing to my parents all summer, and that Christmas was given a pair of EBs. We had started climbing in heavy mountaineering boots. Then I had moved on to wearing my Green Flash. EBs were specialised climbing boots. They had blue and white canvas uppers and a thick black rubber sole. This had no tread, as you climbed by smearing the rubber over a hold, or by digging the edges of the sole onto small holds. This was pretty much the only brand of specialist climbing shoes available. All climbers wore them. If you flicked through Mountain or Crags, the two climbing magazines at the time, all the stars wore EBs. They made my climbing much easier too.

I was at Craig-y-Forwyn with Andrew Henry one day, getting ready for a climb. Suddenly, one of the boys from the climbing club came running round the corner looking startled. He stopped by us, his mouth fell open, and he pointed the thumb of his right hand over his shoulder.

'It's Ron Fawcett!'

He said this in a loud whisper, his voice almost cracking with emotion.

'It's RON FAWCETT!'

My God! We all ran after the boy, and hid in a bush where we could watch. Ron Fawcett was the biggest legend in British climbing. He was in the magazines every month, and did all the hardest climbs. We looked on in amazement. He had a tall, lanky frame, a big bush of black hair and a moustache. He was on Great Wall. Great Wall was the big route on the crag, the hard classic. I tried to top-rope it every time I came here, but hadn't yet managed to do it clean with no falls. Ron was there with his beautiful girlfriend, Gill. He moved easily up a groove. From here the route traverses right to some tiny finger pockets and you must pull up on these with very little for your feet. It was a desperate move, the crux of the entire route.

I wondered if Ron would be able to do the move first time. He traversed easily, and got to the tiny pockets. At this point he took one hand off the rock, and dipped it into his chalk bag. Looking down at Gill, he said in his slow Yorkshire accent:

'Aye, Gill, what are we having for our dinner tonight, love?'

Oh my God, we all thought. He's up there doing the hardest route on the crag, and he's wondering what he's going to have for his tea. Incredible. We had to go back round the corner again to calm down. We talked about how big his arms were, and how strong he looked, and how big he was. I decided I was going to go and top-rope Great Wall. I gathered my stuff, and went round the corner to the route.

I had seen Ron Fawcett once before. I had been climbing on Dinas Cromlech the summer before. It was a big day for me, the day I led my first ever HVS, Ivy Sepulchre. On the same day, Ron Fawcett was there being filmed doing the first ascent of Lord of the Flies. This was one of the hardest routes in the country at the time, taking some hard and bold climbing up the right wall of Cenotaph Corner. Ron had reached the top of the climb, and was making his way down the descent path which skirted around the right side of the cliff. I had just fallen off the crux of Ivy Sepulchre, but before my weight came onto the rope, I had grabbed another hold and caught myself, and managed to battle through the crux to reach easy ground near the top. Just as I did, I looked around. About three hundred feet away, on the rocky hillside below, I saw Ron's distinctive figure. He used to wear bright green Adidas shorts and a vest to match. He stopped, and turned around and looked in my direction.

He looked at me. Ron Fawcett looked at *me*. He turned and walked on, and I floated to the top of the crag.

Back at Forwyn, Ron finished the route and abseiled back down to get his gear back out of the crag. He was sitting on the ground. I walked around the corner, stood in front of him, and said, 'Hi!' He said hello. I stood in front of him for a moment in silence. He looked at me. I stood there, and wondered if he would recognise me as the young gun blasting up the HVS on the Cromlech the year before. He didn't seem to.

'Ah, excuse me,' I said. 'Do you mind if I top-rope Great Wall now, because it's the hardest route on the crag, and I just might do it, and, if you mind then I won't, but I was just wondering, if it's okay. If I do?'

He looked bemused. He must have wondered why I was asking him. He shrugged his shoulders and said he didn't mind, so I set the rope up, and tried it, managing it without falls for the first time.

Ron left soon after, but meeting him blew our minds, and stayed with us long after. From that day on, any time we were traversing on the little wall at school, and we got to a hard bit, we would always stop, chalk up and ask:

'What are we having for our tea tonight?'

In the months to come I would still go out to Forwyn with the climbing club, and Andrew still came along most times. We even went on a climbing trip together to a crag called Millstone, in the Peak District, just outside Sheffield. We got a lift to his parents' home near Macclesfield, and from there we rode over on Andrew's motorbike, a little 50cc scrambler. We set our tent up at the crag, and did some climbing. On the second day I down-climbed an easy route, solo, in order to get back to the ground. I told Andrew to do it too. He hesitated half-way down, but I gave him some encouragement. He went a little further, slipped, fell to the ground and broke his ankle. That was typical of Andrew, on two counts. He was always very accident-prone, and you could always talk him into doing something. The latter quality was something I really liked about Andrew. In this respect, he reminded me of my younger brother, Toby. Not only that, but they both shared the same birthday, 29 October. Later in their lives, both would become keen on horticulture and gardening.

Toby came to St David's the year after I did, and his academic history looked a lot like mine. Simon, my older brother, did well at school. My dad is brilliant at maths. It comes naturally to him. Yet with writing, he wasn't very confident, and would often need help with spelling. My mum reads and writes constantly. She loves it. But I've seen her trying to do sums, or work out figures, and she struggles. Simon had inherited my mum's writing ability, and my dad's ability at maths. Simon had the best of both worlds. And myself, I felt I had what was left. Mum's maths and dad's writing. Toby had been dealt the same cards as me. He too had been diagnosed as dyslexic, and mum had sent him straight to St David's, partly because I was already there, and partly because it had a good dyslexia department. It felt good to be there to look after him.

However, Toby had things a lot harder than I did. He had been born with a rare and extremely serious heart problem. From birth, his life had always been threatened. At first he just looked unhealthy, and in response to my mother's worries, doctors told her it was nothing to be concerned about, and his health would soon pick up. With her background in nursing, however, she wasn't satisfied with their answers, and spent a lot of time seeking the opinion of specialists. Eventually, one of them came back with a diagnosis – Total Anomalous Pulmonary Artery – a very complicated heart condition. Up to that point, it had been a fatal disease, but only very recently a surgical procedure had been developed to treat the condition.

Toby was admitted to the London Heart Hospital, at the time the world's leading heart specialist. Although the treatment had been developed recently, as yet, no-one had survived the disease. It was a terrifying experience for my parents, but at the time I wasn't really aware of that. He spent most of his first four years in hospital, and had to have some serious operations. Surgeons had to remove Toby's heart from his body and replaced it with an artificial one while they worked on his own. They had to do this twice. During surgery the blood supply to Toby's brain was cut, and as a result my parents were told he might develop some sort of brain damage. At sixteen he began to show symptoms of epilepsy. Apart from that he was absolutely fine.

We had gone to the village school together, where I always looked after him. He wasn't allowed to take part in sport because his heart condition prevented him from doing anything too strenuous. His personality was different from mine too. He was very unassuming, not really pushy or competitive, but was always up for anything and keen to get involved in whatever was going on.

At St David's I told him about climbing, and one day he decided he would come out with me to see what it was like. I took him to Forwyn. I explained how it all worked, attached the rope to his harness with a karabiner and I led off, placing and clipping just one runner. I got to the top and set up a belay.

'Safe!'

I took the rope in until it came tight onto Toby's harness and told him to climb. He made steady progress up the lower thirty feet and, below an overhang, just out of sight, arrived at the runner.

'I'm here, what do I do now?' he called.

'Toby, you have to unclip the karabiner from the rope and keep climbing.'

'Okay.'

I heard the sound of clipping. Then Toby traversed out into my view, and looked up at me.

'Okay. I've unclipped the rope. What should I do now?'

I looked down. Toby had unclipped himself from the rope altogether. He had unclipped the wrong karabiner. He had traversed out thirty feet above a rocky landing totally unattached to any safety rope. If he fell now, it would be certain death, and all because his brother had told him what to do.

'Oh no,' I thought. 'Mum is going to *kill* me.'

Toby looked at me.

'Toby, clip the rope back into your harness.'

'I can't. I can't reach.'

His voice was totally calm, and I could tell that he had no idea of the danger he was in. Eventually he managed to move back right again and clip into the rope. I never told anyone about what happened, and Toby never went climbing again. That was typical Toby. Trusting, just like Andrew. Their futures were tragically similar too.

One thing I was mad keen to do was a new route, to climb a piece of rock for the first time. Whoever did a route first got to name and grade it, and send off the details to be recorded in a magazine or guidebook. I read about new routes in my Crags magazine, and thought about how cool it would be to see my name in print. There was an old quarry near the school I visited once or twice, a grotty little place that no one else ever went to. One day Andrew and I managed to do a VS there that hadn't been recorded before, up one of the worst bits of rock at the crag. I was beside myself with excitement, and despite the poor quality, sent the details of my climb off to the magazines. I wrote the name and grade and the date I did it on in a letter to the editor of Crags magazine, Geoff Birtles. I went to write my name under it. At the time people at school either called me Jeremy, like my parents did, or Jez. I thought about it. Jeremy. Jeremy Moffatt. That didn't sound too cool. Jez Moffatt? No. None of the top climbers are called anything like Jez.

Jerry? Jerry Moffatt? That sounded better. I signed the letter, posted it off, and a month or two later, the magazine came out, and there was the route, and after it, my name. From that day on I decided I would be known as Jerry Moffatt.

I stayed good friends with Andrew Henry, but after Mojo I became a lot keener the he was. He didn't want to go climbing as often as I did. One day at Forwyn we saw a tiny boy trying to top-rope Great Wall. He was skinny, dressed all in black, and seemed very young. He had a tiny wash bag on a string around his waist with chalk in it. It was so small, he could only fit two fingers into it at a time, so had to do little double-dips to get chalk on all his fingers. He rested on the rope a few times, but got up the route. The boy was Andy Pollitt, and we got to know each other. He was actually the same age as I was, lived nearby, and was as keen as hell. Andy was just what I needed at that time in my climbing life. We were going to have some amazing times together.

I used to go and meet Andy on my free afternoons on Saturdays. While the others went into town, I got on a bicycle and cycled over to Forwyn to meet him. It was over nine miles away, hilly all the way, and the ride would take me an hour and a quarter. I had to be back for dinner at six, so that left us just over two hours before I had to cycle the hour and a quarter back to school. It was easily worth it; I loved climbing with Andy. He was really keen and very ambitious. He would try anything, and although he didn't always get up everything, his determination was impressive.

After some visits to Forwyn together Andy told me about a route he thought we could free down on Pen Trwyn. This was a limestone crag close to the school, but was too steep and hard to be of any use to the climbing club. To 'free' a route means to do it without 'aid', without pulling on the protection that is in the rock. When sections of rock are too steep or holdless to climb free, just with fingers and toes, climbers, particularly in the 1960s, resorted to aid. So, to 'free' a climb of its aid was a big deal, since it often meant venturing into extreme territory.

'There's a route called Mayfair, and it will definitely go. It looks amazing. Let's go and free-climb it next Saturday.'

Andy made it all sound pretty reasonable, like it was covered in holds. Listening to him, it sounded as though it would be about HVS. I said okay. When I arrived at the cliff next weekend, I saw an overhanging sheet of black and white-streaked limestone. I couldn't see any holds, nor any way of climbing up it.

'What do you think Jerry?' Andy asked as he came towards me.

'Andy. We can't climb that. It's impossible. It's my Saturday off and you've brought me down here to try this.'

'Come on mate, hold my rope.'

The line was blanker and steeper than anything either of us had ever climbed before, by a long way. It just felt like a waste of time, as I really couldn't see any way that it could be climbed, and felt a bit miffed at Andy's over-optimism. Still, he insisted on trying, despite my reaction. He tied onto the rope and set off up the wall.

Every time Andy got to a runner, he clipped his rope into it, told me to hold the rope tight, and rested. Once he got above the runner he would fall onto it. In this way he climbed higher and higher, falling again and again until eventually, two hours later, he got to the belay.

'Safe!'

The rope to me came tight and I followed the pitch without falling. I had seen how Andy had done all the moves, so it was much easier for me. Above was a second pitch. I led off, Andy-style, falling and hanging on the rope. Later we would come to call this 'hang-dogging', and see it as cheating, but back then it was just how we climbed. We hung on the rope because we were 'having a rest,' that's all. In this way I dogged my way to the top, hours later. Andy followed without a fall.

We abseiled back to the ground and chatted excitedly about what we had done, grinning from ear to ear. We looked back up at the rock we had just climbed, and could scarcely believe it. We had just freed a really hard aid climb, climbing something so unlikely that no one had thought of trying it before. This must be one of the hardest climbs around, we decided. It was a week before my seventeenth birthday. I wondered:

'Am I the best sixteen year old climber in the country?'

I thought I might be. And that felt great.

TWO

Crag Rat

'What do you want to do when you leave school?'

When I was a kid everyone seemed to know what they wanted to do and it was usually what their dads had done. 'I want to be a doctor,' or 'I want to be a teacher.' I was no exception. When people asked me what I would be, I also had an answer.

'I'm going to be a crag rat.'

From the moment I became hooked on climbing, I knew the only thing I ever wanted to do was hang around at crags and climb all the time. Even the phrase, 'crag rat' – living in the dirt, having no money, scurrying up cliffs – sounded brilliant. I couldn't wait for school to be over.

Finally my exams came around. Despite the fact I enjoyed all my subjects, my dyslexia meant I didn't expect to do very well. But I inherited an attitude from my dad, an attitude that still holds true. He taught me that if you are doing something, it doesn't matter if you are good at it or not. What matters is that you apply yourself and try your best. It's no good being lazy at school and thinking that when you leave, you will somehow start to work hard and achieve something. You must do your best in the situation you are in. With that in mind I worked hard, and in each exam, had done the best I could do. Finally, the last paper, on commerce, was put in front of me. As soon as I had written all I had to write, I put my hand up and asked to leave. Then I grabbed my rucksack, left by the door of the examination hall and ran down the long school driveway to the road outside. I knew I'd never do another exam again.

I was going climbing. I had agreed to meet Andy Pollitt that afternoon at a nearby crag called Tremadog, so I stuck out my thumb and started hitching. Two hours later I arrived. There was a café under the rocks called Eric's. I took off my rucksack, sat down on the little wall outside and took it all in. A long series of outcrops, up to a hundred and eighty feet high, stuck out of the trees, with fantastic bulges and slabs and grooves winding up the steep, dark rock. The sun was shining, the cliffs looked great and the routes looked amazing. A breeze was blowing along the cliff making the trees rustle. I felt so happy. I was seventeen. I hadn't a care and I was where I most wanted to be.

Tremadog. What a place. As far as I was concerned this was the best cliff in the world. This was how a surfer would feel in Hawaii, standing on the North Shore. The hardest routes in Britain were here, legendary climbs that my heroes had put up. Ron Fawcett, the best climber in Britain at the time, had just done Strawberries, maybe the hardest climb in the country. It had taken him *three days*. It looked mind-blowing, taking thin cracks right up the edge of a drastically exposed sheet of rock high above the road, on a feature called the Vector Headwall. Another superb climber, John Redhead, had added some hard routes on the same buttress, Bananas and Atomic Finger Flake. At the time, these were the hardest routes around. A year or two before Pete Livesey had done Zukator and Marathon Man, and these too were the hardest climbs of their time. Before that were Void and Cream, the two cracks right of Strawberries. Then, of course, there was Vector itself, Joe Brown's original route right up the middle of the big steep buttress, from 1960.

Over the next two months I would climb virtually every day here and do almost all the routes on the crag. As I sat on the wall that afternoon outside Eric's café, I was an ambitious young climber who had battled his way up a few tricky routes. When I left eight weeks later at the start of September, I would have climbed a route considered the hardest in Britain. It was all about to happen for me, sitting there in the sunshine with the breeze on my face. Everything was perfect.

'Jerry, Jerry, where have you been!'

I looked round. It was Andy. He emerged from the bushes across the road and half-walked, half-ran over to me, dressed in tight black clothes and with long messy black hair. He was more or less the same age as me, but looked younger because he was so skinny. I could see from the way he hurried how keen he was to start climbing.

'What do you mean, I've been sat…'

'Come *on*. Grab your stuff. Let's go climb Fingerlicker.'

That was typical of Andy. Fingerlicker was one of Pete Livesey's routes, when Livesey was one of the country's best climbers. Before Ron Fawcett arrived with routes like Strawberries and Lord of the Flies, Pete's routes were the hardest around. Fingerlicker was still one of the top climbs at

Tremadog and probably beyond us, but Andy always had to be getting on the hardest routes. It didn't matter that it was too hard. We had to go and do it. It didn't matter that we hadn't even warmed up. We had to go and climb *Fingerlicker*.

Feeling Andy's excitement, I grabbed my stuff and scampered along the road behind him. We arrived below the buttress and fought through the bushes to the base of the route. Fingerlicker follows a striking line, a perfect finger-sized crack running up an overhanging wall. It has no footholds, so you have to jam your fingers and toes into the crack and pull. We uncoiled our ropes. Andy tied on and set off. Nervously he fought his way up the lower section. He placed a hex deep in the crack, clipped it and climbed on. Higher, as the crack got thinner, he fumbled in a nut. He clipped the rope into the karabiner.

'Take me there, Jerry!'

That was the command for me to lock off the rope and pull in all the slack so that the runner would take all his weight.

'Wow!' Andy pulled his tired fingers out of the crack in relief. He shook them in the air to get some strength back into them. 'This is amazing,' he called down.

'Looks great,' I called back.

'Right, when I say "Now", I'm going to climb again.'

'Okay.'

'Now!'

I spent the afternoon holding his ropes, paying out slack, locking the rope tight as he moved up and placed nuts before resting his weight on the runner. He fought and eventually got to the top. I tied on and followed the pitch with a few rests. We had done Fingerlicker. Or so we thought.

At the time we didn't really understand ethics. Ethics are the unwritten rules for climbing. They are really more about style, what you can get away with and what you can't. Over time they change and things you might get away with at one time you might not get away with in years to come. Your own ethics change too. Andy and I thought that if you did a climb resting on the rope, it didn't matter. It was just resting. You'd done the moves. You'd still done the route. It was a bit like running a mile in five minutes. You might stop for the odd rest, but you'd still run the mile. But climbing wasn't like that. Later we would learn the word 'dogging'. Dogging, or 'hang-dogging', was cheating on a climb – pulling on a runner or resting on a rope – and would mean that you hadn't actually done the climb. Not properly. At the time people often did routes in what was known as 'yo-yo' style, where each time you fell off you lowered to the ground. While dogging a route was not acceptable, yo-yoing was. Nowadays however, yo-yoing is no longer considered acceptable. Ultimately, the best way to climb a route, ethically, is on your first try, without any falls. Yet that day, knowing nothing about any of this, we were ecstatic. We had just done Fingerlicker on our first day. By the time I got to the top it was late, so we made our way back to the car park. Andy ran across the road to Eric's café and I wandered off to find the sleeping barn where we would live for the next two months.

I entered the gloomy building and put some water on to boil on a stove. While I waited I got out my guidebook and by the blue light of the gas flame, flicked through the pages, looking at the descriptions of climbs. I looked at the names of the great routes and imagined climbing them. I was going to work my way through this little pocket-sized book and, by the end of the summer, I would have climbed practically every extreme in the book. Where to start, I wondered, as I read about the endless fantastic opportunities.

All the great crags in Wales have a classic Joe Brown route. Joe was a legendary climber in the 1950s and 60s, putting up tough routes in the Peak District, Wales and elsewhere. He was incredible. He went on to open a climbing shop in Llanberis and a few years before, when I was first getting in to climbing, I wrote a letter to him at his shop, asking for his autograph. A few days later he sent me a postcard. On the front there was a stunning black and white photo of him climbing at Tremadog, undercutting across a bulging slab on a route called Tensor. He was smoking a cigarette. On the back he had written: 'Best wishes, Joe Brown'. Brown's great route at Tremadog and one of the best climbs in Wales, is called Vector. I had read about it and was keen to try it. When Andy came back later, I convinced him that we should do it the following day.

Andy had done it before so it was agreed I would lead it all. The route covers some very steep ground in three pitches. I led the first pretty easily. The crux is the second pitch. It follows a feature called the Ochre Slab, a polished ramp hanging out in space. I led off the belay stance, pulled over an overhang and launched up the Ochre Slab. The exposure and the difficulty kicked in almost immediately and suddenly I felt right at my limit. My feet slipped on the polished rock and I struggled to get good runners in. I began to get scared. At the top of the slab, I reached round a bulge and placed my favourite nut – a number three Clog on a purple nylon sling – into a shallow crack. I gave it a little tug to make sure it was placed securely and with tiredness pumping around my forearms, started laybacking around the bulge above. As I did, I kicked the Clog out of its crack and watched it spiral off down the rope. My next runner was about fifteen feet below that again. If I fall here, I thought, I will take a monster. Instantly, I felt myself switch into overdrive. I kept calm, in a terrified sort of way and pulled and pulled until I arrived at the belay at the end of the pitch. I collapsed, a nervous wreck. Andy had to lead the last pitch after all.

Vector forces an intricate line up a large buttress and, seventy feet from the top, is forced to weave leftwards by a featureless overhanging sheet of rock. This sheet of rock, perched dramatically over a hundred feet above the road, is known as the Vector Headwall and is one of the best bits of rock in Wales. It is split by three amazing cracks. Ron Fawcett's Strawberries takes thin cracks near the left-hand side. In the centre, there are two better-defined lines, Void and Cream. These are two of the best extremes in Wales, and while they are a lot easier than Strawberries, they are both still very hard. We had to get on them.

Void. I was to lead the headwall pitch, the big one, so Andy led off up the first two and got us to the belay below the crux pitch. A steep, hideous-looking crack runs up an acute, overhanging groove, above which a ferocious crack blasts up the smooth headwall. As I was clipping runners onto my harness, preparing for the lead, we heard voices from below. We looked down to see another climber approaching us on the same route. We recognised him as Dougie Hall.

Dougie Hall had been in the magazines at the time and was therefore a famous climber. He was obviously a lot better than us as he stormed up the first two pitches in the time we had just messed around on the belay. He arrived just as I was getting ready to set off. I said hello and squirmed off into the groove. It was steep and awkward and I made slow progress. I fought hard to place a runner and, feeling pumped, called to Andy to give me a rest. Andy hauled back on the ropes. The ropes came tight through the runner above my waist and I took my hands off and started shaking some blood back into them. I looked down at Andy, then to Dougie. I saw him roll his eyes. He tutted loudly.

'Useless doggers,' he complained.

Still not having any idea what dogging was, I just thought, 'Hmm, he's not very nice, is he?' Getting back off the rope, I again started inching my way up the groove. Once more I placed a nut and called to Andy to give me a rest. At the top of the groove I stepped out onto the instant exposure of the steep finger-width crack above; this was still desperate but I managed to battle upwards with no more falls and finally landed, exhausted, on the grassy top of the crag. I had only rested a few times, but had taken over an hour to get up. Andy followed and fought his way up without falling off.

'What was Dougie Hall complaining about?' I asked Andy at the top.

'He said we were too slow and should stick to routes we could do,' he said.

'What does he mean? We did it didn't we?'

'I don't know.'

Before we walked away from the edge, I peeked over to see Dougie nearing the top of the pitch. It had taken him about five minutes.

Not long later, we had a similar experience on Cream. This time it was Andy's turn to lead. I got to the belay below the headwall, and again Andy fought and rested his way up the fierce final crack, doing it with around three hangs. At the top he took the rope in for me to follow, and as I was getting ready to set off, he leaned over and called out at the top of his voice:

'Jerry, whatever you do, don't fall off. Dougie Hall's watching!'

He pointed to the road. There, in the distance below, was Dougie. We were a bit annoyed after his comments about Void, so I knew I had to put a better effort in on Cream. I set off and had the battle of my life, fighting with every jam, pumped out of my brain, but managing to get to the top without falling. That was Cream done.

Over our two-month stay Andy and I were kings of the barn. Other people came and went, but we were there all the time. The barn was a shoddy old building at the base of the crag, with a leaky roof and straw scattered on the floor, where people could sleep for ten pence a night. It was dark inside. At the front were a couple of tables where people laid out their food and stoves. At the back were scattered a load of dirty old mattresses. People would throw their sleeping bags out on the dirty mattresses and sleep there.

At night, when the lights were out, the building came alive with the noise of rats and mice. One night a mouse ran right over my face, right across my mouth and nose and I felt its little feet and tail on my skin. It was horrible. The next day I got a load of bricks and wood to prop up my mattress to try to keep myself safe from the vermin. Another time I wandered over to the barn to find a boy from Lancashire who had been staying there standing outside, looking pale. He said he had seen a rat the size of a rabbit in the barn.

'I thought it was a rabbit.'

I could see he was shaken by it. He said he was going to hitch home the next day and get his tent because he didn't want to sleep inside again. That night, his last in the barn, he slept on the mattresses. The only food he had was a single crust of bread. He was going to have it in the morning for his breakfast before he hitched home, so he kept it that night close to his head. In the morning, he found the corners of the crust had been nibbled. But instead of throwing it away, the boy pinched the *tiniest* millimetres off the nibbled bits with his fingernails. He then fried it in margarine and ate it. That blew me away.

Our dinner was the same every night for the entire stay: curry and rice. I had a big value bag of white rice and would boil a pot of that. I also bought a bag of 'curry sauce' from a chip shop in Llandudno. This was just spicy yellow powder. You put the powder in a cup, added boiling water and it thickened up. Curry and rice. The whole meal cost about fifteen pence.

I was living on 70p each day.

Once, or maybe twice some days, we would have a cup of tea in Eric's café. Eric Jones was a legendary climber from the 1960s and 1970s, who had done lots of amazing alpine climbing, including the first British solo of the North Face of the Eiger. His café was one of the centres of Welsh climbing. He worked there himself and was always very friendly towards us. It was our habit, each time we finished a route, to walk back down to the barn again for a drink of water. When we did, every time we did a route, no matter what it was, Andy would run across the road to Eric and tell him what we had just done.

'We've just done Void! We've just done Fingerlicker! We've just done Vector!'

Eric would always show an interest: 'That's great lads, find it okay?'

'Yeah! Yeah! Yeah!' Andy would reply, and go off into detail about the moves and how he had found them.

From time to time famous climbers would show up at Tremadog. One day Pete Livesey appeared in the car park outside Eric's café. We had never seen Pete Livesey in real life before and he looked and was dressed exactly how he always was in the magazines. He wore dark Helly Hansen pants, a kind of traditional fleece that climbers wore at the time, and had a big curly mop of mousy brown hair and a curly moustache. Spotting him, Andy's eyes almost popped out of his head and he whispered to me in awe: 'That's Pete Livesey! It's Pete Livesey!'

I was star-struck. But not Andy, who marched straight over to him. At the time, we were really in to Ron Fawcett and it was our habit to try to dress like our heroes. Andy dressed just the way Ron did at the time, dark Helly Hansens and Ron's trademark Union Jack woolly hat. He looked like a tiny little Ron Fawcett. I watched him walk straight up to Pete Livesey and start asking him questions. After a minute, Andy came running back.

'Jerry! Jerry! Come on. Grab your stuff, we have to go and do Zukator!'

'Eh?'

'Jerry! Pete Livesey has just told me *the secret* of how to do Zukator! You don't climb the corner at all. You climb a crack on the left of the corner and it's much easier.'

Zukator was one of the big routes at Tremadog, taking a tough line up a steep, shallow corner. We had tried it before, but found the climbing too strenuous and insecure and hadn't managed to get up it. But now Andy had the secret, and with this new inside information, we made our way up through the trees and roped up at the bottom of the route. I led an easy first pitch to a belay below the crux corner. Andy arrived, racked up and led off. He soon got to Livesey's crack, put a runner in the bottom and started climbing it. He struggled up this for about eight or ten feet, ever further away from the corner and his protection until it tapered down, and then just petered out. Andy was clinging on at the end of it with nowhere to go, shaking, arms pumping and totally unable to reverse.

'Watch me! Watch me! There's no holds.'

At the belay I realised what had happened and began sniggering. Livesey had sandbagged him. Sandbagging was the old trick of misleading other climbers – telling them something was easy when it wasn't, or giving them false information – so they would get into trouble and have a desperate time. It was a real art and Livesey was a master. Andy's terrified whimpers grew in volume until, a moment later, he came screaming off the rock. I saw his body in space and he must have fallen twenty-five feet before he came to a halt, crashing into the corner below me. Shaking, he returned to the belay. I had to take over. Without Livesey's 'secret', I continued up the corner direct and managed to climb the route without falls. Andy followed, this time also without falls.

Andy was fond of girls and I was very impressed when he managed to find himself a local girlfriend. She was called Bronwen, a pretty schoolgirl with long black hair tied in pigtails. Sometimes in the morning, as we lay in the barn, Bronwen would show up in her uniform and run in to see him. She would lie on top of him in his sleeping bag and they would sing to each other. At the time, Leo Sayer had a hit: 'Woah woah yaay-yaay, I love you more than I can say...' Andy and Bronwen would sing this to each other, taking turns at the lines, looking into each other's eyes, while I lay right by Andy's side. I found it a bit embarrassing and couldn't see how all this would help Andy's climbing.

In the evenings we would often go to one of the local pubs, an hour's walk away, so Andy could meet up with Bronwen. We would sit in the corner with our half pint of still orange and talk to her about climbing. At the time there was a lot of nationalism in Wales and many locals didn't like the English. They saw them as unwelcome tourists and resented it when they bought property in the region. There were often nationalist slogans daubed on walls in Welsh and they had a reputation for being aggressive to visitors. Sometimes when we were in the pub, grown men would come over and tell us to clear off. We were only seventeen, but we had to get up and go. Another time, walking back from the pub with Andy, an old grey Ford Cortina pulled up alongside and the passenger wound his window down. Andy was wearing his Ron Fawcett-style Union Jack hat. The passenger grabbed it off Andy's head, opened it up, spat in it and threw it on the ground.

'Piss off you English,' he shouted at us and the car drove away.

'But I'm Welsh! I'm Welsh!' Andy called in his squeaky voice. He was from Prestatyn, along the north coast of Wales. That really upset him. 'But

I'm Welsh too!' he muttered, as the Cortina disappeared into the distance.

We knew someone who had a caravan near a crag called Carreg Hylldrem. This was three miles away and we would sometimes walk over for somewhere to hang out in the evenings. There was a little scene of local climbers there that we knew, who would also hang around the caravan. One evening one of the group, Mel Griffiths, said that he was off to Carreg Hylldrem for some bouldering. Bouldering is climbing on smaller rocks and boulders, without ropes. If you fall off, you don't fall far and just land on the ground. That way you can really push yourself physically. I never did much bouldering, apart from on the wall at school, so I said I would go along.

I followed him up to Hylldrem. At the base of the cliff was a short, very steep wall. It overhangs so much it never got wet and the sheep would shelter there when it rained. The wall was covered in holds and these were covered in chalk. Mel showed me some of his boulder problems, pulling hard with his arms, quickly snatching between very sloping, indistinct holds with his feet swinging free as the steep rock pushed him out. I tried them but couldn't do a single one. The wall was so overhanging and the moves were so powerful that I just didn't have the necessary force. Mel was surprised, as by this stage I was doing harder routes than he was. He asked me if I could do a lock-off.

'What's a lock-off?' I asked.

Mel walked over to a tree, grabbed a horizontal branch with one hand and did a one-arm pull-up on it. At the top he stopped, with his arm fully bent at the elbow and his hand locked in to his shoulder, all his weight on one arm. He looked down at his fist, then to me.

'That's a lock-off, Jerry.'

I grabbed the branch with both arms, did the pull-up and let go with one hand so all my weight was on the other. My body sagged downwards. I was unable to repeat Mel's feat. This was frustrating. I bouldered at Carreg Hylldrem some more with other climbers and they all burned me off. On the crag, on routes, I was climbing a lot better than they were. I couldn't understand why they were stronger than me. I didn't like this and decided to apply myself to improve at bouldering.

I can't remember who gave it to me, but at the same time I had a book called *Master of Rock*, about an American climber called John Gill. On wet days I would sit in the caravan and read this book over and over. This was to become my favourite climbing book ever, and Gill was to become one of the most motivating characters I ever learned about.

Born in 1937, Gill began climbing in the US in the 1950s. He had a normal apprenticeship, but as he had a background in gymnastics, he soon saw that bouldering was somewhere he could combine his love of gymnastics and climbing, and became a dedicated boulderer. This was at a time when virtually nobody else bouldered, apart from in the forests of Fontainebleau on the outskirts of Paris. In the US, Gill was unique. It would take over 15 years for the climbing world to catch up with his ideas.

I was struck by Gill's single-mindedness and his determination to do what he believed in despite a lack of comprehension from his peers. There were photos of him doing modern-looking problems – very powerful and dynamic – but wearing the big boots that climbers wore at the time. There were photos of him training on gymnastics rings and doing front-levers on one-inch edges. He would climb really steep rock where he couldn't get your feet in contact, doing jump moves, even double-handed jumps. He was doing lock-offs on small holds, and one arm pull-ups. The book went on to say that most of his problems, years, even decades after their first ascent, hadn't been repeated. He was obviously far ahead of his time. It was well written by another Colorado climber called Pat Ament and sometimes Ament would talk about his amazement at Gill's standard. One time Gill showed Ament one of his problems:

'I could grasp the holds, but not the problem,' Ament wrote.

I understood what he meant and would use that phrase with an American accent myself sometimes.

I found Gill so inspiring. I decided I wanted to improve at bouldering, and if I could, then it would definitely improve my climbing. From then on I would try to make the hour's walk to Hylldrem almost every day and steadily grew more powerful until, eventually, no one burned me off any more. I've never been a natural boulderer; endurance has always been my strong point. But those days that I put in on Hylldrem really helped me improve and helped me early on to realise the benefit of power.

That summer we climbed almost every day. In fact, I can't remember, over those two months, spending a single day without climbing. One morning Bronwen came to the barn earlier than usual and even more excited.

'Aren't you two coming to Porthmadog to see the roadshow?'

Radio 1, the BBC's pop music station, spent the summer hosting events at various destinations throughout the country, where kids would come to see the presenters, hear bands and take part in the programme. Today it was at Porthmadog, the seaside town near Tremadog. It was a big thing and Bronwen told us we had to come along. We all hitched over. There was a couple of open-sided vans with presenters inside, their voices booming out on loudspeakers. They were talking rubbish, but the huge crowd of kids still cheered in all the right places. Some crap band played a song and everyone clapped. They stood around drinking Coke and eating sweets. What were all these kids doing here, I wondered.

'I'd love to try Geireagle,' I said to Andy.

'Yeah, that looks brilliant, doesn't it?'
'Shall we go and do it now?'
'Yeah,' Andy said. 'This sucks.'
We said goodbye to Bronwen and hitched back to Tremadog.

The guidebook was our bible and we read every word over and over again. We read the history and the first ascent list. We scoured every route description and knew the phrases off by heart. There was the all-important graded list, where routes are listed in order of difficulty, and I watched as my pencilled-in ticks reached further and further towards the top of this list. I still have my treasured Tremadog guide from the time, and next to the description of virtually every extreme, I have written in the details of when and how I climbed it: 'Led, 11 June 1980.' 'Led, 23 July, 1980.' 'Soloed, 5 August, 1980.'

Near the back of the book on a blank page, I noted the new routes that had been done since the guide was published. With a blue biro I wrote the route names, descriptions and who had done them. This was partly to keep track of any new activity, but also, as my abilities were starting to out-run the graded list, I wanted to see my objectives written down and to have somewhere to tick them off when I had done them. The Atomic Finger Flake. Climb the hanging flake to the right of the final pitch of Vector. Redhead. Led.

I wore the same clothes for the whole of the summer, a pair of blue corduroy trousers and a football shirt. I never once washed, never brushed my teeth and never shaved. There's a photo of me in Crags from that trip, the first time I ever got my picture in a magazine, wearing the football shirt and with a bum-fluff beard. Underneath, the caption reads, 'Jerry Moffatt bursting onto the scene with an ascent of Strawberries aged seventeen.'

Strawberries. We had done everything else and Ron's big route was the last on the list. I tried it at the end of the two months. I only got to try it for a few days and on the third day, did it with three rests on the rope. At the time we still thought that was a good ascent. I ticked it off in the back of my guidebook. Strawberries. The crack and wall left of the top pitch of Cream. Fawcett. Led.

All too soon, summer ended. Andy went back home to Prestatyn to work for the autumn. I was heading for a place I'd heard a lot about in the Peak District called Stoney Middleton. Andy would come back to do Strawberries, but not with me. We would climb together a lot over the years to come and even live together for a while in Sheffield. He has always been a great friend.

I would only ever return to Tremadog a couple of times: once, the following summer, to do Strawberries properly. The new ethics I would learn in Stoney meant I could not consider my dogged ascent to be valid. The second time, a year or so later, I came by myself on a beautiful day in April. I had hitched over from Llanberis where I was staying. It was midweek and the crag was deserted. Through force of habit I wandered over to the old barn, went in and threw my rucksack on the table. In that frantic summer after leaving school it had always seemed busy and buzzing with people. Now it was empty and felt dusty and abandoned. Had times moved on already? There was only one other boy there, sat on a bench at the back of the barn. I said hello.

He said hello back, smiled and said how nice a day it was. I could tell from looking at him that he was a beginner, mainly from the way he was dressed. He didn't even have proper climbing boots, just big leather mountain boots. I can't remember if I asked him, or just knew, but it was obvious what he was doing. When you're keen and haven't got anyone to climb with, then you can just go to Tremadog and meet up with someone else who wants to climb and get a day in. Sometimes you offer to climb with these people but that day I didn't. Someone else would come along soon and they would hook up. Anyway, I knew I was about to have one of those days.

I put my climbing boots on, walked out into the sunshine and started up the first pitch of Void, moving easily and fast without the hindrance of a rope or protection. This led to the bottom of the Ochre Slab on Vector, where I had the epic a couple of years before. I pulled easily onto it and soloed the pitch, which left me at the base of the headwall pitch of Void. I moved smoothly up the groove where Dougie Hall had once watched me struggle. At the top of the groove I reached out and swung freely onto the steep smooth wall. Below me the cliff dropped away for a hundred feet. I looked down at the drop and revelled in the freedom of not having any ropes or fear to contend with. I chalked up, all alone, the exposure everywhere. Nobody soloed on the headwall back then and I felt fantastic. Thinking back, there are just no words that can describe how this felt. It was almost surreal, magical, feeling separate from my body, yet a part of it at the same time. In this state, I climbed to the top.

After that I kept going. I scrambled back to the base of the crag and did a HVS off to the right. Back down. I did Geireagle, a really hard, off-balance E3. Back down. I did The Plum. The best thing about the day was coming back to the barn after each route. I felt a euphoric whiteness all over me. I've just soloed Vector, I thought to myself. I've just soloed Void, I've just soloed Geireagle, I've just soloed Plum Buttress. Each time, I would see the beginner sitting there, still not with any partner. He didn't know what I was doing between visits, but always asked if I was having a good day. Each time he kept hinting that he wanted to go and do a route.

'It must be fantastic to be up there today. Climbing.'

'Yes,' I replied, 'It really is.'

I had been in such an incredible state of mind, I couldn't think of going off and doing an easy lead with the beginner, but later, remembering what it was like when you are aching to do a route and there was nobody to climb with, I thought I might as well.

'The cliffs look great,' he said, 'Much better than the ones near me.'

'Yeah. Do you want to go and do a route?'

'Oh yeah, I'd love to.' His eyes lit up.

'Come on then, grab your stuff.'

We made our way over to Y Broga, a classic VS on the right-hand side of the crag. We both tied on and I soloed the first pitch, a very polished layback up a slippery slab. I tied onto the belay and called for him to come on up. What followed was awesome. Chatting on the way over, he said he'd only ever done Severe before, so this route was way past his limit. He set off. He struggled and grabbed and fought every single inch of the climb.

'Come on, come on,' I called. 'Hang in there.'

His big boots almost slipped off every foothold and his arms were pumped from the word go. But he wouldn't give in. He was out of breath, his face was bright red but somehow he fought and scraped and battled his way to the belay. Fair play, I thought, that was a terrific effort. I clipped him into the belay as he gasped for air. I climbed on to the top and he followed me all the way up.

That was great. To solo all those routes, then go down and share that experience with that guy. He was buzzing too, he'd just done his first VS. What a fantastic end to the day, my last day in Tremadog. I never got to know his name.

THREE

The Stoney Years

At the end of my summer in North Wales, I hitched back to my parents' house in Leicester. As soon as I walked in, my mum told me to take a shower. She said I stank. I thought she was overreacting, but I took off the blue corduroys and the football shirt, and headed for the bathroom. When I came back into my bedroom where I'd dropped my clothes, the stench almost made me gag.

My parents were glad to see me back in one piece. I told them all about my experiences, about the climbs I had done, about doing Strawberries, and seeing people like Pete Livesey and Dougie Hall. They smiled and said it sounded great, although I think it all went over their heads. I told them too about the barn, about the filth and the rats, and they looked disgusted. The results from my retakes had come back and I had managed to get another three 'O' Levels, giving me six in total. They were proud of that and so was I, considering my severe dyslexia. My original plan had been to go to college and study to get into the Forestry Commission, but my results didn't allow this. My parents asked me what my plans were now. Tremadog had been an amazing experience and I was more sure than ever that all I wanted to do was climb.

It was 1980. Margaret Thatcher was prime minister and the economy wasn't doing very well. There didn't seem to be many jobs about and millions of people were out of work and living on unemployment benefit – the dole. For many people, it became a way of life. For climbers, it was like getting paid to climb full time. Sign your name once a fortnight and a cheque would arrive a couple of days later in a brown envelope. I never thought about whether this was right or wrong at the time and today I am not particularly proud of it, but I was 17 and all I wanted to do was climb. I signed on the dole in Leicester, giving me £15 a week to live on.

I had heard climbers in Wales talking about a crag in the Peak District, the national park in northern England between the cities of Manchester and Sheffield, called Stoney Middleton. This is where the hardest routes in the area were and people said it was one of the few crags that you could climb on all winter. It was steep, so bits would always stay dry. Not only that, I discovered, there were a lot of full-time homeless climbers who dossed at Stoney all the time. The Stoney woodshed was their equivalent of the Tremadog barn. I knew it was where I had to go next. I packed my stuff, said goodbye to my parents and hitched off towards the Peak.

The little map I had finally led me to the small village of Stoney Middleton late in the afternoon. It was really just a main street along the deep-set limestone dale, with a few houses on either side. It had a post office, a café and a pub. A busy road ran through the middle of the village, and lots of heavy lorries and quarry vehicles passed constantly up and down. At the head of the village, more or less above the last houses, were towering walls of rough-looking grey limestone, about a hundred feet high, looking out across the valley. So this was Stoney. It didn't look attractive the way Tremadog looked. The village was dusty and the bottom of the dale had a damp feeling about it. The lorries were deafening as they thundered by.

I stood in the road, alone. I was wearing my big rucksack, containing a sleeping bag, climbing gear, ropes and a change of clothes. I wasn't sure what to do now, so decided to go for a look at the crag. The first bit I came to was an old quarry, which consisted of a series of angular bays with steep, cracked walls above. The ground was muddy, except near to the crag, where it was dry and dusty, sheltered from any rain by the walls above. Lots of trees grew about in the flat ground, casting deep shadows. Further on, I wandered out along a broad ledge with steep walls towering overhead. I recognised it. This was Windy Ledge, one of the famous parts of the crag. And it wasn't hard to see why. The ledge ran out above an abrupt drop, up to seventy feet above the trees and the road. It gave the place instant exposure. The routes above took steeper rock than the angular bays below. The rock above Windy Ledge had never been quarried and was rougher and more featured. I recognised some of the routes from pictures in the magazines – Scoop Wall, Circe, Our Father, Menopause – all big famous climbs with great history. I imagined myself on them, a hundred feet above the busy road, easily cruising the steep walls. I couldn't wait to try.

It was getting late and I was tired from hitching. Back down at the road I saw some climbers walking past with yellow helmets, flared jeans and thick ropes coiled over their shoulders. I asked them where the woodshed was. They pointed towards a building just on the side of the main road. I went over and saw what looked like a half-built garden shed. A few shelves held planks of wood, and above it was a corrugated asbestos sheet forming the roof. There weren't any walls at all. There was a climber there, dressed in torn denims and a shabby woollen jumper. He was in his twenties, a lot older than I was, and was boiling some water on a stove. I said hello.

'Areet, youth,' he said.

I told him I had just arrived and asked was this where people stayed?

'Aye,' he said. 'Welcome to the woodshed. You've got the Vicarage down that way and the Land of the Midnight Sun just over there. Take your pick.'

He made some tea and drank it along with a couple of slices of bread. I looked at the woodshed. Where was the Vicarage? What was the Land of the Midnight Sun?

'Just move some wood around and make yourself some room, lad. The builders come along in the daytime and rearrange it all.'

Finishing his tea, he packed his things back into his rucksack, threw it on his shoulders and wandered off. 'See ya,' he mumbled as he left. It was now getting dark. I sat down on the ground. Later, in the darkness, I rearranged the stored wood to give myself enough space to sleep in and climbed into a two-foot gap in the wood stacks. Some time later more people arrived in ones and twos, and I heard them arrange themselves beds and clamber into sleeping bags. I felt a bit disappointed in the Stoney woodshed. It was nothing like the Tremadog barn. Then it began to rain.

This was to be my home for the next two years.

On the first few days I managed to scrounge the odd belay off climbers waiting around at the crags and tried some of the climbs I had heard of. I got my arse kicked. Everything was desperate, even the easy climbs. Routes were steep and the holds felt small. The footholds were exceptionally polished and slippery. In the first few days I tried some of the famous routes in the E3 to E4 range, grades that I would have had no problem with in Wales, routes like Pickpocket, Bubbles and Our Father. I got nowhere on them, stopped all the time by moves that felt too hard and rock that felt too slippery and steep. I had been used to climbing in Wales where the grades, it was starting to seem, were pretty generous. I wasn't used to the nature of the climbing. As well as that, I later learned, the Peak District has always had a tradition of under-grading routes, which is the way I think climbs should be graded. Between the grades and the routes, I really got burned at Stoney in those first days. Right, I finally decided. I'm going to have to master this place.

Even though it was a popular crag with lots of climbers around, I was so keen that I generally couldn't find enough partners to hook up with. Each day I would scrounge two or three belays off strangers or other dossers I recognised, but it was never nearly enough to satisfy my keenness. One day I was at the crag by myself, desperate to do a route as usual. There was a guy standing nearby, not doing anything and I asked him if he wanted to do a route. In those days I would just ask anybody whether I knew him or not. It was a lot of trust to put in a stranger and I wouldn't do it now. This stranger said yes and he held my ropes as I led Bitterfingers. I was really pleased to do it first try, the first of the tough Stoney routes I had done without falling off. The following day we met up and climbed together again, and the day after that. His name was Neil Molnar. Neil, or Noddy as he was called, was my regular climbing partner for most of the next three years.

I soon got to know all the climbers who hung out there and became part of their group. They were all great characters. There were always at least four or five people there at any one time, all living in one of the various dosses. Plant Pot, Zippy, Dave Chesters, Dirty Derek, Carney, Basic Nick, Super Yorkie, Bullit, Quent, Plod and Doggsy. None of these people worked, although Doggsy had done a short stint at a paint factory in Nottingham. At the time, there was a fashion of wearing white painter's trousers, inspired by the American climbing fashion we had seen in the magazines. Doggsy had come by a stack of these trousers at his factory and kitted us all out. These people were at the crag seven days a week, sleeping, climbing and surviving. Most signed on the dole. There was a real culture of signing on, both in the climbing scene and in the country in general. There was no stigma in it. I signed on for about seven years, did no work in all that time and never got any hassle. Every fortnight, I would go down to my parents' house and sign on for my £15 a week. Because everybody had the same, it never mattered that you didn't have much money. That's what you had and that's what you lived on. Other climbers would come over for a few days. Dougie Hall, from near Manchester, would regularly climb there, mainly with Kim Carrigan. Kim Carrigan was a very good Australian climber, one of those important characters who would travel the world, trying the hardest routes in different countries and often doing them. And that was what brought him to Stoney Middleton.

In the evening, when it got dark and cold, and after we had eaten some food, we all went down to the pub in the village. The Moon Inn was run by a woman called Peggy, a ferocious landlady, who seemed to hate us climbers hanging out in her pub. The first time I went in there, I approached the bar.

'Oh no, not another one of you climbers,' she roared. 'Don't think you're going to spend ten pence on a pint of orange and sit in here the entire night talking about your climbing and not spending any money, okay?'

'Okay.'

'Now, what do you want?'

'*Half* a pint of orange please.'

We would sit down and spend the entire night talking about climbing. Nobody spent any money. Eventually, at closing time, Peggy would tell us all to get out.

From The Moon, we'd make our way to the woodshed, or to one of the other two common dosses. There was the Vicarage. This was beside the graveyard and was being done up at the time. The builders didn't mind us being there since it stopped thieves stealing building materials from the site. The Land of the Midnight Sun was the other popular spot, which was a little shed down near the garage. It was called that because there was a streetlight right outside that shone all night. I found it too bright to sleep there, so usually slept in one of the other two.

The long winter nights were unbearably cold. I would come out of the pub into the bitter darkness. Back at the woodshed, I would rearrange the timber so I had about a foot of space to slide into. My sleeping bag was the cheapest available, thin, with hardly any filling. I would put on two pairs of jeans, a hat, scarf, anorak, any spare clothes I had, get into the bag, cover myself with an old blanket I had found, climb into my berth and shiver the night away. Often it would rain or snow and the cold wind would rattle the sheets of wood.

In the morning, by about seven o'clock, it would have become so cold I would have to get out of bed. There was a café in the village, the Lovers' Leap, but that didn't open till eight o'clock. For an hour I would hang about and try keep warm, doing star-jumps, jogging around, and when the doors opened, race in and have a cup of tea.

The café was run by a woman called Sue, who had a kind nature and was friendly to all the climbers. She didn't mind us being there, even though all we would ever have was a cup of tea and maybe an Eccles cake. We seldom bought food there. Sometimes I would walk down to the village shop and buy a loaf and some sardines, then bring them back to the café. Under the table, I would get Sue's ketchup bottle and cover my bread with red sauce. I would then add the sardines to it, or, if I didn't have any sardines, just have bread and ketchup. Looking back now, I imagine Sue knew exactly what we were up to, but let us get away with it.

Most of the hardest routes in the Peak at the time were at Stoney. Later, as strength, stamina and protection improved, steeper crags like Raven Tor and Cheedale would become the places to push the standards. But in 1980 and 1981, the routes at Stoney were still among the hardest. Bitterfingers, Wee Doris, Our Father, Four Minute Tiler, Kink, Kellogg, Circe, these were the big ones. The hard routes at Stoney were mostly all the work of Tom Proctor. Tom was a Stoney legend and had been putting up by far the hardest routes in Britain in the late 1960s and early 1970s. They were ahead of their time and took ages to be repeated. I had a copy of Crags magazine, and on the cover was a black and white picture of Proctor trying to free-climb a route at Stoney called Menopause. It looked amazing. Tom is bridging up a really overhanging white corner wearing a pair of jeans and a tight striped T-shirt, with enormous bulging biceps. The caption inside said that his next hold was an upwards-pointing pocket above his head into which he had to shove a single finger. To be doing a move like that at that time seemed amazing.

The caption went on to say that while doing the move he pulled so hard that he tore tendons in his left arm and fell off. Menopause was later freed to give a really hard route, and years later was soloed by a Buxton climber called Simon Nadin, an incredible achievement. By the time I moved to Stoney, Tom's routes were still considered the hardest, although he had stopped climbing so much. Still, now and again, he would pop in to the café, just to keep up with what was going on and it was always good to chat to him.

At the time, Tom's route Circe was one of the top climbs, and almost all ascents had involved major sieges, sometimes lasting a couple of days. Circe had a big reputation. It had a vertical wall leading for twenty feet to a severely overhanging middle section, which bulged for another twenty feet before the angle eased off again. The crux was at the top of the vertical bit – a vicious pull on a tiny finger hold. I really wanted to do Circe and one day, as I walked out on Windy Ledge, I met a Sheffield climber, Paul, who was trying it. He had fallen off the crux and was resting on the ground. I asked him if he would belay me on it, and he said he would.

Normally we always belayed with a small, simple device called a Sticht plate, where the rope loops through slots in a thick metal plate and around a karabiner. It provides friction in the event of a fall that stops the ropes from slipping through. They're cheap, safe and easy to use. For some reason, though, Paul decided to use a waist belay. This was the old fashioned method, used before belay devices were invented, where the belayer just wraps the rope around their waist, hoping that will give enough friction if the leader falls. I had never seen anyone belaying like this in real life before and I didn't like the look of it.

I said nothing. Setting off, I moved up the lower wall and clipped the runner below the crux. Reaching up for the tiny finger hold, I placed my right foot on a small nubbin and started easing my weight onto the toehold. At the time, our EB climbing boots always wore out at the toe leaving your socks poking through. The boots were expensive, so the thing to do, when they were worn, was swap them around and put the left shoe on the right foot and the right on the left. This worked, but meant that it was hard to be precise with your footwork. Your feet could slip off holds when you weren't expecting it. As my fingers just reached the tiny hold, my foot popped off the nubbin.

My full weight swung out on the tiny finger hold. I looked down, ready to fall. When I did, I saw Paul was not only using a waist belay, but had left a huge loop of slack drooping down near the ground. He wasn't even looking at me. He was staring off down the valley towards the café. If I fall here, I thought, I'm going to hit the ground. I pulled like a madman on the little hold and, hanging on for my life, stabbed my toe back onto the nubbin. I slapped out rightwards onto better holds on the steep bit and, still totally gripped about hitting the ground, climbed as fast as I could to where it eased. I had climbed Circe on my first try, and with that, I felt that I had started to get the better of Stoney.

Lovers' Leap Café was the big centre of climbing at the time. In the morning all the dossers would meet there and soon be joined by other climbers from Sheffield, Manchester or Nottingham. For the day's climbing, we would either stay at Stoney, or decide in the café to hitch off to one of the other nearby crags – High Tor, Water-cum-Jolly, Cheedale. As soon as breakfast was finished we would wander off individually to stand by the road and start to hitch. This was never too difficult, as we would leave our rope visible so people would know we were climbers and we would often get picked up. Still, two hours was the average length of time it took to get anywhere, even though the crags were usually less than ten miles away.

One of the most famous crags at the time was High Tor, a huge white limestone face towering a hundred and fifty feet above the A6, just outside the town of Matlock. I was climbing with two really experienced climbers from Bolton and led a route called Lyme Cryme. At the top of the crag, I tied myself to a large tree and started to belay up the first climber. He arrived and also lashed himself to the tree. I pulled the rope in to belay the second climber and started chatting to the first.

They had both just come back from Yosemite and he described it to me. I had seen pictures in the magazines; it was pretty much the centre of the climbing world at the time. It had huge, 3000ft walls of perfect golden granite with routes that took climbers days and days of effort to climb. They would have to sleep on nylon hammocks tied to the rock face. Yosemite also had short, one-pitch climbs as hard as anything in the world, and some of the world's greatest bouldering.

'It sounds mind blowing,' I said.

'Yes,' he answered, smiling. We both looked down towards the road below, content.

When I was little, only three years old, my mum recalls an incident that happened as the family was driving back from the shops. Going round a roundabout, I was playing with the door in the back seat and opened it. Propelled from the car, my body went tumbling across the road and landed in the verge. The car stopped and my parents rushed over to find me totally unhurt, only crying.

Another time, I was in the back seat again, a few years older, and dad was driving. It was snowing heavily and our car unexpectedly lost control. Skidding onto the opposite lane we went straight into the path of an oncoming bus and collided with it, head on. It was in the days before back seat seatbelts and the force shot me forwards. My body, airborne, flew through the windscreen, bounced on the bonnet and off onto the road. I lost consciousness, only recovering it again later in hospital. My dad was there and was relieved to see me open my eyes. He told me that I was basically unhurt, only a few scratches.

'You went right through the windscreen, son,' he said, shaking his head. 'You must have a charmed life.'

Back on the top of High Tor, staring at the world below, I felt a tug come on the rope. The climber who was still seconding had fallen off some sixty feet below and his weight was starting to come onto the rope I was holding. I waited for the belay on the tree to support my weight, but I kept sliding towards the edge. Suddenly, more weight came onto the rope with a jolt and pulled hard at me.

The jolt whipped me right off the top of the crag. I hadn't tied onto the tree properly. I accelerated into mid air and fell at full speed down the cliff, head first. I screamed, certain I was going to die. Then the rope attached to my harness started to come tight. I came to a springy halt after falling over fifty feet, sprung back up and came to a stop. I was alive. I looked up, and not far from me, a young climber was mid-way up one of the other classics, Darius. Our eyes met. His were bulging out of his head. I felt myself collapse into gales of laughter and laughed until I was rescued from above. When seconding the route, the first climber had removed my runners from the rock and had brought them up with him, as was normal practice. However, for some reason he had left one still clipped into the other climber's rope. It was an old faded nylon sling he had found in Yosemite, attached to an old piton, placed during Lyme Cryme's first ascent twenty years before. This sling had caught the weight of the two of us falling through the air and somehow held the both of us. Why did he leave it in? How come it hadn't broken under such force? That night, I lay on the shelf in the woodshed, wide awake.

'I should have been a gonner today,' I thought to myself in disbelief, looking up at the night sky and the stars that shone in it.

Around this time I started to do new routes. Being the first person to climb a particular piece of rock means you get to name it and grade it, and your achievement is recorded and printed in a guidebook. New routes are how the sport moves on, and by doing them you're really adding something new to climbing. What's more everybody can compare themselves to what you've done. Nearly all the great climbers added new routes, and the climbs from each era can tell you what the standard was like at the time.

In the 1950s and 1960s Joe Brown's and Don Whillans' routes were the hardest of their time. In the early 1970s, Tom Proctor and Pete Livesey's routes showed where the limits were. After that, Ron Fawcett's routes were top. If you wanted to be great you had to do new routes. I did a couple at Stoney and really got a taste for it. Doing new routes held extra challenges in terms of the time it took to find and prepare a climb, but they had extra rewards too. I loved the idea of adding my name to the history of the great crags, especially if it was with a hard route.

Down at one of the local crags, Cheedale, I spotted an unclimbed groove that looked good enough and hard enough to be worth trying, and got stuck into it. This meant a lot of hard work. For three days I got up early in the morning, leaving the woodshed, hitching and walking for two hours, cleaning the line, and the same back again. Everywhere I went I carried an enormous rucksack. Everyone did. Even though I always stayed at Stoney, on our trips out we packed up everything we had, sleeping bag and mat, spare clothes, ropes, gear, shoes and any food we had, and lugged the backbreaking load all the way to the crag, and then, after a day of climbing or cleaning a route, lug it all the way back to Stoney. I have no idea why we didn't just leave our stuff at Stoney. We just didn't.

The route required a lot preparation, abseiling down with tools and brushes to clean the rock and remove any loose holds, before it was even climbable. Eventually it was ready and I went down one day with a fellow woodshed dosser, Carney. I knew it was going to be a dangerous route, with a real chance of hitting the ground. I set off and got a runner at about ten feet. I climbed on through the crux and pressed on to about thirty feet. Here it was possible to place some good runners. I fought one nut into a thin crack and was trying to fiddle in another. My arms were getting very pumped. I didn't have much energy left.

We had a motto at the time: 'When in doubt, run it out.' A run-out is the distance a climber is above their last runner. The idea behind the saying is if things are getting a bit much, don't waste time arranging protection, just press on and climb higher to easier ground. That's how you got up things. Right, I thought, on I go. Abandoning more runners, as I already had a good one in, I climbed on and then, with my arms pumped, came across some dirty rock. It was filthy and I couldn't do the move with the rock as it was. I decided I would need to clean the route some more. If I lowered off here, with yo-yo ethics, I could go to the top and give it a clean, then climb up again with the ropes clipped through the runners, avoiding the need to lead the dangerous lower section again. I warned Carney I was going to jump onto the runner. I let go, felt myself sail through the air, but the expected support from the nut and the rope never came. The nut had pulled right through the crack.

I fell free for nearly forty feet and landed on my back, right in a patch of stinging nettles, my head just missing a big rock. I sprung upright onto all fours and blood started pouring out of my mouth. Carney looked at me in horror. I was gasping for air, but was so winded I couldn't actually breathe. I felt terrified, but, looking at him, I managed to croak one word before passing out.

'Monster!'

When I came to, Carney was shouting manically: 'Fucking hell! Fucking hell! I thought I had a stiff on my hands. I thought I had a stiff on my hands!'

I just lay there. Another climber, Al Rouse, a famous mountaineer, came round the corner. He had heard the thud of my body hitting the ground from the other side of the dale and had rushed across to see what had happened.

'Bloody hell, youth, that sounded realistic,' said Rouse.

'Really?' I asked with pride.

Somehow I was okay. I was almost totally unscathed. A few chipped teeth and a cut tongue had caused the blood from my mouth, and not internal bleeding. I stood up and checked myself out. Not dead yet. My back smarted from landing in the nettles all the same, and I could feel myself starting to stiffen up.

I hobbled out and hitched back to Stoney. I limped into the café and saw the shock on Sue's face. She took me into the kitchen where she cleaned up my face and arms while she told me she had had a dream the night before that I took a serious fall. That explained her shock. Even weirder, in the café that morning, I'd glanced at my horoscope in one of the papers. This was something I almost never did. It read: 'Today you will seriously think about changing your sport.' Perhaps someone was trying to tell me something. I never read a horoscope again.

That afternoon, feeling sorry for myself, I phoned Andrew Henry and told him what had happened. Andrew told me to come over to his house in Macclesfield, which was an easy hitch from Stoney. His mum took me to hospital, where it turned out I had a broken sternum and a bruised hip. Needing more rest, I went back home to Leicester the following day.

Andrew's family has always been very kind to me. Andrew and I obviously became lifelong friends at school, and he later ended up moving to Sheffield, not long after I did, to set up a landscape gardening business. It was great to have him nearby. We used to go out together in town, and the night before Christmas Eve I dropped him off outside his house.

The following day I went to visit my parents. When I got there, I could tell something was up.

'Sit down, Jeremy,' my dad said. 'We have some terrible news. It's Andrew Henry. He's dead.'

'Oh no he isn't, I saw him last night. I dropped him off.'

In the night, with no warning, Andrew had a brain haemorrhage and died. For some reason I had to get back to Sheffield that evening. I set off from Leicester but halfway, on the motorway at midnight, my car ran out of petrol. I had to phone the breakdown assistance and wait for an hour in the cold dark night for the truck to come along and fill me up. I stood there in the darkness, by the side of the motorway, thinking over and over about my friend. It was horrendous to think that Andrew was gone, one of my best friends, no longer there.

I quickly recovered from my Cheedale fall. My legs unstiffened and my chest felt fine. I returned to Stoney a week after the fall. In the meantime another local climber, Johnny Woodward, had gone to Cheedale to try the route. This was something people just didn't do. It was an unwritten rule that if someone has put time and effort into cleaning a route, then he or she is allowed reasonable time to complete it. Everyone knew I was going to go back to Cheedale, but Woodward ignored that and actually hammered in a peg to improve the protection. People try to avoid pegs in rock if possible because, unlike nuts, they are permanent and scar the rock and lower the challenge. I had shown that the route could be climbed without a peg, but still he went down and hammered in a peg and did the climb, and named it Ninth Life as some sort of comment about my fall. He had stolen it and I was livid. A couple of weeks later he came into the café. When I saw Woodward, I felt real anger towards him and almost felt like attacking him physically. I've never spoken to him since.

As time passed and I continued to live at Stoney, it began to feel like home. I had gotten over the early struggles and was in tune with the crag. At the time, in Britain and America, there was a cult of soloing amongst climbers. Climbing without ropes, the most dangerous game in climbing, expressed their sense of freedom and acceptance of risk. I read about soloing experiences and felt enthralled by the accounts. I thought it would be good to solo a lot of the big Stoney routes one day. I loved the place and had a real personal history there; the routes were really important to me. I thought about the idea and knew it was coming. I woke up one weekday morning in the woodshed and felt perfect. The sun was shining, the air was cool and the crag was practically deserted. At about two o'clock, I put my boots and chalk bag on and wandered out along Windy Ledge.

Kellogg, Kink and Circe were the big three routes there at the time. Kink and Circe both had really hard moves on them, putting them too close to my physical limit at the time, so there was no way I would try to solo them. That left Kellogg, E4. I had done it before quite a few times and knew the moves well. I did a bouldery start up the lower wall, then tenuous crux moves over a bulge into a groove. The groove was easier, but just above it the climb became horrendously loose. I knew I could easily pull a crucial handhold off and at that point I was almost seventy feet above the ledge, with another sixty feet below that. Carefully, I climbed to the top, buzzing.

I soloed Dies Irae, E1, and having done that, Proctor's classic E4, Our Father. The last time I had led the route I had fallen off it, but this time it all felt so certain. After that came Scoop Wall, another steep long E2 corner. Next I did Special K, which was also quite loose in its upper half, and then finished with Kingdom Come, both E3. These were all big, hard routes, and I had cruised them all, solo. Less than two hours after starting, I sat down on Windy Ledge, my face turned to the evening sun.

I felt incredible, invincible, and a feeling like that stays with you forever. I had known what I wanted and had risked everything for it. In that situation, make one mistake and you're dead, no doubt about it. You're playing with the ultimate card. It's a crazy card to play in some ways and I can't imagine doing it now, but then, on that day, it was right and perfect – and amazing. More than twenty five years later, that feeling I had sitting on Windy Ledge in the evening sunshine is as fresh to me as it was on that day.

From time to time I returned to my parent's home, not just to sign on, but to catch up with family and friends. At one of these gatherings, a friend of my dad asked me what I most wanted to achieve in climbing. My dad had told him I'd become obsessed, and he thought I'd say Everest or something.

'I want to free the first pitch of Little Plum,' I told him.

Little Plum was a Stoney route that Tom Proctor had tried to free-climb. It was a two-pitch climb at the end of the crag near the village. It had first been done in the 1960s, but, as was the style at the time for very big, steep loose limestone routes, it was climbed using aid. The climbers had hammered in pegs and expansion bolts, and used these to pull themselves up the rock. It was a style of climbing nobody did any more. In fact the vogue at the time among leading climbers was freeing the routes of their aid, using the pegs and bolts only as protection and, in a way, showing how they had moved beyond the previous generation.

I tried to explain free-climbing and Little Plum to my dad's friend, but I don't think he understood. If he had actually seen it, he still wouldn't have understood. A vague groove up a hundred feet of dusty limestone above a busy road in a narrow Derbyshire valley with heavy lorries speeding along the road below doesn't seem much like the Himalaya. It's often hard to explain rock climbing to non-climbers, who are used to hearing about summits and views and adrenaline. How could I explain how important it was? The crux was a single lunge to catch a tiny fingertip hold. How could I explain that to someone who wanted to hear about walking up the side of Everest for thousands of feet in the freezing cold? It wouldn't mean anything to him that Tom Proctor had put loads time into trying to free Little Plum, but hadn't succeeded. Fawcett had tried it. Dougie Hall had tried it and Kim Carrigan had tried it. None had done it, and the fact that it had repulsed them all made it massive. In fact, Kim and Dougie, who had both recently been to America, had compared it to some of the hardest routes there.

'I think it's harder than Psycho,' Dougie said.

Wow, harder than Psycho. Psycho, in Colorado, was one of the world's top routes at the time. I had seen pictures of it. So far, despite the efforts of the world's best climbers, no one had managed to repeat it. And here, in Stoney Middleton, was a climb that might be harder than Psycho. If I were to do Little Plum, it would be incredible.

I spent a couple of days trying Little Plum's crux move, a long, dynamic throw for a little edge of limestone, about the size of the small side of a matchbox. On the second day I was getting close to holding the edge, which led to easier climbing above. Noddy was belaying me, and after another fall, he lowered me down to the belay, where we were chatting.

'Look,' he said, pointing to the road below. 'It's Kim and Dougie.'

Kim Carrigan and Dougie Hall had come out of the café and were walking up the road towards the crag. They spotted me and stopped for a look.

'They're watching you, Jerry.'

'I know.'

'Get up and try it then.'

'I don't know, it's…'

'Go on Jerry!'

'Right then,' I said to Noddy.

I moved up to the crux, squeezed a pathetic under-cling with my left hand, got a vicious little pinch hold with my right, ran my feet up the wall below, then launched my body, at full stretch for the matchbox edge above.

My fingers touched it. As the upward momentum of my body came to a stop, I fastened the tips of my fingers around it. When my body then sagged down again, all my weight came onto this tiny hold. I started squeezing, squeezing on the hold. Somehow I managed to hold it. I got my falling body under control, sorted myself out and quickly finished the pitch.

I screamed with joy at the belay. I had done it. I looked down. Dougie and Kim called up to say well done and turned to continue their walk up the road, chatting. I lowered off, and to fulfil the promise I had made to myself if I ever did this, we ran down to the café and I ordered us both a full-set breakfast: eggs, sausage, bacon, tomato, beans, fried bread, black pudding, toast and tea.

If Kim and Dougie hadn't come along and watched, I'm not sure I would have done it. At least not that time anyway. But having them watch really brought out something in me. I suppose that sense of competitiveness, a desire to impress my peers, has always been something that brought out something extra in me.

The second, still-aided pitch of Little Plum had always looked impossible and people hadn't really tried to free it. It had a six-foot overhang, which didn't appear to have any holds on it. One day, some time after doing the first pitch, I was having a rest day, and just out of curiosity, went up for a look. With Noddy belaying again, I had a few tries. Some holds at the back of the roof allowed me to stretch for the lip, but any attempts to hold this just resulted in me swinging off out of control onto the rope. It didn't look like it would go.

Sitting high up on our belay, we could see the road and café below. When I looked down, I saw someone and recognised him as Geoff Birtles. Geoff had actually done the first aided ascent of Little Plum in 1963. He didn't climb so much any more but he was now the editor of the great British climbing magazine, Crags. He recognised me and gave me a wave.

'Get on with it, stop messing about,' he called up.

Geoff Birtles is watching, I told myself. He had written about me in his magazine a few times but had never seen for himself what I could do. I wanted to show Birtles that I was the man. I moved up and surged through the moves. At the overhang, with one hand at the back, the other far away at the lip, my feet cut loose as usual, which usually meant I fell. Instead, I summoned every muscle in my body to squeeze, locked myself rigid and somehow got the swing under control. I instinctively threw one of my legs out to the lip, over my head, and used my toes to catch a hold above. This gave me a moment to get my other hand around. With the good hold in both hands, I quickly pulled up and was soon at the top of the crag. I looked down. Geoff gave me a big thumbs up and I could see he was smiling.

I had done it. I had free-climbed both pitches of Little Plum. My dream had come true. It must have been the hardest climb in the country at that time. Stoney Middleton, with Tom's routes, had once possessed the hardest climbs in Britain, and now, with my ascent, I had once again put Stoney at the top of the heap. The history of climbing ran through all the big climbs of previous generations, the great routes of Brown and Whillans, the creations of Proctor, Livesey and Fawcett. Now, it included Little Plum. I felt I had started to put my name on that list.

FOUR

American Dreamer

As soon as I got into climbing I started to read the magazines. I was given a subscription to Crags magazine for Christmas and soon sent off for all the back issues. The school climbing club had a little section in the library and that had a subscription to Mountain. I devoured these magazines, absorbed all the articles. They were inspirational, telling about the great climbing areas in the UK and the rest of the world. From reading them it was obvious where the centre of the universe was as far as climbing was concerned.

America.

Everything about it seemed cool. There were huge granite walls in Yosemite Valley where climbers would sleep in hammocks as they spent days climbing thousands of feet of overhanging rock. There were beautiful desert crags such as Joshua Tree with its magical golden boulders. There were sandstone walls with cracks that split blank faces for a hundred feet without changing width. The stories about these places blew me away. One of my favourite articles was by two Californian climbers, Mark Hudon and Max Jones. They described their efforts to free-climb some short, desperate climbs around Yosemite. In their accounts they would try these climbs repeatedly, sometimes day after day. They would climb till they could climb no more, forearms screaming in pain, fingers bleeding from being forced into tiny cracks, taking huge falls as they were unable to stop even to clip into protection. Reading their accounts, my palms sweating from excitement, I was amazed at their efforts. I thought, that's what *I* want to do. I wasn't even climbing VS at the time.

Americans even looked cool. They wore white karate pants, with tanned upper bodies, their long hair tied up in headbands. They had big chalk bags hanging from their waists, hands and wrists coated in the magical white powder. Meanwhile in England, we had Pete Livesey with his odd-looking moustache, dressed from head to toe in dull Helly Hansen fleece or old woollen jumpers to keep out the cold. I wanted to look cool. In school I would wear my white cricketing trousers, put on a John McEnroe sweatband and shiver my way shirtless along the little traversing wall behind the playing fields on cold March days. Around my waist, my wash bag hung from a piece of string, but instead of a toothbrush and bar of soap, it was filled with French chalk. French chalk is a kind of talcum powder, and while it might have looked like climbers' chalk it certainly didn't work like it. Climbers' chalk – crushed up light magnesium carbonate – is the same as gymnasts and weightlifters use to absorb sweat and improve grip. My French chalk was a horrible, slippery powder that fell off the rock and smelled funny. At the time, English climbers, influenced by the Americans, were starting to use proper chalk, but its use was very controversial. Some people said it was cheating and that the white marks it left behind destroyed all sense of adventure because it revealed where all the handholds were. A group calling themselves the Clean Hand Gang, set themselves up to oppose the use of chalk and to preserve the adventure in British climbing. On the back of the school wall, as my fingers slipped around in French chalk, I couldn't see what all the fuss was about.

Because I had absorbed magazines in my early days and was so inspired by what climbers were doing in other countries, I had always seen climbing as a global thing. I didn't see my peers purely as other British climbers, but wondered how the routes I was doing compared to those in Germany, France and America. At the time, top climbers would travel a lot. If you were going to be good you had try and do the hardest routes in other countries. It doesn't seem to be like this quite so much any more, with people spending longer and longer on a climb, often on their home turf, but in the 1980s that was the state of play in climbing. After my time in Tremadog where I climbed Strawberries, and then at Stoney where I had freed Little Plum, I felt that I had done the hardest climbs in Britain. When I decided that I should travel to try to test myself on a worldwide scale, there was only one place to go: America.

A friend from Sheffield, Chris Gore, was also keen on the idea, so we made plans to travel together. Chris was the perfect person to go with. First, he was a terrific climber who I respected. At 23, he was also a bit older than me and he had a driver's licence. He had been to America before and knew about some other great venues. A plan was soon made: we would go to America and try their hardest routes.

In the late 1970s, Jim Collins was one of the great American climbing legends. I had read about his routes in the magazines and they really stood out for me. I read about his training regimes. He would climb up the undersides of flights of steps without using his feet in order to strengthen his arms. He would do mammoth stamina traverses on outdoor walls, carrying a pin between his teeth. When his fingertips became blistered from so much traversing, he would hang on with one hand, and burst the blisters with the pin and carry on. Wow! On the fingerboard at the Polytechnic gym in Sheffield where we used to do pull-ups, someone had written in felt-tip pen: 'Jim Collins was here.' Every time I did a pull up, I would struggle to pull my body up to the top, and would see the message in front of me: 'Jim Collins was here.'

There were two routes that Collins had done in 1978 and 1979 that sounded like the living end: Psycho and Genesis, both in Colorado's Eldorado Canyon. Both had taken the super-strong Collins a lot of work, Genesis supposedly needing over a hundred attempts. A hundred attempts! Since this had first been climbed, no one had managed to repeat them, despite the efforts of many great climbers. I knew that Dougie Hall and Kim Carrigan had tried them. When I saw them at Stoney I asked them what they were like.

'Bloody desperate, Jerry. Horrendous.'

Psycho was a very short roof climb. Almost a boulder problem, it crossed an enormous overhang, with just two holds in the middle of it. I loved this sort of climbing, thuggy and powerful, and really fancied a go at it. Genesis was a slightly overhanging wall climbed on tiny fingerholds. I pored over the pictures of the climbs in Mountain. Collins looked very tall, and he was stretched out on Genesis, making it look very reachy. He wore a tiny little pair of shorts, a white flat cap and long white sports socks that came really far up his legs. He looked like a proper athlete. Jim Collins was The Man and I became obsessed with doing his routes.

Another climb I wanted to do was Supercrack at a crag in upstate New York called the Shawangunks, or the Gunks, as climbers called it. Supercrack was graded a bit easier than Psycho and Genesis, but it was one of the most beautiful lines I had ever seen. A single thin crack split a steep clean wall perfectly for a hundred feet. I had always been inspired by finger cracks and this looked like one of the best.

A friend of mine from Sheffield, Pete O'Donovan, or Pod as we called him, had tried Supercrack recently. He just missed getting it on his first attempt, but had done it second go, a brilliant effort. Previously, the quickest ascent had taken three days.

'You could flash that, Jerry,' he told me.

Flash Supercrack? Climb it on my first try with no falls or rests? Really?

Pod was sure that with the right training, it would be possible. As the idea grew in my head, I probed him for every piece of info about the route. He told me about finger stacks, a way of curling your fingers around in certain sizes of crack to make a good hold, that are crucial on the pitch. What size are the jams, how steep is it? Where are the rests, where are the easiest runners to place? What sizes of nut do I need? Questions, questions. He told me everything he thought I would need to know, and from then on I dedicated myself to preparing for America.

I went to the Peak and trained every day. For Supercrack I tried to do as many fingertip cracks as I could. I looked everywhere for any climb that would push my stamina or technique on cracks. On Curbar Edge there is a climb called Insanity with a steep crack that you climb by leaning to the right. I worked out that doing this face-on, jamming straight into it, would make its grade harder, so I continually top-roped this, up and down, never taking rests.

For Psycho, I worked out at Tom's Roof. Tom's Roof is a small, dirty bouldering cave halfway up the crag at Stoney Middleton. It was named after Stoney legend Tom Proctor who did the original problem there. Proctor was a real visionary, and this problem, like so many of his climbs, was largely unrecognised, but ahead of its time. The roof of the cave has one hold, enough for the tips of the fingers of two hands. Tom's original problem stretches across the roof to get the hold, then uses it to lunge for a good hold on the lip of the cave. It covered about seven horizontal feet with just one fingerhold. From the pictures I had seen of Psycho, it seemed perfect training, so I began to work out lots of hard eliminates based on Tom's problem. These 'eliminates', problems that eliminated good holds to make the original a lot harder, allowed me to focus on the difficulties of Psycho.

I gave all the eliminates I invented different names, like the Swing Thing and God's Golden Power Allowance That He Gave Unto Me. I worked out a long sequence that linked many of the problems together. I'd start at the back of the cave, with a problem called The Womb. I'd climb out on this, go into Power Allowance, reverse Tom's Roof and finish on Swing Thing. This link-up was called Jerryatrics and it was perfect training. I would spend ages there by myself – at the time, nobody else was bouldering in order to train – and I felt myself getting stronger, fitter and more powerful. I followed the same process for Genesis. One of the best bouldering areas at Stoney is Minus Ten Wall, a thirty-foot-wide wall of vertical limestone, covered in small, polished fingerholds. It was possible to work out endless desperate problems on this, which trained my fingers for the style of climbing on Genesis.

It's hard to put across how motivated I was and how hard I trained, but looking back, one day in particular summed it all up. Chris, who had a car at the time, had arranged to give me a lift to Raven Tor. We were to meet at the Polytechnic gym at ten next morning. I spent the night before with a friend in Sheffield, and in the morning marched through cold, heavy rain to arrive at the Polytechnic at 9.30, excited and in a great mood. I knew Raven Tor was steep enough to stay dry in the rain, and what's more, I had a lift there. Lifts to the crag were rare, and Raven Tor was desperate to get to by public transport. Eventually Chris showed up and I ran to his car to get in. However, he said he had changed his mind. It was too cold and wet he said, and he couldn't be bothered going.

I was gutted. I had been looking forward to this so much. Chris drove off, but I wasn't going home. I walked in the rain to a roundabout at the edge of the city, began hitching, and within an hour, arrived at Stoney Middleton. I knew of a little cave there, not Tom's Roof, which I knew would be wet, but another, just beside the main road. I knew it would stay dry, as I'd spent a lot of time there the previous winter. I was dropped off in the main street near the café. The day was dark, and by now sleet was starting to fall. I ran up the dale and into the shelter of the roadside cave. One of the things that I always carried in my rucksack was a blowtorch, which I used to dry out damp holds. Having dropped my bag, I searched around outside the cave and gathered up a bundle of sticks. I piled them up and blowtorched them until they caught light and soon had a blaze going. I was cold and wet, so I dried myself off in front of the fire. Once I was warmer I began to do laps on a traverse at the back of the cave, forward and back, over and over again. At one end there was a large flat hold, with no good footholds, where I would practice recovering my strength between traverses. Each time I got back to it, I would shake the blood back into my arms until I had recovered enough to do another. After a few I would go back and sit in front of the fire and warm myself up again.

It was brilliant. I remember thinking: 'I'm the only one who is training; I'm getting an edge over everybody else. Everybody else is in Sheffield, nobody else is climbing. Everything's wet. I'm the one who's found a dry bit of rock, I'm the one who has found the motivation to get out here. This is why I'm going to be the best.' I happily spent the day there, a freezing cold October midweek day, as the rain and sleet lashed down outside, sitting by the fire, warming my hands up, doing some more traverses. This is so much fun, I thought to myself. I was completely happy.

Chris had a job at the time working on the buses, so was usually busy during the week, and he was having problems with his girlfriend. Because of this his preparation wasn't that good. I wasn't going to let anything get in my way, women, work or anything like that. Maybe that was why I never had a girlfriend, but at the time I was confused by Chris's attitude: 'What's all that about? Why isn't he training?'

Finally, in September 1982, it was time to leave for America. We had a big party in Sheffield, so I'd gone to the supermarket for a case of Pomade, the cheap, fizzy wine drink we had been fond of at school. The following morning we got the bus to Sheffield Parkway, from where we were to set off on our journey to London. While Chris hitched, I leaned over the crash barrier, puking my guts up. No one gave us a lift and eventually we had to get the train. We flew out of Heathrow the next day, arriving in New York late in the evening. We took a taxi through Times Square and, looking out the window, I was blown away by the fact that I was finally here. My brother Simon had been in New York the year before, and I had loved his stories of the place. We got the last bus to New Paltz, a university town close to the Gunks, and collapsed, exhausted, in a motel late that night. I woke up next morning, still exhausted, aware of some funny noises and voices in the room. I sat up to see Chris sat on the edge of the bed watching cartoons.

'Fifty-two channels,' he said in amazement. In England at the time, we only had three.

The trip didn't start too well. It rained all that day, and for the next two. Instead of doing anything sensible like relaxing or getting over our jetlag, we found a bridge that we could climb under and spent the three days training. I can't remember why that seemed like a good idea. Keenness, I suppose. On the fourth morning, when it eventually dried up, we raced to the crag.

It was autumn and the trees were changing. Red, yellow, brown, orange, just the way I had imagined it would be, only more beautiful. We had already heard of some classics to try and wasted no time in having a go at them. However the climbing was hard, and to start with, we got our arses kicked. I had never climbed on this kind of rock before, so even routes of 5.11 felt desperate. The American grading system is different from the British; everything is 5.something, 5.8, 5.9, 5.10 and so on, which are then divided into a, b, c and d. In the Gunks, 5.11b, which should be about E3 or E4, felt really hard. I didn't mind this, because in a way that's why I had come here, to challenge myself on different types of rock and different styles of climbing, to see what I could learn from them. I really had to fight on routes that should have been easy, but after a few days we began to get used to it.

We tried a 5.11d one day. It had a desperate rockover, one neither of us could do, despite a bunch of tries. Two climbers came along and introduced themselves as Harrison Decker and John Sherman. They tried it, but they too had no success. There was some gear left in the climb, and as we had all decided we had failed, and Sherman had been last to try it, he offered to climb out along a big ledge and get it back.

Walking out on the ledge, he clipped an old peg for protection. Further on, he held a large flake of rock. But the flake wasn't attached and he pulled it off. He fell. His weight came onto the peg and it ripped from the rock. He went thirty feet, crashing through a tree and smacked into the ground. Sherman looked badly hurt and Decker ran off for help. After a while John opened his eyes.

'What happened?'

'You fell off. Don't move. Decker has gone for help. How do you feel?'

'Oh, I gotta pee.'

'Don't stand up, you might be hurt.'

He stood up for a piss, but couldn't do one, so sat back down again.

'What happened?'

We told him. And again he wanted to stand up for a piss. Nothing. He sat back down again.

'What happened?'

Then, after a minute, he looked at me.

'Hey, I know you. Don't I know you? You've been in the magazines, right?'

He's seen me, I thought. I've been recognised. Somebody's recognised me. I tried to be cool.

'I've seen you,' he repeated, 'What happened? I gotta pee. I've seen you.'

I was getting more and more excited.

'Yeah, maybe you have seen me in climbing magazines,' I said, grinning with pleasure and pride.

'Yeah,' he said. 'You're Gary Gibson, right?'

Oh god no, I thought. He thinks I'm Gary Gibson.

Gary Gibson was another British climber renowned for doing loads of new routes in Britain, nothing exceptionally hard, just hundreds and hundreds of new routes. Bloody hell, I thought, that's a kick in the teeth.

Sherman recovered. He wasn't known then, but went on to become one of America's more prolific boulderers. Gary Gibson went on to do thousands of new routes.

At the campsite we met a guy called Skip Guerin, who was one of the best climbers in America at the time. Although he kept himself to himself, we became friendly, and he wanted to do some of the routes that we did, so we began climbing together. He was a tall, skinny Californian with long blond hair, and had a super-relaxed air about him. Skip was never in too much of a hurry. He stretched a lot, which was weird because nobody stretched in England. I would stand there talking to him and then he'd throw his leg over the top of a table and start bending down and doing the splits. He'd be chatting to me and stretching and I was thinking, 'Weird. Stretching for climbing? What's that for? You just need to be strong and do pull-ups!'

During our two-week stay, we ticked our way through lots of classics. One day I took a walk over to look at Supercrack. The reason I wanted to do it was because in the photos I had seen, it was a beautiful line. In reality it looked even better. A thin, finger-width crack split a huge white wall with no other features apart from an overhang at half-height. I sat there by myself for nearly an hour looking at it, feeling my desire to climb it grow stronger and stronger. I wanted to climb it, but more than anything, I wanted to flash it, climb it first go, with no falls.

Talking to Skip that night, it turned out that he was returning to his home in Colorado in a couple of days. That was where we were heading next. I hadn't known how we were going to get there, so when he said he'd give us a lift, we were delighted. This was perfect, but it meant it was crunch time – I had to go try Supercrack in the next two days. I had planned to have rest days before trying it to recover some of the strength I had lost from so much hard climbing in the weeks before, but I felt like I was climbing really well. I thought: 'I feel good. I'll not bother with a rest day. I'll just try it.' In the morning Chris, Skip and I made the hour and a half walk to the crag, and soon I found myself tying onto the rope at the base of Supercrack.

It reared above me. The pressure just to get on it was great, and I felt impatient, so I made myself sit for a while longer and let myself relax. It was easy to become overwhelmed, to think: 'This is it. This is what I've trained for, now is the time – I'm going to have to flash it.' But I had to focus: 'I'm going to try my hardest. I'm going to give it my best shot and just see what happens.' It's tough when you've dreamt about something and you've trained so hard for it, and the time finally comes.

At last I felt ready: 'Right, come on, let's try it.'

Hard moves came at me from the start. Feeling determined and fully focused, I rammed my fingers in and jammed up the bottom of the crack. At about fifty feet, beneath the mid-height overhang, I saw a tiny finger-hold on the wall just left of the crack and grabbed for it. It was small, but was a welcome change from the savage finger-jamming below. I quickly placed a good nut and pulled around the overhang above, to where I knew there was a large flat hold. By now I was badly pumped. I just about got to this hold and my right hand curled around it. It was square-cut and flat-topped and had a cool, smooth texture. As soon as I touched it I flipped back to the damp cave at Stoney Middleton, to the smooth flat-topped hold where I would spend ages hanging on while I recovered strength between traverses. It wasn't a great hold, by any means, and there were no footholds, but I knew immediately I could shake out on it and recover, because I'd spent the whole year hanging on this jug. 'I'm back at Stoney,' I thought, and my body relaxed. I knew how long I could hang on here for, and knew that in doing this, I would get all my strength back, and doing exactly that, recovered almost completely.

The crux was now to get stood on the flat hold, but with the strength I had recovered from shaking out, I scraped through it and stood up. I placed one more nut. I've done the hard bit, I said to myself. Above, the route was there for the taking. I readied myself for the remaining battle above. Stay calm, relax and concentrate, I thought to myself. Every climber knows that feeling. It's no different from doing your first VS or your first E1. When you know you're through the crux and it's yours for the taking and you're pumped and fighting. The muscles in my forearms were bulging with blood and lactic acid, and screaming in pain. I grasped hold after hold, almost coming off every move. Come on. Come ON. My feet slipped on the rock, fingers just about uncurling from the holds. In this way, I clawed my way to the belay.

'YES, I've done it!' I surged with joy.

Later Chris tried. He did really well – I think he might have got to the flat jug first go, then fell off. He lowered down, but didn't rest long enough. 'I'll give it another quick go,' he said impatiently. He got near the hold again and fell, then tried again a bit too quickly before he had rested. Up again, his fingers slipped, making less ground each time.

That's all part of climbing. You fall off and come down and because you are feeling psyched and annoyed at yourself for making a mistake, you want to go straight back on it. As soon as you start climbing like that you won't get anywhere. If I ever fell off, I would come to the ground, get a stopwatch out and make sure I rested for half an hour. It's hard to do. But you've got to stay calm, not get angry, and keep a level head. I wasn't always like that – plenty of times I was up there screaming, kicking the rock, cursing and flailing – but that doesn't get you through the route any quicker. It just makes it a lot worse.

In the end Chris gave up. The next day we were heading to Colorado, so we packed up our stuff and headed to the parking lot. Skip had a nice car, a sporty red Lancia and we squeezed ourselves and our stuff into the back. On the back seat of the car was a large shoebox. I opened it. It was full of music cassettes, and as Skip got in, he pointed to the box. 'Before we get to Colorado we're going to have listened to all of those tapes at least twice.' I was looking at it and thinking that's impossible. But we did. It was almost all Grateful Dead and a few other equally dire groups. There were one or two tapes of The Doors, which was a bit of a relief, and then it was back to the Grateful Dead. Skip drove day and night. It was a long, hot journey. Three days across America. Finally we arrived in Boulder, entirely knackered.

Skip had said we could stay with him, so it was with tired relief that we staggered in late at night to collapse on his living-room floor. Skip's place on North Twelfth Street was a great house and we were to end up staying there for two months. It was an hour's walk to the bouldering crags at Flagstaff that I had read about in my John Gill book, and a short drive to Eldorado Canyon, home of Psycho and Genesis. The house was full of climbers, who either lived there or who popped round and it was always really good fun.

But first things first:

'Come on, Chris, let's go shopping.'

We had to go shopping for white tube socks and tiny sports shorts. The Colorado look, pioneered by Collins and his friends, was where it was at, and we wanted to get with it. The tube socks, long sports socks, parallel sided, without any knitted heel, had to come half-way up the calf. The ultimate was to try to get the tube sock tan line, a deep bronze that went from the crotch area, where the tiny sports shorts finished, to a point mid-way between the knee and the ankle, where the socks finished. We wanted to look cool like Americans, not with baggy tracksuit trousers and big red socks like British climbers. As I walked out of the shop that morning into the Colorado sunshine with my new socks and shorts, I felt like a million dollars. Funnily enough, I have a British climbing magazine from the following year where I made a front cover, climbing Master's Wall in Wales. There I was, in the freezing shadows of a north-facing Welsh mountain crag, still dressed in the tube socks and sports shorts. I think by then the tan had faded.

Back at Skip's house that day, I saw a familiar face.

'Hey! Hi Jerry.'

'Hi Jack. What are you doing here?'

'Man, I live here.'

I had known 'Jack' from the UK, where he had visited the year before, and it was great to see him again. I had met him at Stoney where I saw him leaning against Minus Ten Wall looking at the trees and, as was usual for me at the time, I went up and asked him for a belay.

'Fancy doing some climbing?'

Yeah, he said, and that was the beginning of a great week for me. Every day he came out with me, always happy to belay, and never seemed to want to climb himself. Yet he was content and always seemed really mellow. He'd say strange things, like: 'Isn't this place so beautiful,' which was strange, because Stoney was a bit of a shit hole, or say, 'The leaves are on the trees.' Of course they are Jack, that's where they live. Or I'd be fighting my way up a route, and I'd come down, and he'd say, 'Oh man, up there, you were soooo pumped, huh?' At the time, I just thought Americans were a bit odd, in a really nice way, but still a bit odd. When I met him again in Boulder, it all started to make a bit more sense.

Every morning Jack would get up and take LSD. This powerful hallucinogenic drug set him up for the day and he would then just go about his 'normal' routine in a fairly content manner. I recognised this manner from before, and when I asked him, he said yes, he had smuggled a bottle of liquid LSD into the UK when he visited the year before and would consume some every day before going to the crag. Looking back, my first thought was that if I had known, I would not have been so content with him belaying me. But then on second thoughts, if that's what it took for someone to be happy to belay me for an entire week, then it was worth the risk.

Boulder was a real party town. Everyone seemed quite well off, lots of sports cars and enormous trucks. Even the climbers seemed pretty rich, at least to Chris and me. We were still living on as little money as possible, and despite the party atmosphere, we could never afford to drink. For food, we sussed out how to eat for free. There was a place near where we lived that made bagels, and any bagels they hadn't sold would be put outside the back door at the end of the day. This was great – free bagels. They were a bit stale, but we didn't care. After climbing we'd go to bars where there was a happy hour. We'd have one drink – our usual still orange – and get free food. Not proper food, but little blocks of cheese, peanuts and a bit of salad. We would bring a plastic bag and fill it with cheese and peanuts and any other bits of food, and go back and have cheese and nuts on toasted bagels. We ate well and spent virtually nothing.

Skip lived with a climber called Bob Horan. Bob, like Skip, had tried Genesis and Psycho without success. He and Skip told us tales of desperation, tiny holds, footless climbing, about Jim Collins trying the routes hundreds of times, and about the legends of Eldorado. Eldorado was a steep, narrow-sided valley, the vertical red and gold walls only about three hundred feet from side to side. It was one of the most historic climbing areas in the States, where standards had always been pushed. Climbers like Layton Kor, Steve Wunsch and Jim Erickson had all created masterpieces here. Jules Verne, T2, The Naked Edge, all amazing climbs, the Psychos of their day.

Climbing on the diamond-hard Eldorado sandstone, bouldering at Flagstaff and Horsetooth, we grew stronger and more into the groove of the local rock. The time felt right to try what I had come here to try. Skip, Chris and I went to Eldorado one day and warmed up, then we climbed an easy first pitch that led us to the belay below Psycho.

Above, the roof loomed enormously outwards for what must have been almost ten feet. My mind raced back to the wet cold days at Stoney where I imagined myself being in this position a million times. At the back of the overhang, just above us, were undercut holds. In the middle of the roof there was a small fingertip edge. Round the overhang and out of sight, I knew there was an enormous jug. The problem was to link the three holds together. We huddled on the belay, chattering excitedly. A cold wind was whistling down the canyon, its chill adding to my nerves. I climbed easily to the overhang and clipped a bolt runner in the roof and returned to the belay to ready myself. Time to get on.

I had seen pictures of Collins climbing the route and knew exactly how he had done it. I moved up to the undercuts, ran my feet up the steep wall. In a bunched position, I locked off my left arm and reached out to get the fingerhold in the middle of the roof with my right hand. Now, as Collins had done, I swung my feet off the back wall and rotated them around 180 degrees to the lip of the overhang and hooked my toes around to try to get some grip. Hanging upside down under the roof my body felt like it was crucified onto the overhang. It was an incredible position, but not one I could move out of very easily. Trying desperately to control the swinging of my body, I took my left hand off the undercuts. I then had to reach all the way through and try to get it onto and around the lip of the overhang. I tried, but I just couldn't get my left hand near the lip. Everything felt awkward and tied up. I fell off and my weight sagged onto the rope. I tried again, but couldn't get my hand anywhere near. Off. Try again. Off.

Cold and dejected, I lowered down to the belay. The other two had a go, also without success, and eventually we all returned to the ground. As we walked down the canyon that evening, I was quiet. This is going to be a lot harder than I was expecting, I thought.

That night in Skip's house, I decided that it would help if I were more flexible. I had half-watched Skip do his stretches, but I had never stretched myself. I put my left foot up on a table, grabbed the edge of it and cranked my body down towards my foot with all my force. This was the equivalent of trying to get strong by bending over and attempting to pick up a two hundred pound load. As I stood up, it felt like my hamstring had been used to tow a truck. I limped off to bed.

Next day we went back. I warmed up and climbed to the belay. Once again I tried executing Collins' contorted sequence, stabbing my toe out to the lip of the overhang. And once again, when I tried to reach my hand through, I felt my body about to swing off. Then, hanging there, it occurred to me that this was just like one of my eliminates in Tom's Roof. On Power Allowance, I had swapped hands on the roof hold, just like this one, before reaching through. It seemed like a much more natural way of doing Psycho. Quickly I managed to swap the fingers of my right hand for the left. I then started reaching out for the jug around the lip.

I can remember it as clearly as yesterday. Almost in slow motion, I saw my right hand going forward. My mind raced. I'm going to do this. I'm going to do this. I'm going to do Psycho. This is impossible. Only Jim Collins can do Psycho. I watched my hand go round the lip, it grabbed the jug and that was it. I pulled up and clipped the belay and lowered off. I had done Psycho. First try of my second day. It blew me away.

After that I tried Genesis. This was a very different climb, only slightly overhanging, but made difficult by having very small hand- and footholds. The first time I tried it I really struggled. The climb had a definite crux that involved a massive reach from a big, but not particularly good hold, with feet pressing hard off tiny footholds, to a small hold miles up and left. Time and time again I tried this move but just couldn't get the distance. I wasn't sure what to do, and the move really baffled me. At the end of a lot of attempts, I lowered off. That night I was talking to Boulder climber, Bob Horan, who had attempted Genesis on numerous occasions. He told me how he had tried it, using the big hold in a different, less obvious way, making the long reach possible. I went up the next day and, using Bob's sequence, fired it off. I had done Psycho and now had done Genesis, two of America's hardest climbs.

After that I spent the rest of the trip mainly bouldering at Horsetooth and Flagstaff, often doing second ascents and repeats of John Gill problems. I had borrowed a copy of *Master of Rock* from the Boulder County Library and would wander the hillsides with the book, using the pictures to identify problems, repeating anything I found – The Capstan, Traverse of Hen Cloud, Just Right – amazing problems, all really tough. I did this for about a month, every day, walking from the house on North Twelfth Street, fingers in shreds from constant climbing, tape holding my skin together. Interestingly, I remember that before leaving on the trip, I had tried to do a one-arm pull-up and couldn't. One day in Skip's house, there was a gymnastics ring, and out of curiosity, I decided to try one again. I hung straight from one arm and pulled myself all the way into the lock-off position. With each arm. Beside the ring was a pull-up bar with a loop of climbing webbing through it. I hooked the middle finger of my right arm through this, hung off it, and again, straight away did a one-finger, one-arm pull up. Something was working right.

Over the month Skip and Chris had continued to work on Psycho and both did it. One of the last days of the trip we were all in Eldorado canyon. It was a Saturday. The crags were busy with local and travelling climbers. I belayed Chris as he had a go at Genesis and, impressively, he managed to do it. After he had clipped the belay I lowered him to the ground. Looking again at the great climb, I decided to have a go at top roping it.

At the time our EBs were expensive and precious, and to preserve them, I had done a lot of bouldering in my trainers. I decided to do Genesis in my trainers, despite it being a route that required the use of tiny footholds. They were white, with a blue Nike flash on them. I tied on and shot up the route. In front of all the other climbers.

I have a video of an American climbing TV programme made at the time called *On The Rocks*, about climbing in the area. I am on it, and at one point the interviewer asked me what I liked about climbing? I looked into the camera:

'I like burning people off.'

I don't remember thinking like that, being so competitive, but there it is, on film. I like burning people off. I had gone to America and in front of everyone, I had top-roped one of their hardest routes in a pair of trainers. Brilliant.

If the trip had ended there it would still have been a trip of a lifetime. But there was one more climb I wanted to do. The previous year, the British Mountaineering Council had organised an international climbing meet in the Peak District and I had gone along. There was an American climber there called Randy Vogel. Randy had written the guidebook for Joshua Tree, a major climbing area in California. I had heard about a desperate route there called Equinox, a fierce crack climb first led by Tony Yaniro. I asked Randy about it.

'You know what, man? Don't even bother. Don't even *bother*. That thing is sick. It's desperate. It'll cut your fingers to shreds and you won't get up it. It's *hard*, man, like, *real* hard. It took Yaniro *days* to lead that thing. Hell, it even took *Bachar* three days to *top-rope* it. *No* chance.'

I just nodded in agreement, but Randy's attitude got me fired up. Who the hell is Bachar, I thought. What makes Randy think he's so much better than me? So he thinks I can't do Equinox, eh?

Right, I thought, I'm having that.

Back in America, with Psycho and Genesis done, it was time to go to Joshua Tree. In Boulder, once again, luck was with us. Jack wanted his VW bus delivering from Colorado to LA, only three hours from Joshua Tree. Chris and I embarked on a three-day drive west. We got to LA and took a bus to the small town of Joshua Tree. From there, we spent a few hours hitching to the crag, pitched our tent and once again began the process of struggling desperately with a new style of climbing and a new kind of rock.

The crystalline granite tended to give two particular types of climb: desperate, holdless slabs where you would scratch with your fingernails to try to claw onto anything at all to help you while your EBs slipped around ineffectually on poor smears, or steep cracks, where you would mash in your fingers, hands or fists and pull, with no footholds either side of the crack to help you. Both felt nearly impossible. I battled up 5.9s and 5.10s, trying not to let my pride take too much of a battering. Chris, who had been before and had great footwork, was climbing well on the slabs and ended up doing all the leading. I struggled even to follow.

On the third day there I was roping up below Spiderline, a 5.11 hand-sized crack, for what I knew would be a fight. A figure appeared around a nearby corner: white karate pants, tanned skin, a flat cap turned backwards, long flowing blond hair, and a pair of light-coloured rock shoes, different from the EBs that everyone else wore. I looked at Chris.

'It's John Bachar!'

I had seen pictures of the American climbing legend and recognized him instantly. He seemed to be walking in our direction. He seemed to be coming right up to us.

'Hi!'

'Hello.'

'Are you... Jerry... Mullett... Mufflett...?'

Word of Supercrack, Psycho and Genesis had obviously spread, even as far as Bachar. The name thing was obviously deliberate.

'Yeah. It's Moffatt.'

'Sure it is. Good to see you.'

And with that, of all the routes at Joshua Tree, of all the thousands of routes, he squeezed between Chris and me, and soloed the one climb we were about to try. With ease. He disappeared over the top and was gone. I led it and almost puked with the effort.

John Bachar. The legend. Over the time we were to spend there, I was going to get to know Bachar really well and climb with him a lot. He is an amazing character, intelligent, funny and capable of displays of the greatest generosity and the most frustrating behaviour imaginable. In years to come he would pay out of his own money to have me see specialists to help me over a terrible injury and then he would later chip the holds off one of my best ever problems out of frustration. Over the weeks to come he would explain to me all his hard-earned knowledge about climbing and training to help me improve, while at the same time not even tell me how to do a boulder problem.

For example, I was trying a Bachar problem at Cap Rock one day and getting nowhere. The man shows up.

'This is hard, John, how did you do it?'

He wouldn't tell me.

'What? What do you mean you won't tell me?'

He wouldn't tell me. Bachar reckoned he had got this trait from John Gill; never tell anyone how to do a problem. Let them figure it out, because *it's part of the problem*. I kept trying different methods and getting nowhere. All the time Bachar stood there in silence, watching me flail. I couldn't believe it. A few days later I was there again with a friend of Bachar's, Mike Lechlinski.

'Oh yeah,' Mike said. 'Bachar hooked a heel around the corner there.'

I tried it. With the heel hooked, supporting some of my weight, the holds all worked, and I soon did the problem. Later that week, I went up there again. Chris was there. He had heard me talk about the problem and had fancied a go.

'Hi Jerry. How did you do this, I can't quite work it out?'

'Can't tell you, I'm afraid, Chris.'

'What!'

I wouldn't tell him. What an idiot. Sorry Chris. It was the only time we fell out in six and a half months.

When I look back on my time there, of course I remember the climbing. But the really special thing about Joshua Tree, by far the most amazing thing about my time there, was the simplicity of life. We had no car, but once every week we could get a lift into town. This was an hour's drive away and the only source of water. Otherwise we stayed in the park the whole time, in the campsite or on the crag. We would get up an hour or so after dawn, when the sun had taken some chill out of the cold desert air, then sit around for an hour while we heated water and ate breakfast. As the day warmed up, we would stretch and chat, do some pull ups to warm up and joke around. Then we'd go to climb, in large groups or as a pair, or alone to solo. In the evening we would return and cook dinner. When night fell we would build a fire and all gather round and chat or drink tea staring at the flames. We did this every night, and I remember lots of the time just staring into the flames or looking upwards at the stars. The stars in the sky above Joshua Tree are mind blowing. I'd never seen so many in my life.

Joshua Tree National Park is a beautiful place, a real wilderness. It's a desert, with rocky hillsides covered with huge golden granite boulders and outcrops, all scattered about to create a complex and interesting landscape. The stumpy black Joshua trees were everywhere. We were to stay here for three months, and I would get to know the place inside out, every tree, every boulder. In secret places you would find ancient Indian rock art, and sometimes I would spend all day wandering, lost, discovering things.

There was a great group of climbers hanging out there. There was a guy called John Long, one of America's most famous climbers in the 1970s. Night climbing was one of his things and he would lead us off on amazing easy climbs by moonlight, taking exposed routes to the tops of the outcrops. Sitting on top and with us gathered round, he would then tell stories. He was a great storyteller, really funny, fantastic, barely-believable stuff. They might have been exaggerated, but it didn't matter, they were great stories. Long went on to become one of the great climbing writers in America.

Chris and I continued to work our way through the classics, getting stronger, fitter, and most of all, used to the Joshua Tree granite. I said to Bachar that I was going to try to do Equinox. Hopefully, with enough tips from him I would be able to do it in less than three days.

'No, man. You should flash that thing.'

Flash it? When it had taken him three days to top-rope it and Yaniro even longer to lead it?

'Sure man, that thing can be flashed.'

Captivated by the idea, I decided I would try to flash Equinox.

I knew I was not good enough to do it just then. I would have to make myself a better climber, really move myself on to a point where doing it might become a reality. But I knew I could. I still had lots of time left in Joshua Tree, but most of all, I had Bachar.

From the moment I met John Bachar, I knew he was someone I could really learn from. Apart from being a brilliant climber, I soon realised he was very analytical about his activities. He read books on diet, training, movement – anything that would have a bearing on how well he climbed. In that sense he was a real pioneer, as no one had approached climbing like that before. He devoured these books, understood their principles and adapted them. And now, with his help, I was going to train and develop my climbing, and move it on to a new level.

Bachar told me about diet. Up to that point I would eat whatever filled me up for the least amount of money. This would be free peanuts, sliced bread, curry sauce, ketchup, white rice, stale bagels. I almost never ate vegetables or fruit. He always ate really well, mostly a vegetarian diet. He gave me a book called *Diet for a Small Planet*. It talked about eating different types of food groups together so you could release the amino acids and utilise them to get all the proteins out of the food. It explained how this would give you the energy needed to recover after training and how this would mean you could train more.

Bachar explained the importance of training power over stamina. Stamina, or fitness, is the ability to do forty pull-ups. Power is the ability to do two pull-ups loaded with a one hundred pound weight belt. Raw strength. Being stronger meant that moves would feel easier and so, on a long climb, all the moves will take less out of you. This means you will get less pumped, meaning in a way, you gain stamina. However, no amount of stamina will help you do a really hard move. For that you need brute power. The other benefit of training for power is that it is harder to gain, but stays with you longer. The last time I did a one-arm pull-up, the classic test of power, was in 2002. I know that with a little bit of training I could do one again in a month. That power will still be in there.

A particular thing Bachar was in to, was soloing. He used to solo a lot, go on huge circuits around Joshua Tree, often on really hard and high routes.

'Soloing is the *ultimate* form of climbing.'

He was never short of a strong opinion and it was quite like him to say something like that, telling me what the *ultimate* was. He was very good at soloing and had a really good climbing style for it. He moved in a very precise, assured way. He never messed around with his feet, always placed them perfectly and smoothly. He could do the splits and was able to use all sorts of bridging moves. Bachar had one of the best climbing styles I have ever seen. Even today, I don't think I have seen anyone climb better than him, smooth, flowing, certain.

I remember once asking him about his soloing, if he ever got scared. He looked at me.

'Death is a gift,' he said. 'Without it, life has no value.'

It's a Bruce Lee quote, and it *almost* sounded ridiculous, but when I thought about what John had said, I saw the truth in it.

Bachar studied martial arts, read books like the *Tao of Jeet Kune Do* by Bruce Lee for ideas and ways of thinking that were applicable to climbing. A lot of the time when you're climbing, John explained, you really want to be letting go of holds, not gripping them harder. Find ways of applying just the right amount of force to a hold, he suggested, instead of wasting lots of energy. Relax the entire body. Flow.

Bachar lent me *Zen in the Art of Archery*, a book about a guy from the West who goes to Japan and meets with a monk who is going to teach him archery. When he first meets with the monk he cannot draw the arrow back. Physically it is just too hard. He would struggle with the bowstring, never able to budge it. By the end of his apprenticeship, he's not even pulling the arrow any more. It seems to draw back of its own accord.

Bachar also thought a lot about the Chinese idea of chi and told me about some of its ideas. By making a ring with his thumb and forefinger, he explained, he could channel energy from the ground. It would come up the body, down the arm, create a vortex in the ring formed by the thumb and finger. By relaxing into it, he explained, it is impossible to split the thumb and finger. In this way John could summon enormous amounts of energy from the earth. He used this method once on a desperate boulder problem in Joshua Tree, The Anglo Saxophone. He summoned the energy, created this force from the earth within him, stepped on and applied the energy to the problem.

He fell off.

I bouldered on slabs a lot, often no hands, to tune my sense of balance, as well as to save my skin, shredded by daily climbing on the harsh granite. I would stand on one leg close to a wall or slab, and pick out imaginary points on the rock that I would touch with my toe to train accuracy in my footwork. I tried one of the classic boulder slab problems there, Stem Gem, smearing and palming up into a steep rounded groove. But there were no holds and it was all on the feet. It always felt hard.

Bachar wore different boots from everyone else. Absolutely everybody climbed in the old blue and white EBs, the only boots that the shops sold. Bachar said his boots, Fires, pronounced *fee-rays*, were a Spanish design. Their Spanish manufacturer, Jesus Garcia, approached John to see if he would distribute them in America. After trying a pair he said yes. They still weren't in the shops yet, and wouldn't be for some time, so Bachar was very precious about them. The soles were very sticky and he gave them to me to try Stem Gem. In these boots I walked up it, almost no handed. The boots practically stuck to the rock, and when they finally appeared, were probably the biggest technical advance in rock-climbing history. I scrambled back to the base of the boulder, raving about how great they were. He took them straight back off me.

I started doing a lot of soloing, especially on rest days. Prior to that I never took rest days, just climbed hard every day, but I started to learn the value of recovery. With Bachar's influence, this would often involve 'active rest'. Not total rest, but days of doing the activity at a much-reduced level. For a sprinter, on a rest day, you would go out and do a bit of a jog. As a climber, I would go on easy soloing circuits. It keeps coordination and flow intact.

Bachar had a training area called Gunsmoke. There was a very fingery traverse there. Alongside this he had a wooden finger board, and he had set up a ladder, with long sections of rope and solid rungs. You would climb up the underside, feet hanging free, and lock off each arm to reach for the next rung at full stretch. Bachar was incredibly strong on these, really made them his own, so much so that the ladders ended up being called Bachar Ladders. We would do a set of these, then immediately do two sets of the traverse. The ladder worked the shoulders, and the traverse worked the fingers. It was a sort of circuit training and it was really effective, and I soon noticed a great improvement in my fitness.

Equinox. I don't think I've ever been so prepared for a route as I was for that. The day came. I felt ready. I warmed up that morning, soloing a good circuit of routes, and I felt confident, smooth and strong on everything, moving perfectly. John, Chris and I walked across to the route. A crack split a huge, golden granite shield, a thin, black curving line on an otherwise perfect sheet of rock. As a line it was pure and inspiring. At the base I put on my EBs, tied onto the ropes and racked some gear onto my harness. I climbed up as far as I could, placed some protection, then climbed back down to ready myself. My secret weapon was a half-sized Friend. Number one was the smallest they made, too big for Equinox, so we dismantled my number one, photocopied the parts and had the copier reduce the image by a third. I cut the shapes out, stuck them to my cams and filed them down to match – reducing the size but maintaining the all-important cam angle. This, I was keeping for the top.

I stood relaxed, preparing my thoughts and emotions. When I was ready, I got on the rock and just stormed it. I moved perfectly, not hesitating, yet not rushing, always keeping my momentum, putting in only the runners I needed. Near the top I felt unstoppable and so within my abilities that I felt that I could just keep going and do the same again. I didn't even place the Friend.

A week or so later, I was on the long flight across the Atlantic to London. Chris had gone back a few days earlier so I was by myself. I sat in the middle seat, between two American tourists. The stewardess was moving up the aisle offering free drinks to passengers. I was dirty, dressed in filthy clothes and my body felt worked from head to toe. I stank. The stewardess was moving closer. I looked at my skinny knees. I looked back up and stared down the aisle.

My mind kept going over and over the same thing. I had just done Genesis and Psycho. I had flashed Supercrack and Equinox. These were some of America's hardest routes – the world's hardest routes. I had done them. It could have gone either way, but I had tried and I had succeeded. Nothing could possibly make this any better, nothing. Cars, money, fame. None of that mattered. I felt like I was going to burst out of my body. I felt amazing. The stewardess was moving closer. I stared down the aisle. I was twenty years old, and here I was, arguably the best climber in the world.

'Would you like anything to drink, sir?'

I am the best climber in the world.

FIVE

Master's Wall

In 1983, if you'd asked me what I wanted to achieve in climbing, the answer would have been easy: 'The hardest, most dangerous new routes possible.' Britain has always had a great tradition of bold, dangerous climbs. It leads the world in this style of climbing and there are many incredibly difficult climbs where, if you fall, it means serious injury, or even death. This was where it was at in Britain in the early 1980s. Brown, Whillans, Livesey, Fawcett, Redhead. They had all been masters of bold climbing, and had all carried forward this great tradition. I now wanted to put my name on that list and to take things even further.

At the time there were two styles of climbing that were pushing the limits of boldness on British rock. The gritstone edges in the Peak District, on the outskirts of Manchester and Sheffield, had many thousands of routes on some of the most popular cliffs in the world. Gritstone – dark, rounded, heavily weathered – is one of the best rocks to climb on. It has incredibly high friction, perhaps the highest of any rock, and the moves on it are beautiful, often more to do with balance, technique and dynamism than brute strength. Some climbs are well protected, but many have absolutely no protection, and on the harder routes, the moves are extremely difficult and the climbing insecure. Sometimes, sixty feet can feel a long way up.

The other Mecca for dangerous climbing was the mountain crags of North Wales and the Lakes. Here, for decades, the best climbers in the country had come and pushed the boat out on hard, beautiful climbs, with huge run-outs above sketchy protection, where leaders had to keep their heads together in terrifying situations. Unlike gritstone, where you can solo a cutting-edge route in under a minute, the mountain routes often meant slowly inching up a hundred and fifty foot pitch in a terrifying situation for an hour or more.

These two styles were where I wanted to leave my mark when I returned from America. I arrived back in the country, fit and as motivated as ever. And in my luggage I had hidden something very special.

Before I left, Bachar offered me a deal. He was trying to set up a company to distribute the Fire rock boots and needed some start-up cash. In return for a loan of a couple of hundred dollars, which he soon repaid, he gave me a pair of the precious Fire boots. These were the incredibly sticky-soled shoes that Bachar would let me try every now and again, and with them, I could almost walk up steep slabs where the hard rubber of my old EBs would have scratched and slithered. As one of the biggest technological advances ever made in climbing, I knew that when I got back to Britain, they would give me a great advantage on many climbs.

Back home, I was living again at Stoney, often dossing in Tom's Roof, but more and more I would go back to Sheffield in the evenings. Noddy, my old Stoney climbing partner, lived in a tiny bedsit in the Broomhill area of Sheffield and often let me sleep on his floor. His single room was a little box, about ten feet by ten feet. There was a small sink in the corner and a little cooker with two rings on top. His bed took up most of the room, and in what was left, I could just about roll out my sleeping bag. It was great to have a room to stay in.

Noddy was a great climbing partner. In my position, ambitious and single-minded, I needed someone who would be happy to come along to wherever there might be a climb I wanted to try. He was very obliging in this, sometimes going back to the same venue day after day while I worked at a climb. He was an interesting character. I liked him and found him funny. Not funny in a joking sort of way, it was more his attitudes and manners that amused me.

But he had a dark streak in him. I would often hear him talking about the people he hated. He hated the police. He hated teachers. He hated climbers who tried to get recognition beyond what they deserved. There was a climber at the time with very long arms, which allowed him to do routes other climbers couldn't. Noddy hated him because he had long arms and never missed a chance to criticise one of his routes. He hated people who worked in shops, and if the assistant did anything at all to annoy him, even in the slightest, even if they misheard him – he would mumble deliberately – he would become incredibly rude and aggressive towards them.

'Pint of milk,' he would mumble.

'Sorry?' an assistant would ask.

'I said a pint of M. I. L. K.'

He hated anyone who had a job. 'Sell-out tossers,' he called them, and had a very low opinion of them. 'I'll never get a job,' he used to say. And he never did. There was obviously a lot going on inside his head, although he usually kept it bottled up.

For the time, he did some fairly hard routes – not quite the hardest, more the bolder ones. In Cheedale once, he tried a route that started with twenty feet of unprotected climbing, leading to a peg. At ten feet he started shaking. He pushed on, above a terrible landing, and the shake got worse. I couldn't look. I was muttering under my breath, 'Please, Noddy, you're going to die. Please get the peg clipped and lower off.' By now he was convulsing. He moved up and clipped the peg, but instead of lowering off, as I would have done, and with his body now only in a mild tremble, he carried on. Three feet later, Noddy was wobbling again.

That's what he was like. He climbed in dangerous situations very close to what he was physically capable of, and sometimes I worried about his judgement. At the time, if he were leading E4, he would solo E3, always in his same shaky style, wobbling and scratching up them. I remember thinking that you can't do that all the time. Climbing like that you are in a lot of danger and luck can always play a part. But that was Noddy's thing. I never understood it.

In the evenings, when the climbing was finished, we would hitch back to his bed-sit and eat a sandwich. After that we would walk for half an hour down to the Polytechnic and chat to the climbers at the gym, do a few pull-ups, or go to the bar and watch TV. The bar was often empty and we would sneak behind the counter and help ourselves to orange juice from the pump. One night I suggested we went to Stanage the next day so I could try Ulysses. He knew what Ulysses was and he just shrugged and said okay.

Stanage Edge is the three-mile-long gritstone escarpment on the outskirts of Sheffield. It's the most famous of all the gritstone crags and has a climbing history stretching back to the 1800s. Right in the centre of the crag are the Plantation Boulders, a collection of perfectly sized blocks of gritstone sat amid beautiful beeches and pines, that hold some of the country's hardest and best boulder problems. On the cliff above this are some of the crag's best routes. On one particular section the rock zigzags in and out at right angles to the base, these sharp angles stretching upwards for seventy feet. On the inside corners are cracks and these attracted the first ever climbers to Stanage in 1880. It's incredible to think of climbers doing these big steep corners so long ago, before any proper equipment, climbing routes totally solo because protection simply wasn't invented and wouldn't be for decades.

The outside corners of these features form arêtes, much like the corners of buildings. Arêtes tend to give very striking lines, jutting out from the crag and are highly prized first ascents. The way to climb them is to hold onto the outside corner with both hands, lean off to the side and try to walk your feet up. It requires balance, co-ordination and sometimes the ability to move quickly, as the forces on your body are trying to swing you off and out of balance. They also tend to be bold, as there are no cracks to place protection, so they are often climbed solo. The section of rock above the Plantation has three of the best arêtes on gritstone. On the left is Archangel, first climbed in 1972 by Ed Drummond. On the right is White Wand, a sharper arête than Archangel, but steeper and more technical, first done by John Allen in 1975.

Right in the centre of all these lines was the last of the arêtes, still unclimbed in 1983, despite attempts by many climbers. It was what was known as a Last Great Problem, a line just beyond the abilities of the day, a line so famous and unclimbed, that everyone knew about it. It was blunter than the other two, making it less positive to hold and it was almost vertical, making it much more powerful. Its line was so beautiful that climbers had had to give it a name, even before it was ever climbed – Ulysses' Bow. I was desperate to try it.

To get to Stanage, we would take the bus up through Crosspool, along Sandygate Road, past the Hallamshire Golf Course, to the terminus near a reservoir at the back of the crag. From there it was almost an hour's walk. It would take two hours in total, although it meant that we didn't have to make the difficult hitch from Noddy's bed-sit. The walk was beautiful and we would wander across the dark moors, chatting about climbing, taking the piss out of people and having a laugh. We got to the crag where I soloed Archangel a few times to warm up and then had a go at Ulysses on top-rope. It felt desperate.

In the funny way of climbing ethics, what you are allowed to do depended on where you are. On gritstone, top-roping was allowed. The practice of setting up a rope from above, allowing a climber to practice the moves on a route in safety, had been common on gritstone since the 1800s. Perhaps it was because routes on gritstone could be hard and unprotected, making them too dangerous to lead. Perhaps it was because, as they were so short, it was very easy to walk round to the top and set the rope up, something that you couldn't with a mountain crag or in a heavily wooded limestone dale. But for whatever reason, top-roping was a common practice on gritstone, especially before a first ascent. Later, when climbers improved, or on later ascents when they know that something was possible, they would try to do them starting from the ground without top-roping. However, while top-roping was considered fair play on gritstone, it wasn't on mountain crags or on limestone. On these, you could abseil down the route and clean it, feel the holds, check the runners or pull your body into the right positions. The difference probably seems marginal today, but at the time, these were the ethics and people followed them.

I top-roped Ulysses about five times on my first day, the Fire boots sticking well to the rough gritstone. It still felt hard and the thought of lead-ing it was too scary. I returned another day, again top-roping it another five times. The third day, I came back, top-roped it a couple more times, and finally soloed it. Ulysses was mine. A photo of me on the route made the front cover of a climbing magazine, which was great. But the best thing was doing a state-of-the-art first ascent, right bang in the middle of the most popular crag in the country.

The following year a young climber called Johnny Dawes soloed Ulysses without top roping it first. When I heard about this, I was impressed. It was a phenomenal achievement. I would climb with Johnny a lot over the years to come. He was tremendous fun to climb with and moved really well on rock. Genetically, he wasn't cut out to do the hardest, most physical things on limestone, but on the stuff he was good at, dangerous, technical ground, he was superb. He later went on to add some of the top routes on Derby-shire gritstone and on the slate quarries of North Wales.

The traditions of climbing in Britain stretch back over a hundred years, and if there was one cliff that represented the very heart of those traditions, it was Clogwyn Du'r Arddu on the flanks of Snowdon in North Wales. 'Cloggy' flanks the northwest corner of Snowdon's huge bulk, an hour's walk from the old quarrying village of Llanberis. Climbers had been doing great deeds here since the turn of the century and it dripped with history. There were lots of stories of pre-war climbers struggling up wet dirty cracks on wild winter days, or making unprotected hundred foot run-outs on mossy slabs with hemp ropes that could barely hold a fall. It is a big, complex cliff and its north-facing aspect means that it is often sombre and foreboding. Of all the Last Great Problems in the country at the time, the biggest, boldest and most famous of them all was at Cloggy.

Right in the centre of the cliff is a slab of rock, a full rope-length high, and two hundred feet wide, known as Great Wall. It is the centrepiece of Cloggy. In the 1950s, Joe Brown – the Master – had tried to climb a crack on the left-hand side of the wall. At the time Joe's personal ethics allowed him to place no more than two pegs in a pitch, so when he got to the half-way point having already placed his two pegs, he decided to retreat and leave the route incomplete. Pegs are tricky things. Metal spikes hammered into cracks and used as aid or protection damage the rock the way nuts don't. They also tend to be left in place, so they change the nature of the rock and of the challenge it presents. In Brown's day, nuts were still rudimentary or non-existent, so pegs were more logical. But despite this, Joe left the chal-lenge for future generations.

That only made the legend of Joe Brown all the greater and the Master's Wall more tempting. In the early 1960s, Pete Crew abseiled down the route and inserted tiny pebbles into the crack above Brown's high point. Before nuts, climbers would rely on pebbles that they carried in their pockets, fiddled into the cracks. They would then thread string behind the pebbles and clip their ropes into the string. This would be their protection on these enormous, difficult routes. By comparison, Brown hadn't abseiled the climb. He merely had a pocket-full of pebbles, hoping somehow to find the right pebble for the right place as he went. Thanks to Crew's tactics, he was able to climb the line that Brown had failed on, using the threaded pebbles both for protection and for aid. Still, it must have been an incredible effort. The wall had become known as Master's Wall in honour of Brown's effort, but Crew called his climb Great Wall. It was one of the top routes in the country.

In the 1970s, people began to think about free-climbing Great Wall and in 1975 a young gritstone genius called John Allen finally succeeded. Allen's ascent was controversial because he used chalk, which, ridiculously in my opinion, was seen as giving an unfair advantage. Time moved on and Great Wall became a popular classic. People began to look towards the big, blank, crack-less expanse of rock on the right side of the huge slab.

John Redhead was one of the major characters in the North Wales scene at the time. When Andy and I were young, Redhead was one of the climbers we thought was cool. He often wore a red neckerchief, so we both got a neckerchief. I wore mine every day for a year, until it eventually rotted off my neck. Redhead had been neck and neck with Fawcett in North Wales at the time, and he added some great routes, some of them extremely dangerous. He had a reputation for being a wild character, and his routes being totally mad, although from climbing with him, the thing that impressed me was how shrewd and prepared he was about things. I once saw him, prior to a first ascent, abseil down a route and mark with chalk where the crucial footholds were, or the exact spot where a piece of protection might fit. I had never seen that done before. The practice shocked me when I first saw it, but it wasn't long before I used it myself.

Redhead started to give the great, unclimbed wall at Cloggy some serious attention. Without cracks, the line, a long, near-featureless slab, was very thin on protection. What there was – tiny nuts, buried half-in, half-out of poxy cracks – gave only the hope of security, and the line just screamed danger. He gave the route some very brave attempts. Once, he got very high, but gripped with terror, retreated off a tiny skyhook, a curled metal claw, sitting precariously on a flake of rock. John lowered seventy feet back to the ground with all his weight hanging from this marginal protection. Another time he got even higher, only to take a huge fall, rag-dolling down the slab, somehow being held by one of the tiny nuts. As if to draw a line under his efforts, Redhead abseiled down the wall, drilled a hole in the rock and placed an expansion bolt runner at his high point. He gave the climbing up to this bolt a name – The Tormented Ejaculation.

It seemed wrong to put bolts into mountain rock. Bolts are a way of protecting blank sections that could not be protected in any other way, but were only used on some kinds of limestone, not in the mountains or on gritstone. That was the ethic then and still is. That was generally accepted. Bolts had no place on Cloggy. To prove the point I decided I would go up there myself and try the route without the bolt.

I made the long walk up to Cloggy to have a look at the wall and then abseiled down the line, checking handholds and footholds, trying to get an idea of how to climb it and sussing out any place where protection might go. The year before I had watched Redhead prepare his route on abseil and knew exactly where it went. The featureless rock has no obvious line, so knowing where to move at various points was a big help. Redhead's bolt marked his highpoint and above this, I could see, was the crux. I felt the holds, and taking my weight off the abseil rope, tried some of the moves to get an idea of how I would climb this section. It looked hard, and more than that: extremely serious. The only protection I could get for these moves were two little nuts below the hardest moves. I couldn't imagine them holding a proper fall. The route had death written all over it.

At the time, I knew I had to get my head in gear. I knew I had to become used to the situation where, if I fell off, I would die, and learn to stay calm in the face of this fact. So between abseils down the route, I would solo a route to get back to the top. I soloed Great Wall, a really spooky solo and a route I had only led once before years ago when it was right at my limit. I soloed The Boldest, Curving Arête and others, all just as hard as Great Wall, often having never climbed them before. Despite this, I felt solid and in control.

I had a rest day and decided to climb the route the next day. My Fire rock boots were by now getting old and badly worn, so I sat them out in the sun all day as I relaxed by the lake below the cliff in the hope that the heat would shrink them a little, to make them feel more snug on my feet. The following day I walked back up to the cliff with Paul Williams. Paul was a local climbing enthusiast who had also belayed Redhead on some of his attempts. I was in good company. I warmed up, went round to the top of the crag and abseiled down the wall, removing Redhead's bolt. At the base of the route, I pulled the abseil ropes back to the ground, watched them tumble down the hundred and fifty feet of wall and land, crumpling at my feet.

Quietly, in the shadow of the wall, I clipped the few pieces of protection to my harness, tied into the ropes and slipped on my boots. I breathed deeply, emptied my mind and stepped onto the rock. I climbed up the wall for thirty feet and placed a good nut. From here I traversed right towards a line of flakes. I had cast my eye over these on abseil, but as the climbing didn't look too hard, I never gave them much attention. I got there on the lead and started moving up them. Suddenly it all started getting a lot harder than I had anticipated. I lay-backed higher up the flakes and was soon a long way above the one good nut. I began to feel totally out of control. My feet smeared on little holds I hadn't taken the trouble to clean fully while my fingers crimped desperately on barely-adequate flakes. By now, I was facing a monster fall, perhaps even hitting the ground. I carried on, terrified.

Unprepared for this difficulty, this danger, I now felt way out of my depth. My forearms were pumped from gripping too tightly and I was fast losing strength in my fingers. Retreat was not an option, so I clawed onwards, higher and higher, seventy feet above the rocky ground. I was alone on this huge wall of death and I felt out of control. I didn't want any part of this any more. I had in my mind the two tiny nuts just below the crux. While the placements didn't look like they could hold much of a fall, I could probably lower off them in safety. I only wanted to get off the face alive.

I got to the footholds below the crux and threw my weight onto them, taking some strain off my pumped arms. I wriggled the nuts into the cracks. I stood there, panting, with my body leant against the rock. I could feel my heart thumping against the wall. I gave the nuts a gentle tug to make sure they were seated properly and had a final think about lowering off. But I rationalised that if I ever wanted to do this route, and I did, then I would have to climb that section again, and I knew I never wanted to do that. So. Think. The next moves were the crux. I had looked at them properly on abseil and had a good idea of how to do them. The route was there for the taking. I tried to relax, recovered my breath, got my mind to the place it needed to be and made the decision. I set off. Almost automatically, the crux moves flowed by, relatively in control compared to the lower section. I climbed smoothly, moving up and rightwards to a crack on the right side of the wall where I could finally place another good nut. My relief was incredible. From here a final fifty feet of climbing led up and left. This top section was hard and still terrifying – it would have been possible to take a hundred foot fall down the slab – but the knowledge that I wouldn't hit the ground made all the difference, and I scraped my way to the top.

I had done it. I had climbed the route; this was the biggest thing on British rock. It was absolutely massive and I had done it. In a notebook in the famous Llanberis climbers' café, Pete's Eats, I recorded the climb, and Paul Williams came up with a name for it, De Torquemada, the leader of the Spanish Inquisition. I wasn't bothered what it was called, but nobody else liked the name. Just like Ulysses had already been named before it was climbed, so too had the Cloggy line, and the traditional name had to stay – Master's Wall, in honour of Joe Brown's attempts on it twenty-five years earlier.

Three years later Johnny Dawes did a more direct route up the wall. Where Master's Wall moved right at Redhead's old bolt placement,

Johnny's route, Indian Face, continued more or less straight up the wall, giving a harder and more dangerous route. It was a terrific lead.

Master's Wall had scared me. Afterwards, I decided not to risk my life again like that for some time. Climbing can be dangerous and at the end of the day, you have to think of what you are risking and make your decision according to what your values are. I knew that life was precious and I knew about risk. That was the thing about climbing. Even from early on there were always reminders of what could happen if you were overambitious, careless, or just plain unlucky. We had a friend at Stoney, Simon Horrox. Simon was a lovely person and a really talented photographer. One summer, he decided to go to the Alps. Before he went, we were taking the mickey out of him, saying how dangerous the Alps were and be sure to wear your helmet.

I was sat in Stoney café one day, when Noddy came in.

'Have you heard about Simon?' he asked.

On Simon's first day in the Alps, he was crossing a snowfield when he was hit by a stonefall and killed. Such a great person. Gone. Just like that. He was the first climber I knew well who died and it really shook me up.

Despite all this, you make your own decisions. Even though I'd made a promise to myself when I reached the top of Master's, the very next day I went alone to the Cromlech and had my incredible day soloing hard routes, such as Right Wall, in an incredibly risky situation. But I knew the score and made my decision. Just like Noddy, who, about two weeks later, decided to go to Carreg Wastad, only a half a mile from the Cromlech, and set off on one of his edgy soloing missions.

I was sitting in the Stoney café later that week, flicking through a climbing magazine, when a friend, John, came in. He looked upset and came straight over to my table.

'Have you heard about Noddy?' he asked.

SIX

World of Sport

After the dangers of mountain routes in North Wales that summer, I felt ready for some fun by the seaside. In 1983, that meant Pen Trwyn. Pen Trwyn is a long band of limestone that runs above the Marine Drive, a tourist toll road just on the outskirts of the seaside town of Llandudno, only a few miles from my old school, St David's. Its white and black streaked rock is never more than seventy feet high, very solid, and generally steep, sometimes extremely so. As such, it lends itself perfectly to very hard, fingery, but usually safe climbing, and it felt like the perfect place to push the physical standards at the time.

Llandudno is a real tourist town. It always has been, ever since Victorian times. There is a seafront with hotel after hotel and lots of people come for their summer holidays from other parts of Wales, and from English cities such as Liverpool. The main street is filled with amusement arcades, candyfloss, shops selling little trinkets and postcards. Grown-ups and children wander up and down all day, usually sunburned and stuffing chips or sweets into themselves. There is an enormous pier that sticks out just below the start of the Marine Drive. This has lots of kiosks where people draw cartoons of tourists, sell chips and hamburgers or sticks of rock. At the end there is an amusement arcade with dodgems and a merry-go-round, and all the time organ music, which drifts along the crag in the sea breeze. In the evenings holidaymakers get drunk in the pubs and walk around the streets shouting at each other. Chips, sunburn and alcohol. It's a classic British seaside town.

In the years since Andy Pollitt and I had free-climbed Mayfair, Pen Trwyn had exploded in popularity as climbers realised its potential. In 1983 a lot of the top climbers visited. Fawcett was there, Andy Pollitt, Mel

Griffiths, Tim Freeman, Basher Atkinson, Stevie Haston, John Redhead, all doing hard new routes or second ascents. It was a lot of fun. The sun shone almost every day. The local Welsh climbers – Mel, Redhead and Stevie – would come over for the day. Fawcett stayed with friends in Llanberis, and the rest of us, Basher, Andy, Tim and myself, slept in a dusty cave, right beside the road at the start of the Marine Drive.

The cave was always dry, but the floor was dusty and covered in sheep shit and usually smelled of piss. Still, it provided shelter and that was all we wanted. Life was simple there. Sleep, climb, eat, climb, sleep. We would get up in the morning and sit for a little while in the sun to wake up. From there, it was straight down to Parisella's Café for breakfast.

Parisella's Café was right at the start of the Marine Drive. It specialised in ice cream and sold trinkets and sweets to the tourists. Andy had befriended the woman who worked there, and through him we all got to know her. Every morning, as we were always up early, we would wander the few hundred metres down to the café and help her lay out the chairs and tables and give the place a sweep and tidy up. It must have taken about two minutes. In return for this she would give us free breakfast. Anything we wanted.

From the café we would head back to the crag, climb for a few hours, then meet up at Parisella's for lunch, again free. She never charged us for anything. I don't quite know how that worked – breakfast, lunch, ice cream, sandwiches, chocolate – everything free. In the whole month we stayed there we spent almost nothing on food. After lunch it was off again for another session of climbing.

In the evenings we would wander into Llandudno to hang out in the bars and talk about climbing. These were busy, so if you only bought a half of still orange, or maybe didn't buy anything at all, you could still sit there all night and no one would notice. After, we would stroll back to the cave again, fish out our sleeping bags and mats and lay down in the dirt. I can remember, every night, being totally exhausted from climbing. I would lie down and look up into the black night sky and stare at the stars. Within moments the stars would double up in my vision, my eyes would close and I'd be asleep.

Our cave not only gave perfect shelter, but it was also a great bouldering spot and a perfect place to warm up in the morning before going off to the crags. The long, near-horizontal roof was covered in holds and it was possible to make up some very difficult problems on it. I worked out a hard sequence of moves through the cave. It was long, covering almost fifteen feet of roof, with a fairly high finish, and for a long time I was the only person who could do it. I called the problem Parisella's Roof after the café. From then on the cave, which had previously just been known as 'the cave', became known as Parisella's Cave.

I was bouldering there one day with some of the local climbers and one of them, Tom Jones, who had been to Yosemite recently, told me a story about John Bachar.

'Bachar does Midnight Lightning almost every evening in the summer, at exactly the same time. And every evening a crowd gathers to watch him,' he told me.

This was impressive. At the time, Midnight Lightning, in California's Yosemite Valley, was one of the hardest problems in the world. It is the best line on an enormous boulder, sat in the centre of Camp 4, the climbers' campsite. I had wanted to do the problem on my visit to America earlier that year, but when we got to Yosemite, the place was deep in snow and climbing out of the question. Still, I had seen the problem and was impressed, as it was not only desperate looking, but also fairly high, with a crucial final mantelshelf high above a bad landing.

'And when I saw him do it,' Tom continued, 'as he did the last move, he looked down at me and said: "Pretty cool, huh!"'

That amused me. One morning as I was messing around and bouldering in the cave, I saw a man, aged about fifty, walking along the road with a dog. This was my chance. With Tom's story still in mind, I immediately jumped on my problem, Parisella's Roof. I had the moves wired and I yarded across the roof like a god, climbing out to the lip of the cave. Just here, before the move to pull through onto easier ground above, I hung off one hand and chalked up with the other. I made really heavy breathing noises in order to attract the dog walker's attention. He looked over. So did the dog.

'Pretty cool, huh?' I called to him.

The man and the dog both stared for a moment and then, without a word, turned their heads away and carried on, leaving me hanging.

Climbing at Pen Trwyn was always fun and very relaxed. There was the constant sound of organ music coming from the pier, seagulls, parents and kids walking and chatting. Basher had a Citroën 2CV, a little French car whose back seat was removable. We would lean this against the wall on the opposite side of the road from the crag, and while someone climbed, the rest of us would slump on our couch, shouting and heckling.

One day, as we were lounging, we saw a little boy come along the crag. He was a pale-skinned punk-rocker, dressed in tight black clothes, wearing colourful bangles, with long, dirty black hair. He looked about fourteen. The boy went over to a classic E5 called Axle Attack, tied on and set off up it with a friend of his belaying.

He made good progress, getting past the crux. But a little higher, he was obviously getting pumped. Higher again, his body started shaking like a jelly. He got to a bolt runner, put a karabiner in and tried to clip the rope in. Yet each time he pulled up slack, he shook and dropped the rope again. From our armchair, we all started to take an interest and shout encouragement.

'Don't clip it, just go. Run it out! Run it out!'

Too pumped to clip the rope, he took our advice and pressed on. At the next bolt, he was even more pumped and once again tried to clip the rope. By now his body was wobbling hard, and as he pulled up the rope to clip, his other hand uncurled from the rock. The kid went for an enormous fall, screaming at the top of his voice. He fell for miles. The rope got wrapped around his leg and as it came tight, flipped his body upside down, and he came to rest about five feet above the ground. All of this made for great viewing.

The lad was Ben Moon and he was in fact sixteen years old. Ben would go on to become one of my best friends, as well as one of the world's top climbers. It's not surprising, because even from that first climb it was obvious that he had the one thing that is needed more than anything else. He had tried his hardest. He had pulled and clawed and wobbled until he could do no more. He just kept going and just kept fighting. It is that, above everything else, that gets people to the top.

Ben had just left school. He had read in the magazines that Pen Trwyn was the place to go that summer, just like I had gone to Tremadog three years before. He had left his home in London and headed straight to Llandudno with one thing in his mind: climbing. From then on he stayed with us in the cave and became one of our group. His leg had a bad rope burn, caused by the friction and heat from his fall off Axle Attack, and in the filth of the cave, it soon went septic and took a long time to heal.

In the 1960s Pen Trwyn had been used to practise aid climbing. At the time people couldn't conceive that rock this steep could be free-climbed. On these aid routes, if there were no cracks or pockets in which to place nuts, climbers would drill holes and place an expansion bolt, pulling on these to cover blank sections. Historically, bolts were against the ethics of British climbing. British climbing has always valued danger and commitment as one of its most important aspects. Bolts meant anything could be made safe, in a way ruining the challenge.

However, at the time people considered Pen Trwyn, along with several other very steep limestone cliffs in Yorkshire and Derbyshire 'impossible', so the climbing scene wasn't too bothered when aid climbers drilled a bolt into these cliffs. By the 1980s, things had changed. These 'impossible' aid climbs often made brilliant, desperate and well-protected free-climbs. A lot of the new routes we were doing at the time were actually first free ascents of the old aid routes, and the expansion bolts gave welcome protection for the hardest, blankest sections.

I had already freed a route called Oyster to make a very tough pitch of

E6, one of the hardest routes around at the time. Just left of Oyster I had spotted a steep, blank wall. I abseiled down and saw there were just about enough holds to climb it. I drilled and placed two bolts, practiced a few of the moves and soon felt ready to lead it. Pete Kirton, a very strong boulderer from Northumberland, was belaying and a few people stopped to watch me climb. One of these was the German climber, Wolfgang Güllich.

Even by then, Wolfgang was a famous character. He was probably Germany's top climber and had been over to America and repeated some of the top American routes. He was incredibly muscular, with enormous biceps, shoulders and legs. He was so muscular, in fact, that he was a stunt double for the American Rocky actor, Sylvester Stallone, when he made the climbing film, Cliffhanger. I chatted to him at the crag a bit. He was very friendly and had a really modest gentle manner.

Right, I thought, watch this. I knew the route was going to be very difficult, but with Wolfgang watching, I was determined to climb well. I pulled on and cranked the route out in moments. Brilliant. Later, Pete said that I should call the route Masterclass. I asked him why, and he said because I had just given Wolfgang a Masterclass in how to climb. I liked the joke and liked the name, so Masterclass became the hardest route on the crag, probably the hardest route in the country at the time.

A few days later I bumped into Wolfgang in the Peak District where he was trying a route called Linden, a huge, bold E6 at Curbar, that took a flake-line for sixty feet up the biggest wall at the crag. We chatted about Germany. I had seen a magazine called Boulder, a German publication that only came out for four or five issues. It focused a lot on a limestone area called the Frankenjura, which was near where Wolfgang lived. The pictures, by Thomas Ballenberger, were the most amazing I had ever seen in a magazine. I told him how fabulous I thought his local area looked, and he told me about some of the routes. He said he was driving back to Germany in an hour's time and I asked could I come back with him. I was still dossing, so I had all my stuff with me. I pointed to my big rucksack. He was in his little Volkswagen Golf and already had four people and all their climbing and camping gear to carry. But he said yes, no problem. Of course he would. That was Wolfgang.

In my excitement I said I would show him where the crucial nuts were on Linden. Dressed only in my jeans and without warming up, I put on my climbing shoes and soloed up to a flake at twenty feet. I had been to this point before in a previous attempt and knew where the runner went. Stood on the flake, I felt great, and decided just to solo to the top of the route, straight off, as a warm-up, in my jeans and sunglasses. Having watched me, Wolfgang decided he didn't fancy it. It's a terrifying route. We went to his car, all piled in, set off and drove, stopping only for the ferry, almost twenty hours direct to Obertrubach, a village near Nuremberg and Wolfgang's house. Crawling from the car, I staggered into the street in the cold early morning and into the house. Inside the steamy kitchen, sitting at the table, was Kim Carrigan.

'How's it goin', mate?' he said in his loud Australian accent with a grin on his face.

Another enormous German sat at the table, slowly stirring a great big mug of coffee with a spoon. I recognised him from Boulder magazine as the German climbing legend Kurt Albert. He had massive shoulders and arms, a big mop of blond hair and a bushy blond moustache. Kurt stirred the coffee, looking at me. Then his face broadened into a huge grin and he pulled the big silver spoon out of the cup. He held it in his fist, turned it round so the bottom of the spoon was pointing towards me, then, holding it right up to my nose, said:

'Hup! Look at your funny face!'

I looked down at the spoon. It still had coffee on, but I could see my reflection. My head looked really small apart from my nose, which looked massive. I started to laugh and I knew I already liked this person. Just like Wolfgang.

While everyone laughed at my funny face we were given a coffee and some pastries. I sat, spaced out from the journey, neither awake nor asleep, wanting only to lie down. Kim finished his coffee, stood up and said he was off climbing to Grossweinsteiner and did anybody want to come. Grossweinsteiner was where Sautanz was, one of the routes in the photographs in Boulder magazine. In the picture, Kurt Albert was climbing an immaculate white wall of overhanging limestone on tiny one and two-finger pockets, his toes just touching the surface of the rock.

Kurt was an absolute climbing legend. In Germany, for years, he pushed grade after grade, keeping pace with the developments of Fawcett and Livesey in Britain. Only recently had Wolfgang started to take things on, and would push them to incredible levels. Their local climbing area, the Frankenjura, is a large area of forest, an hour north of the German city of Munich. Millions of square miles of dense, ancient rolling woodland is latticed with narrow country roads. Here and there are lovely ancient villages and small white limestone cliffs are scattered throughout the forest. They are not very high, a hundred and fifty feet at the very most, and where the rock is solid, it tends to be steep or overhanging. It was very like the limestone I had climbed on in Britain.

Because of this, it was also used for aid climbing in years gone by, just like Pen Trwyn. Before guidebooks, aid climbers would paint a red ring at the base of a piece of rock, to let others know that it had been climbed. Then later German climbers, and Kurt in particular, worked through endless aid climbs to produce state-of-the-art free-climbs. To let the aid climbers know that he had freed the climb, Kurt would get a pot of red paint and fill in the red ring that the aid climbers had used to tag their climb. Kurt's tag became known as a 'rotpunkt' – a 'red point'. In years to come, the phrase redpoint would come to define the massive push in standards that took place in free-climbing in the 1980s.

A redpoint was an acceptable ascent, and was when a climber went from the bottom of a climb to the top, clipping all the runners as they went, no matter how much practice had gone in to it beforehand. It was a way of saying that yo-yoing wasn't acceptable any more. Despite this, Kurt was still yo-yoing his free-climbs at the time. But that didn't matter, the phrase was named after him. In this way, as much as for his new grades, Kurt was one of the most important climbers of his time.

I told Kim I'd come with him. Despite being knackered, I knew I had to try Sautanz. We set off and weaved around the windy roads through Hansel and Gretel forests, taking loads of junctions, eventually coming to a parking spot. We got our stuff and followed a path through birch and fir trees, little uphills and downhills, and got to the crag. It looked beautiful, much blanker looking than I was used to. I recognised Sautanz.

Sautanz was the hardest route in the country when Kurt did it in 1981. Kim told me he had done the quickest ascent of the route so far, spending only three days on it. I hadn't seen Kim since before I had gone to America and was keen to impress him. After the briefest of warm ups I asked could I have a go at Sautanz. I set off, fought like a bastard, almost falling off every move, pulling like crazy and got to the top having climbed it without a fall.

'I don't think you're going to have any problems with the routes here, mate,' Kim said as I lowered down.

The next day, we went to a crag where Kim was trying to free an old aid climb. He had already spent several days on it. I tied on and fired it first go. In 1981, John Bachar had visited and climbed a route called Chasin' the Trane. This had taken Bachar several days' effort to do and Wolfgang several days to repeat. Again, I did it first try.

Only a couple of months before, Wolfgang had added his own testpiece, Heisse Finger. This was the same grade as Chasin' the Trane, but Wolfgang believed it was the harder route, probably the hardest in the country. Wolfgang hooked me up with a friend of his for the day, Tony. Tony had heard that I had been climbing really well, and climbing their hard routes without falls, and wanted to see for himself.

'You climb this first go and I buy you a beer,' he said. If he thought that would make a difference, then he obviously didn't know much about me.

The route took a groove up a very steep white wall, about a hundred feet high. I tied on and did it first try. At the top, as I clipped the belay, I let out a scream, half in triumph, half pain. I had just done Germany's hardest route and I felt great. Sautanz, Chasin' the Trane and now Heisse Finger, all without a fall. It's not that I was doing these routes easily. They all were overhanging, viciously powerful climbs, with gnarly little finger holds, sharp and hard to see, and the moves were never obvious. On every route I had barely fought through the moves, really ugly stuff, and just about got to the next hold. But that didn't matter. I had done them. I felt great and wanted to do some more climbing. Tony said no.

'First I must buy you that beer.'

He took me down to an old bar in the local village, ordered me a huge litre of Bavarian pils and got me to drink it. At the time, I seldom drank, but I downed the whole glass and instantly felt leathered. I told him I had to go home. We got back to Wolfgang's house and I tried to make a coffee, but I knocked over the glass coffee pot. It smashed and I tried to go and say sorry for breaking it, but fell down on a bed and was soon fast asleep.

Flipper Fietz was another German climber I had heard of. He had really long straight black hair, was short, about five foot two, and incredibly strong, like all the Germans seemed to be. All muscle. Even back then, in 1983, he could do a one-arm pull-up on a piece of wood less than a centimetre deep. The best I ever managed was on a one-centimetre edge. Once you go below that they become desperate. Flipper was strong ahead of his time.

Fietz had his own thing going on. He was totally obsessed with John Gill, much more so than I ever was. He was very creative and artistic, and the walls of his apartment were covered in his drawings and paintings of the American bouldering legend. He was really a boulderer, but his thing was bouldering on routes. All he was concerned about were the moves. For years he would free the hardest routes or create his own. Yet while he would free all the moves, he never bothered actually doing the route. If he climbed, resting on the bolts, as long as he had done all the moves, for him, he had done the route. He wouldn't get credited with doing the first ascent, because for that you had to climb the route without resting on the bolts. That didn't matter to him.

Flipper took me to a crag just above a village playground. The main feature of the crag was a long overhang about fifteen feet across. The underside of it was covered with small pockets, and at the time no one had managed to free-climb the overhang. Flipper had bolted a route across the roof, which he had called Ekel. He had tried it, but hadn't managed to do the moves on it yet. I gave it a go and managed to dog my way across the overhang, resting on the bolts, but doing all the moves.

Flipper went berserk.

'Oh my God. Das ist krazy! Das ist KRAZY!'

He was beside himself with excitement. I was hanging off the belay, thinking, well, all I have done are the moves. To me that was good, but not really a big achievement. I hadn't done the route. But to Flipper – 'Krazy! Krazy! *Krazy!*' – I had done it. I had never seen someone so excited. I returned with another climber a couple of days later. Flipper had placed the bolts so that they were hard to clip on the lead, so I drilled some more in better places and after a couple of tries, led the route to do the first ascent. I did it in my bare feet so I could use my toes like fingers, and hook them into the little pockets. This might have been a daft idea. This route felt as hard as the climbs I had been doing in Britain and was a new level of difficulty for Germany, the first 9+. Two days later I saw Flipper and excitedly told him the news.

Nothing. Flipper shrugged his shoulders without much interest. He couldn't see the point in what I had done, when to him, I had already done it. He was a funny guy.

There are two main areas in the Frankenjura: the north, close to Munich, and the south, which is a longer drive away. For the last week of the trip Chris Gore had flown over, so Wolfgang took us to the southern Frankenjura one day, where he showed us a steep, white face in a beautiful wooded valley. He told me about a route of Flipper's there called The Face. It had a crucial hold on it, shaped like a smiling face, with two one-finger pockets for the eyes. As usual, Flipper had bolted the climb, done all the moves, named the route and left it at that. It had still not been redpointed. Wolfgang suggested I tried it.

I spent the day yo-yoing it and eventually got three-quarters of the way up the route. Back in Obertrubach that night at Wolfgang's, I found myself becoming obsessed with it. The climbing was stunning, with lots of moves on tiny finger pockets, with long and technical moves to link these together. It felt like the hardest route I had ever tried, much harder than Masterclass, but I knew I could do it. For the next couple of days we climbed in the northern area, but all I wanted was to travel to the south again and try The Face. Chris and I had no transport of our own however, and lifts there were hard to get. We managed to get a ride down there another day. The sharp pockets cut my fingers badly, and despite my best efforts, at the end of the day, I had still not managed it.

My trip to Germany was almost over. The night before we left, I was almost in tears from the frustration at not getting back on The Face. At the time, I was running every evening, so went for a long run by myself to come to terms with it all. I was gutted. It was one of the best and hardest things I had tried, it was there for the taking, but I needed the opportunity.

When I got back from my run, I discovered that Chris had managed to borrow a car for the following day. I was ecstatic. In the morning we drove up and I made no mistakes. The Face, Germany's hardest route, at X-.

Three hours later I was leaving Germany, heading first to France on a photo shoot for a Munich outdoor shop catalogue, then back again to England. I had come to Germany, done almost all their hardest climbs without a fall. I had advanced their top level by two grades. And just as important, I had made two really good friends. Kurt and Wolfgang had brought me to their country and shown me all the best routes. They had showed me unclimbed lines and when I did them, were gracious and happy to see them done. In the years to come I would spend a lot of time with them. I would climb and boulder with Kurt, one of my favourite climbing partners ever, with his friendly, relaxed enthusiasm, and with him do some of my best ascents. I would hang out and train with Wolfgang, and watch as he progressed to become one of the world's most important climbers, who would push forward the boundaries of world climbing. Wolfie combined the talent and dedication of a top athlete with one of the friendliest and most charismatic personalities in climbing.

Phil Davidson soloing Right Wall (E5 6a), Dinas Cromlech, Wales. On Friday 15 July 1983, the day after making the first ascent of Master's Wall (E7) on Cloggy, Jerry soloed 7 routes on Dinas Cromlech: Cemetary Gates (E1), *do wn* Ivy Sepulchre (HVS), Left Wall (E2), Cenotaph Corner (E1), Memory Lane (E3), Foil (E3) and Right Wall (E5).

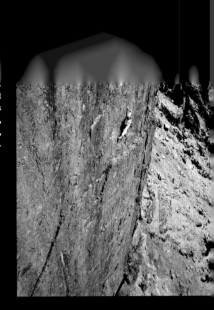

The Moffatts: Tim, Jerry, Christine, Toby and Simon in 1971.

(L-R) Simon (7), Jerry (6) and Toby (4) in Cromer, Norfolk in 1969.

The rugby first XI at St David's. Jerry is fourth from left on the back row, stood on tiptoes. "Went back to school. Traversed." *Diary entry, Tuesday 11 September 1979.*

The St David's College Climbing Club in 1978 – (L-R) Jerry, Andrew 'Henners' Henry, Mark Cole and Paul Stanfield.

This classic photo of Joe Brown climbing Tensor (E2) at Tremadog was on the post-card Joe sent Jerry. "Sent letter off to Joe Brown." *Diary entry, Thursday 10 May 1979.*

Hitching back to Sheffield in 1984.

(L-R) Mark Leach, Jerry, Luke (Quentin's son), Mark 'Zippy' Pretty, Quentin Fisher and Ben Moon watching the calories in Stoney Café.

Making a fast repeat of Ron Fawcett's route The Prow (E7) in 1982, at Raven Tor in the Peak District.

A youthful Jerry training in Tom's Roof at Stoney Middleton. Note the tube socks and Fire rock boots.

Making *the* move on the top pitch of Little Plum (E6) in 1982, at Stoney Middleton in the Peak District.

Jerry ecstatic after flashing Equinox (5.12d) at Joshua Tree and (inset) going for broke on the lead.

The legendary John Bachar, deep in thought.

John Bachar demonstrating the 'secret' heelhook move on the boulder problem Pumping Monzonite at Joshua Tree.

1982. Jerry and Chris Gore in the Grand Canyon.

Sporting the Colorado look on the first ascent of Master's Wall at Cloggy. "Abbed down Master's [Wall], took bolt out then led it. Gripping E7 6b." *Diary entry, Thursday 14 July 1983.*

Jerry interviewing Ron Kauk while in Germany for the UK climbing magazine *On The Edge*.

Kurt Albert making the impossible possible in Fontainebleau.

Danny, living the dream at 124 Hunter House Road in 1981. It really was that bad.

The fearless Neil 'Noddy' Molnar soloing Millwheel Wall (E1) at Burbage.

Ben Moon sleeping rough at Saussois in 1984.

1984. The first ascent of Papy On Sight (F7c+) in France's Verdon Gorge. "Jerry's influence was absolutely MAJOR in France in the early days of free climbing." *Verdon climber and photographer, Marco Troussier.*

Jerry and Andy Pollitt at Stoney Middleton in 1990.

Making *"great moves"* on Revelations (F8a+) at Raven Tor in 1984.

Soloing Fern Hill (E2) at Cratcliffe. *"A great solo on positive holds."*

SEVEN

The French Connection

Of all the places I have ever lived, of all the caves and cellars, the asbestos shacks and rotten tents, none came close for wildness, filth, and pure disorder to 124 Hunter House Road.

The house was a Victorian terrace with five bedrooms in Hunters Bar, Sheffield, an area popular with university students. Lots of people lived in 124, amongst them, Tim Freeman and his girlfriend, Mandy. I knew Tim well from my time in Wales. When I got back from Germany, I didn't fancy another winter sleeping rough at Stoney, so I invited myself to stay in Tim and Mandy's room. I moved in, rolled my sleeping bag out on their bedroom floor and spent the autumn and winter there.

It was a madhouse.

Nobody worked. Everyone signed on the dole and the council paid the rent. The house was a pigsty. If you made a cup of tea, you would take the teabag out of the cup and throw it on the floor. You wouldn't dream of putting it in a bin. The floor was the bin. There were usually around ten people living at 124, a few of them climbers, the rest living a similar sort of life. There were two guys there, Danny and Nick, who were essentially nocturnal, and apart from the fact that I hardly ever saw them leave the house, they lived a lifestyle very similar to that of a climber. They played guitar and listened to music, and they loved to party. One time they went on a three-day session, from Sunday evening till early on Thursday morning, where they hung out in their room, never going to bed. There were constant shrieks of hysterical high-pitched laughter and really bad guitar strumming. At the time, New Order had just released their single, Blue Monday, and for the three days they played that record over and over again at top volume. Three days. I would go to bed hearing it, get up hearing it, go out training and it would still be on when I got back. They would latch onto particular lines and shout them out over and over again.

'I see a ship in the harbour. I will and shall obey.'

On Nick's birthday another guy from the house, Ian, was walking up the main road that runs through Hunters Bar, lined with posh shops. As Ian passed an up-market bakery, he spotted an enormous birthday cake in the window. The shop assistants were busy with a queue of customers, so Ian ducked into the shop, grabbed the cake and took off up the road at top speed with the beautiful cake in his arms. At home he presented it to Nick, who seemed touched.

'Happy birthday, Nick.'

We all came down to the kitchen for the ceremony. Ian lit the candles; Nick made a wish and blew them out. He then attempted to slice the cake with a huge knife but found he couldn't. He pressed harder, but the knife still wouldn't cut through the icing. Frustrated, he clasped the knife in his fist and stabbed downwards into the cake. Finally a small lump of icing broke off. He picked it up. It was made of wax. Ian had stolen a display cake.

People would often doss in 124 for a week or more, sleeping on the couch or on the floor. These would be friends, or friends of friends. You would ask their name, chat to them or give them some food. Once, after a climber had been staying for a while, I became curious about him.

'Who's that guy?'

Nobody knew. Nobody even knew who had asked him to stay. Perhaps no one knew him and he had just found his way in. This in itself wasn't unusual.

There was a climber called Chipper who rented one of the rooms. One evening, as he was in bed with his girlfriend, Alice, the stranger burst in to the bedroom and started attacking him. 'Get away from my girlfriend you bastard!' the stranger shouted, punching Chipper in the face. We were downstairs watching TV but when we heard the noise charged upstairs and pulled the stranger off his victim. He was livid, spit spraying from his mouth. It was clear the stranger had been having delusions that Chipper's girlfriend was in fact with him. Having dragged him off, we didn't know what to do with him.

So we marched him downstairs to the front room of the house where there was an old bed frame. Using rope and tape, we tied his hands and feet to the corners of the frame and left him in a star position on the floor. We then all settled back down to watch TV, while the madman groaned. Some time later, at about two in the morning, a neighbour called round. John had left a guitar at our house a couple of nights ago and wanted it back. The guitar was in the corner of the room and John had to step over the bed and its occupant to reach the guitar.

Then he said thanks and cheerio, and left. At no stage did he pass comment on the man tied to a bed frame in the middle of the floor. Looking back, it's this fact – that a groaning stranger tied to a bed with everyone sat around watching TV wasn't worth mentioning – which says most about 124 and the life we led there.

In early March 1984, a man from the council came round. There had been complaints. When he saw the house, he said it was the filthiest dwelling he had ever seen. Given the poverty that existed in Sheffield then, this was saying something. Later that day, workmen came round to board the house up as unfit for human habitation. Everyone had to take their stuff and move out immediately. I wasn't too bothered. I was off climbing to France in two days' time anyway.

After my trip to Germany the year before, an outdoor shop, Sport Scheck, who produced a major catalogue every year, paid for me to go on a photo shoot to the south of France. We were taken to a crag called Buoux, where the top French climbers, Patrick Edlinger, brothers Marc and Antoine le Menestrel, and Jean-Baptiste Tribout, had been adding hard new routes. We arrived there in the blazing late summer heat, and although it was too hot to climb properly, I was impressed, and decided I wanted to come back to try their routes. From there I had hitched back to England, stopping off in Fontainebleau, an hour south of Paris.

Fontainebleau is one of the world's most amazing bouldering areas. Set in wild forests that were once the hunting grounds of the kings of France, are tens of thousands of grey sandstone boulders. No one knows for sure how these boulders got there. Scattered throughout the forest, in small groups or alone, they are the perfect height for bouldering, usually between eight and fifteen feet tall, often with flat sandy landings underneath. It's bouldering heaven. At the time, I hadn't heard much about the area – bouldering wasn't something that most climbers did much; it was usually Parisians who visited the boulders for afternoons out.

I spent an amazing week there. The problems were fantastic and hard. I was sleeping under a cave at an area called Bas Cuvier, when I bumped into Marc and Antoine le Menestrel, and Jean-Baptiste 'Jibé' Tribout. Antoine kindly invited me to stay with him in Paris. He was studying there and had a tiny, beautiful apartment near the Louvre. Every morning of my stay I would get up, take the Metro to Porte d'Orléans and hitchhike to the forest. I couldn't get enough of it. Some days I would climb by myself, on others I would hook up with one of the French climbers. I climbed until my fingers bled, then made the easy hitch back to Paris. It was good to get to know Marc, Antoine and Jibé, and I would see a lot of them over the years to come.

Back in the UK, I told Ben Moon all about the crags and convinced him to come to France with me the following year, in the spring of 1984. He was still a relative beginner at the time, but I could tell he was keen and it was hard to find people who would come on a long trip like this. I also invited him to come and live at 124, to sleep on Tim and Mandy's bedroom floor.

'There's a pull-up bar in the bedroom, Ben, so you can start doing pull-ups as soon as you wake up,' I told him.

He moved in and we spent that winter training for France.

We trained hard. I had lots of techniques I could pass on to Ben, who I soon realised was a very good listener and a good learner. We really put the hours in. We would have long sessions down on Broomgrove Road, a little vertical wall of a college building, where there were tiny features on the bricks that you could hang on. We worked out some ferocious traverses and went there almost every day. Often too, we went to Stoney. I had a rope ladder, with wooden rungs that you could climb footless, as Bachar had shown me, and set this up above Minus Ten Wall. We did traverses, or top-roped routes, then ran over and did sessions on the Bachar Ladder. We turned the crag into a gymnasium. Sometimes climbers would come along and see us and you could just see them thinking: 'What the hell is going on here?'

I always have a goal in mind when I am training. A couple of years before, Andy Pollitt and Ron Fawcett had gone on a French exchange trip to a crag a few hours south of Paris called Saussois. Andy talked about a route they had all tried there, Chimpanzodrome. This had been the hardest route in France when first done by Jean-Pierre Bouvier two years before. He graded it 8a, the same as The Face, although it had since been downgraded to 7c+. Andy had tried the route, Güllich, Edlinger and Fawcett all tried the route too without doing it. It sounded desperate and I decided Chimpanzodrome would be my goal for the trip. Not only that, I wanted do it on my first try. March came and we left for France.

We hitched out of Sheffield, crossed the channel and made it to Fontainebleau, where we set ourselves up under an overhang at Bas Cuvier. The winter cold still hadn't given way to springtime yet and while the climbing was good, our frigid existence bordered on unpleasant. When we couldn't take the cold any more, we packed up and hitched to Saussois.

Saussois is in the middle of nowhere, over a hundred miles south of Paris, and a long way from any large towns. Hitching there was a lot of trouble. We arrived and set up camp in a little cave. It was still bitterly cold. The crag was deserted. In the mornings we would have to walk an hour to the nearest shop to buy bread and then walk back. We never once managed to hitch a lift. It was all pretty miserable.

We did some classics and Ben began to try Chimpanzodrome. To the right of this, Marc le Menestrel had done a new route, Bidule, which he had given 8a+, the hardest route in France. I was trying this, so Ben and I took turns at working out the moves on our routes. The crux of Bidule was quite short, but very difficult, climbing on small finger pockets, and very different from the climbing we had in England.

At that time the French were doing routes in a different style from climbers in the UK and Germany. We were still climbing yo-yo style. With yo-yoing, if you fall, you lower to the ground, but leave the rope clipped through the runners for the next attempt. This could mean that you had to clip very few runners on the next attempt. Within this approach there were also variations, with some people believing that when you fell off, you could climb up as far as the next piece of protection, but not place it or clip it, and then jump off. At the other end of the scale were people who believed that once you fell off, you had to close your eyes and lower to the ground with them shut, so you wouldn't gain any extra knowledge.

With the French method, on the successful ascent, the climber had to clip the rope through all the runners as they went. If you fell off you lowered back down and had to untie, pull the rope back to the ground and start again. This was obviously harder than yo-yoing, but they practised moves beforehand, and would often top-rope climbs a lot before trying to lead them, which we didn't really do. They also typically spent longer working the moves. Marc had spent a long time that winter working on Bidule.

Their style, climbing a route from the bottom to the top, clipping the rope into all the runners as you went, became known as redpointing, from Kurt Albert's painted tags in Frankenjura. In years to come, this method would be accepted all over the world as the standard way of climbing the very hardest routes. It was better in some ways, as it was easier to quantify. Yo-yos were all a bit of a grey area. Sometimes, on a successful yo-yo ascent, you wouldn't clip any runners at all and essentially top-rope the route. Having said that, yo-yoing definitely wasn't any easier than redpointing, it was just a different style, and in some ways, because you never top-roped routes first, it was harder, and there always seemed to be more of a fight involved.

As well as redpointing, the other new terms that were coming into use in France at the time were 'flashing' and 'on-sighting'. When a climber flashes a route, he does it first time, without falling off at all. However, he might have watched other climbers trying the route and know where the holds are and what moves to do. On a hard climb this can make a great difference, because you don't waste precious energy searching for hidden holds. On-sighting means flashing a route with no prior knowledge of where the holds are or how to do the moves. This is much harder than just flashing it. In years to come, when climbing competitions became big, on-sighting was a popular method of climbing, as it is a great test of a climber's skill. Up to that point I had made very little distinction between all these methods. I always wanted to climb a route first try, without falls, and you either climbed it like that or you didn't.

The year before, while staying with the le Menestrels in Paris, I had had an argument with them over dinner. I had heard mention of the term 'on-sight', although I had misunderstood it. I thought that to climb 'on-sight' meant going to the bottom of the route and climbing up it, as long as you hadn't abseiled down it or top-roped it before. Even if it were yo-yoed, as long as you started from the ground and hadn't abseiled it, it was an on-sight. Of course, for them, 'on-sight' meant doing it first time, knowing nothing about the route and without falling off, so it had come as some surprise to them when I said over dinner:

'I am going to on-sight your hardest routes.'

'There's no way,' they said, 'You can't.'

'Yes I am. I am going to on-sight *all* your hardest routes.'

They thought that I was declaring that I was going to go and do all their hardest routes first try, but of course, that wasn't what I meant. Months after that dinner, when it was all explained to me, it dawned on me what they had meant. They must have thought I was pretty arrogant.

Nevertheless, with some of the climbs I did on this trip with Ben, I raised the level of what could be flashed and on-sighted in France. Previously, Edlinger had had the country's hardest on-sight with 7b+, and I would raise that level to 7c+. When I think about this, why I was climbing routes on-sight so much harder than the French on their own rock, I think British style was a big part of the reason. Almost every route I climbed yo-yo style involved a massive amount of fight, always battling hard above a runner, try-ing to get to the next one. And that fight feels very like the fight you need to put in during an on-sight ascent, hanging on for grim death, frantically trying to find a hold good enough to pull on while being pumped and above runners. So although the redpoint ethic meant ultimately you could climb harder routes, the way we climbed in Britain prepared me very well for on-sighting in France.

Plus, I was actually climbing better than everyone else.

It took me three days to do Bidule in yo-yo style. I was happy. This was the hardest route I had done yet. In the meantime, Ben was working on, and finally did, Chimpanzodrome. This was amazing. Ben's previous hard-est climb had been a 7a+. Now it was my turn to try Chimpanzodrome. I had watched Ben try it and knew where the holds were and how to do the moves. I was desperate to try to flash it, but as Bidule had taken so much out of me, I decided to have a rest. So next day, a Saturday, we both hung out and read.

Sunday dawned. 18 March 1984.

'Happy birthday, Jerry.'

It was my twenty-first. Most people, on their twenty-first birthday, think about having a big party, or getting presents. I was on a dusty crag in a deserted corner of France, drinking water with just one friend. But I wouldn't have been anywhere else. I had decided to flash Chimpanzodrome on my birthday and was beside myself with excitement. If I could pull this off, it would be the ultimate birthday imaginable. At the same time, failure would be horrific. The pressure was on. We got up early, walked the hour for bread and back, and on our return, were stunned to see the crag heaving with climbers.

Sunday climbers had arrived from Paris and the normally deserted crag looked like a different place. The French were immaculate, with beautiful matching tops and bottoms, hair coiffured, perfect suntans and towelling headbands. Their karabiners all matched. They were also clean. We mingled with the Parisians like two dogs. Ben, with his pasty white skin, looked about fifteen. His long, black hair was starting to mat into dreadlocks. His clothes were filthy. I too had scruffy clothes, holes in my trousers, my hair dyed into black and red patches, punk style. We looked more like refugees than climbers.

We went over to our cave and got our gear on, and I warmed up by doing a 7b overhang, first go, which attracted some attention from the French. They watched us go over to Chimpanzodrome. At the time, I always climbed in my lucky swami-belt, a simple ribbon of webbing with no leg-loops, to keep myself light. I tied on to a single rope, 9mm in diameter, and fired the pitch off, first try. I ripped it to bits. Straight after, Ben too went up it once more, like a rat up a drainpipe. From there we went to L'Ange, a three pitch 7b+. I on-sighted that too. We came down. The French were stunned. We wandered to the sleeping cave, and as we had done everything that we wanted to do, packed our bags. We might as well head south. *Au revoir.*

As usual, hitching wasn't easy. We made our way to the péage kiosk at the start of the Autoroute du Soleil. No one gave us a lift. The evening passed. It started getting cold and dark, and then, very quickly, a dense freezing fog descended. Within moments we were shivering, and with little chance of getting a lift, we unrolled our mats and sleeping bags and crawled in under the shelter of the péage. That was my twenty-first. In bed, sober at seven o'clock at night, with cars buzzing by at high speed fifty feet away, shivering in a freezing fog.

I was just so happy. It felt like the best climbing day I ever had, and, looking back on my career, if I were to pick one day that stood out above all others, then it would be this one.

Buoux was the crag I had visited on the photo shoot the year before. It's a beautiful wooded valley in the Provence region, with slopes covered in small oak trees and lots of little shrubs, which change to beautiful colours in autumn, capped by amazing, bulging, orange and blue-streaked walls of limestone. Since my visit last year, I had heard that the Parisians, Marc, Antoine and Jibé, had been adding hard, top-level routes here. It seemed the Buoux crags were the new place to be.

After an epic hitch and riding trains for free we finally got there. After a couple of nights sleeping under the bridge in the local town, Apt, menaced regularly by police Alsatians, we decided to move out and slept instead in a cave near the crag. Then we were told about a little hut in the woods at the base of the crag.

'You can stay there if you like, just no mess,' said a young French woman who gave us a lift from Apt to Buoux.

She worked in the ancient auberge at the foot of the valley, in the village of Buoux itself. The hut she showed us was a beautiful little cabin, with nothing in it but a bench and a table. We rolled our sleeping mats and bags out on the floor in what was to be our home for the next four weeks. Each morning we would take the short walk down to the auberge and buy a loaf off her, then spend all day climbing. After that, it was back to the hut. It was still March or April and it got dark and cold early in the evening. In the darkness, all there was to do was eat the bread and crawl into our sleeping bags. We had brought a Sony Walkman with us and we sat side by side with an earphone each. We had a Dionne Warwick tape, a Diana Ross tape, Killing Joke and a load of other punk tapes. Each night we just sat there, wrapped in our sleeping bags, cold and hungry, listening to music.

I started repeating the new routes that had been added to the crag, like Marc's Rêve d'un Papillon, one of the country's first 8as. There were lots of other climbs around 7b+ that I was consistently climbing on-sight. The hardest climb there at the time was Antoine's route, Elixir de Violence and over a few days I started learning the moves.

Then I got really sick.

We had been drinking water straight from the stream that ran down the shallow valley from the farmland above, through a village and fields of horses and cows. One day, because of the water, I got terrible stomach ache and diarrhoea. I started to vomit violently. This lasted three days and all that time I lay curled up in the corner of the hut, feeling like there was a knife in my guts. I was still drinking the stream water, as was Ben, who never became sick. On the third day Ben hitched into town and came back with a little cheap stove and a packet of soup. He heated up the soup, passed it to me and I took a sip.

It tasted amazing! I felt the thick warm flavoursome liquid go down my throat and it was like heaven. This was the first warm food I had tasted in six weeks.

Every day of the trip so far, we ate, for breakfast, half a large baguette, covered one side in Nutella chocolate spread, the other in a squashed banana, divided between two. For dinner, we ate the other half of the baguette, with a layer of cheese and a layer of tomato, again divided between two. To drink, all we ever had was cold stream water.

I did own a camping stove back in Sheffield, but to save space we hadn't bothered bringing it. When hitching, too much equipment and too much weight make travelling awkward. Anyway, I needed all the space in my rucksack I could manage. At the time I was so obsessed by training that I wasn't going to lose my edge on this trip. So I had brought my Bachar Ladder to France, taking up more than half my rucksack. I had set it up at the crag, Stoney-style, and would sometimes spend days laddering, doing laps on routes and running down to the football pitch in the village below to do pull-ups.

After a week of being sick, I finally felt well enough again to try Elixir de Violence. After all the vomiting and diarrhoea, I was as light as a feather and shot straight up it, redpoint style.

After a few weeks, Marc, Antoine and Jibé arrived to do new routes. Until they arrived we hadn't seen another climber there. It was great to have a chance to climb with the French climbers. Despite an obvious sense of competition between us all, it was always positive and brought some great efforts out of everyone. I liked the fact that these top French climbers managed to climb together. It was something that myself and Ben would manage to do too over the years to come, as Ben grew to be a world-class climber. Not every country does this, and I think it is to their detriment. There's a lot to be gained from friendly competition, and I learned a lot from the differing styles and strengths of these three.

Marc and Antoine were superb boulderers, with good technique and finger strength. Antoine was really relaxed and had an artistic air about him. He seemed very creative. I thought he moved really well, with a superb controlled style, very fluid, and he also had incredible stamina. Of the two brothers, Marc was the more powerful, with a more explosive and determined style, and fingers of steel. He was the more proud, and very competitive, not in a nasty way, but you certainly felt it.

Top climbers, as in any other sport, can get competitive. This is usually a fairly healthy thing. I am competitive myself, but I hope I'm good-spirited about it. It's aimed at bringing out the best in everyone and not a wish that the other person won't do well. This sort of very aggressive competitiveness isn't something you come across much in climbing. It certainly wasn't there in 1984 with the French lads. The closest I ever came to it was a few years later in Germany.

Kurt Albert and I had wandered up to Klagemauer, a bouldering area in the Frankenjura. I had been there a couple of years before and met a young, up-and-coming German climber. We had chatted and climbed a bit together and when I arrived at Klagemauer the second time, he was there again. I said hello, asked how he was and how his climbing was going.

'Ach! I think in the moment I am stronger than you.'

Wow. Right. I didn't know what to say. It almost felt funny but it was also kind of heavy. I wasn't too bothered, because I had been doing some routes lately, so I knew where I stood and where my place was. But he wasn't giving up.

'Have you ever climbed The Electrical Storm in Hell, footless and statik?'

Electrical Storm was the classic boulder problem at Klagemauer, the young climber's local crag, linking small holds up a thirty-degree leaning wall of silver limestone. I had done it loads of times years before, when it was hard for its time. I walked over, not warmed up. I took the holds and locked my way up the crimps, with ease, first go. I dropped off and stood there. A range of emotions crossed the young German's face. He was obviously thinking. Finally, he looked triumphant.

'Ach,' he said. 'But I did not say it was hard!'

Marc was nothing like that.

Jibé Tribout would go on to be one of the world's most important climbers. He would bring top grade climbs to countries throughout the world, including America. In 1986 he introduced the grade of 5.14 to America, with To Bolt or Not to Be at Smith Rock. But at the time, in 1983, he still hadn't reached his potential. He was nowhere near as strong as Marc and Antoine, yet he went on to achieve just as much. He had the most amazing motivation and desire, and even though people say natural talent is important, I think it's desire that gets results.

People are often unwilling to acknowledge or give credit to hard work, seeming to prefer talent, even if it's wasted. People often talk about the much-loved Belfast footballer, George Best, as being a great talent. George was a brilliant footballer with Manchester United in the late 1960s. He had real flair and a great personality, and never gave off the impression that he was particularly interested in hard work. He went on to become a playboy. He famously said: 'I spent a lot of my money on booze, birds and fast cars. The rest I just squandered.' At the time, people held him up as being easy-going, but just amazingly talented, which is why he was such a good footballer. But I remember an interview on the radio with someone who used to play football with George in his youth.

'Oh yeah,' he said. 'George Best was always the first on the training pitch and the last off, whatever the weather.'

Of course he was. He worked hard. Jibé was like that. He wanted it and he got it.

In years to come we all remained good friends and I was always welcome at their family home near Paris, just as they were always welcome at mine.

Even their sister, Severine, stayed at my house for two months, and she wasn't even a climber.

Amongst the routes I did at Buoux was a recent 7c of Antoine's. It took a long, sweeping overhang on one of the biggest walls there, named after the original route on that sector, La Mission. One day the three French climbers were all sitting on top of the crag, overlooking the Mission wall, and they watched me climb it on-sight. Antoine later told me that to see someone climb a route at that level, first try without falls, blew them away. He was very gracious and it really seemed to inspire him. It showed him what was possible in the on-sight style, and some years later, Antoine went on to be the first person to on-sight 8a. This was the great thing about travelling, where you don't just have a chance to learn from the routes and climbing of other countries, but you can also bring your attitudes and ideas to them.

A week later, Wolfgang showed up with his friend Helmut, and we hung out. Helmut owned a Mercedes estate car. Ben and I were agog. A Mercedes estate! He drove us into town and we went to a café, where Helmut ordered coffee and croissants all round. We were eating these thinking, 'Cool! A croissant!' When Helmut offered to buy the round, we were psyched out. Wolfgang looked at the rope we were climbing on. It was an ancient pink rope, nine millimetres in diameter, to be used as a pair in the British style. It was frayed and tattered. It had hard and soft bits, and bits where the precious kernel poked through the protective mantle. He was shocked and gave us one of his better eleven millimetres. Wolfgang and Helmut were driving from Buoux to the Verdon Gorge and offered us a lift. We took it.

The Verdon Gorge was the classic venue in the south of France in the mid 1980s. It wasn't far from Buoux, but was much higher and had a more rugged feel to it. There were big, grey limestone mountains everywhere, and the air was cooler and much cleaner. Through these mountains ran a huge gorge popular with tourists. They would pop out of their cars and come and stare over the edge, and it would take their breath away. It took *our* breath away. It was almost a mile across and its walls were vertical or bulging sheets of the most beautiful silver and blue and yellow rock. These walls dropped for a thousand feet to the depths below. At the bottom, dusty slopes ran down to a turquoise river at the base, thin and cold looking, having flowed far from distant snowy mountains. It was funny to compare the hugeness of the gorge with the tiny river that made it.

The gorge had a long climbing history and was one of the world's great climbing destinations. There were long and serious routes that went from the bottom, fifteen pitches long covering two thousand vertical feet. It also had shorter routes on the upper hundreds of feet. The road from the local village, La Palud, led to within feet of the lip of the gorge, so for convenience, most climbers would abseil in from here and climb out on routes that were usually between one and six pitches long. This allowed for harder and more technical climbs than the longer, more serious ones that started on the valley floor.

The gorge had been the birthplace of French free-climbing. Years before, aid climbing had been practiced here, but in the 1970s, Ron Fawcett and Pete Livesey had visited, and seeing the potential that the steep hold-covered walls held, started to free-climb the French routes. This was a revolutionary step for the time and really influenced the French climbing scene, showing them what was possible on their own crags. Since then great French climbers had really developed the crag, none more so than Patrick Edlinger.

Edlinger was a contemporary of Fawcett's and pushed standards in France. He had long blond hair and climbed in a really slow, elegant, controlled way. Very French. There were loads of photos of him doing amazing climbs in the Verdon, super looking routes on one and two finger pockets, the floor miles below. Sometimes he climbed them solo, sometimes barefoot. 'Le Blond', as he was known, gave off a romantic sense of freedom, making him a bit of a hero in France, way beyond the climbing scene, in a way that no one was in England.

We had a great time climbing here. Kurt Albert turned up to meet Wolfgang. He had brought an enormous rope, two hundred metres long, which he raved about. With this he would lower us for hundreds of feet down multi-pitch climbs to top-rope them, sometimes with both Ben and me tied on, a few feet apart. Down we went, down forever it felt like, with no control. Gripping. We would then spend ages climbing continually for hundreds of feet back to the summit rim.

In Verdon, I tore into repeating some of the routes in good style. I on-sighted a 7c that a top French climber called Jean-Marc Troussier was trying. I shot right up it in front of him and he was absolutely stunned. He had never heard of people on-sighting at this level. He took photos and got me onto the front cover of the French climbing magazine, Alpinismo, which was great. I also on-sighted a 7c+ called Pol Pot, the first route of that grade ever on-sighted, anywhere. Years later, when I was competing, one of my main friends and rivals was Didier Raboutou. Didier later told me that he had watched me on-sight Pol Pot, which had inspired him to take a look at his own climbing. He went on to become one of the best, and *the* person to beat in the climbing competitions that would soon start taking place across Europe.

Where the road met the crag there were thick green metal railings that the tourists would lean over. Right beneath the most popular viewpoint were some classic one-pitch routes, as well as a famous open project. A route had been bolted and despite the efforts of Marc, Antoine and Patrick Edlinger, it had not yet been climbed. Since it was now up for grabs, I decided to have a go.

Ben and I threw our ropes over the edge to abseil down to the belay. We only had one abseiling device between us, so Ben used this to go down first, sliding down a hundred feet of rope to arrive at the belay. Because the walls are so steep, these belays often had no ledges to stand on, so the belayer would just tie directly into some bolts and hang on his harness, with hundreds of feet of exposure dropping away below your feet.

With no belay plate or abseiling device of my own, I descended on a sliding friction knot, with the rope simply wrapped around a karabiner to slow my descent. The exposure in Verdon is incredible and you normally grip your ropes pretty tightly when abseiling here. Which was lucky, because somehow I managed to cause the rope to become unravelled from the karabiner. I heard a click and looked down to see the rope hanging free, not attached to me in any way. I was now hanging off the rope by one hand with hundreds of feet below me. I did a one-arm lock-off and with my free hand wrapped the rope back into the karabiner. Oops! I got to the belay, tied on in relief and relaxed. A few people have been killed in this way.

'Bloody hell, Ben, that was close.'

'Jerry, look,' said Ben.

I looked up. There, on the rim of the gorge, were about a hundred faces peering over the edge looking at us. Some climbers must have shown an interest and once that happens, tourists aren't long in joining in. They were aware of the reputation of the route we were about to try. No pressure then.

First time up I battled through the steepness on little fingerholds and tiny pockets, clipping bolts as I went. Higher, there was a desperate jump out rightwards to a sloping sidepull. This was the crux and I almost got it first try. I flew off into space and the rope caught me. I lowered down. Deciding that, as a first ascent, I should do it French style and not yo-yo, I pulled the rope back down. After a quick rest, I set off again. Once more I fell off, but closer to the sidepull. Third time, I got it and immediately locked it in to grasp better holds above, leading to an easier sprint to the top of the crag. All the tourists gave a round of applause. I had managed the first ascent of Papy on Sight, a superb new classic 8a. It was a fantastic first ascent to get because it was in Verdon's most popular location and was a known project tried by all the stars. I was ecstatic.

By now, Ben and I were starting to get burned out. After Papy on Sight, we spent a day hanging around the campsite in the sun with Wolfgang, Helmut and Kurt. We had been climbing non-stop for months, always going hungry, and we felt worn out. Still, we were fit, and for once, Ben's pale skin had actually gotten a pretty good tan. As it was the last day, he decided to go and have a shower. He hadn't washed once during the whole six weeks on the basis that if you haven't washed for two weeks, then you might as well keep going, because another four weeks won't make any difference. When he returned from the shower however, he looked like a ghost. All his tan had gone. He stood there, once again that pasty blue-white he had always been. His tan had all been dirt. Wolfgang almost choked with laughter. Tired, but clean, we set off the following day to make the long journey back to England.

When I look back over my climbing career, I think that these were possibly my best years. During those trips to the USA, France and Germany, with the new routes, solos and on-sights I was doing in Wales and England, I pushed world standards. It was a chance for me to compare myself with the other top climbers at the time, and I would say I was probably a couple of years ahead of them all in 1983 and 1984. It would be some time before the world caught up with me. I was young and very ambitious, I worked hard and I had some luck. Things had gone my way. It was a great time.

EIGHT

The Phoenix Burns

By 1985, I had been climbing constantly for seven years. I had gone from being a total beginner to putting up the hardest routes in Britain. I had travelled to some of the best climbing areas in the world, had done their hardest routes and added my own. Things had been going really well and it meant absolutely everything to me.

To do this I had pushed my body to the limit, every day of every year. I had climbed the hardest climbs and boulder problems. I had trained as hard as I could at every opportunity. Every day, I had worked to become a better climber – I was doing pull-ups in my parents' garage on Christmas Day – and I knew what physical exhaustion felt like. I had demanded a lot from my body, and, in 1985, it finally broke.

For years I had been getting used to constant pain in my elbows. All through my first trips to America, Germany and France, I had felt shocking twinges running up from my elbows when I straightened my arms. I had paid it little attention, always training harder and harder, telling myself that sooner or later, this pain would go away. I took a lot of aspirin.

In the summer of 1984, I had arranged another trip to America. I was going to go back to Yosemite Valley where there were a couple of things I wanted to do. I wanted to repeat Midnight Lightning, the world's greatest boulder problem, and do The Phoenix, the hardest crack-climb in the Valley. I got psyched, and as usual, stepped up my training another notch. I worked like an animal in preparation, blinded by my determination to succeed.

Once again my training was paying off. In the summer of that year, before going to America, I added a new route to Raven Tor in Derbyshire that was to set a new standard. This fierce, overhanging limestone crag, right beside a narrow dead-end road in a secluded valley, had been the forcing ground for hard climbing in the last couple of years, blowing the Stoney routes out of the water in terms of difficulty. In 1982, Ron Fawcett had freed routes like Sardine and The Prow to give climbs as hard as any at the time. The Prow was big news, but Ron's climb had avoided one major issue.

The old aid line of The Prow followed a very steep groove, and unlike a lot of the rock at Raven Tor, appeared to be totally holdless. Ron had traversed in to the route from an easier start on the left. This was still accepted as a free version of The Prow, because no one believed the true start would ever go free. Some people had tried, but seldom got any further than running their hands up and down the smooth-sided groove, confirming to themselves that there really was nothing to pull on. It had a very futuristic look about it, and some of those who had tried it – and many who hadn't – said it would never go free. I never thought it would either, although every now and again would have another try at it.

One time I was trying an overhanging route in the middle of the crag. I had previously tried this, but a lot of the holds were loose. Tom Proctor, who had developed the notoriously-loose routes at Stoney Middleton, had told me about some of his tricks. He had told me he would sometimes pour cement behind the holds to make them solid. I tried this on the Raven Tor route, but it hadn't set, so I spent another day scraping it off again. I spent another day again securing the holds with Araldite, and this time they were solid. Returning to do a first ascent, for some reason I allowed Tim Freeman to try it first, and after several attempts, he did it. He named it Weedkiller.

I was really annoyed with myself. I did it straight after, first go, but was still annoyed. In this mood, I went to have another try at the impossible groove of The Prow. I tried something no one had thought of before; I put my knee into the groove. Somehow the friction of my thigh against the smooth rock held me in place perfectly and I climbed it. Wow! I was so psyched. Below this section there was a very powerful and fingery entry into the groove, off a tiny finger pocket. However, this suited my strength perfectly and I was able to crank through this move too.

'This is going to go,' I thought to myself. I could barely sleep that night with excitement.

I spent a day preparing the route and returned a few days later and led it. There was no doubt about it: this was a different level to anything that had gone before. Not only did people imagine it would be hard, they thought it was *impossible*. It was the hardest route in the country. I named it Revelations.

Not long after, Ben Moon, who was climbing better all the time, added a tough new route on the Pen Trwyn crags in Llandudno. When we had developed the crag in 1983, we had mostly climbed on the crags above the Marine Drive. Beneath the road was another band of cliffs, Lower Pen Trwyn, dropping steeply to the pebble beach below. This had a very overhanging wall, with beautiful brown and orange bulges blasting out for almost sixty feet. Its central section overhung by almost thirty degrees. It was gobsmacking, and in 1983 was beyond the levels of the time. In 1984, Ben climbed a route called Statement of Youth, taking less steep rock at the right-hand side of the bulging section. He graded it E7 6b, being towards the end of the time when the traditional British grades were still being used for sport climbs. In French grading, it turned out to be 8a, the magical grade, and the first in Wales. However, besides the difficulty and quality of the route – it was a tremendous pitch – what marked out Statement was its use of bolts.

For the first time, a route that had not previously been an aid route had been fully bolt protected, French style. Ben had abseiled down and drilled and placed eight bolts to protect 80 feet of climbing. And not only that, he had placed them in places where it would have been possible to place natural protection – nuts or Friends – in order to make an entirely bolted-up climb. It raised a few eyebrows at the time among the ethics police, but ultimately what won through was the quality of Ben's route. I fancied a go at this. I told him I was going to go over to Wales to give it a try.

At the time we still didn't have any transport and were still hitching to get around. I got the bus from Sheffield that led to the top of the Stoney valley with Ben. He was going to get off and walk down to Raven Tor, while I was going to get my thumb out and hitch over to Wales. I asked him about the route.

'It's hard, Jerry. It took me six days to do it, but if you get good conditions, you might do it in three,' he said.

I think I might do it a lot quicker than that, I thought to myself.

By late that evening, I had arrived in Llandudno. The following morning, I scrambled down the rocky descent path to the boulder beach and did some easier routes to warm up. I then got on Statement of Youth. The moves weren't super-desperate, but the route was long and very strenuous. I was climbing the route yo-yo style, which, although it was quickly going out of fashion, was still an acceptable way of climbing. By mid-afternoon, I was getting high on the route. However, this part of the crag is tidal, and twice a day the water comes in and immerses the lower section of the cliff.

At about half past three, with the water lapping at our feet, I was forced to abandon my attempts and go for a stroll along the pier. I watched the water rise and fall, and as soon as the level was low enough, in the cool of the early evening, I was down there again and tying back onto the ropes. On the next try I succeeded. I'd got the second ascent in a single day. But only just. It had been a lot harder than I was expecting. That was probably the last route I ever climbed yo-yo. It is a fantastic route, one of the best 8as in the country.

In spite of the pain in my elbows, I was fit and strong, and in October 1985 I arrived once again in Yosemite Valley where I met up with Bachar. It was good to see him again. I told him I wanted to do Midnight Lightning.

In the dead centre of Camp 4, the climbers' campsite, there is an enormous block of the finest granite, more than thirty feet high and forty square. It has been bouldered on by generations of great climbers. It is beautiful and has vertical tiger-stripes of black and light grey where running water has changed the colour of the rock. Some of the faces are easy-angled slabs, but some are steep. One face is so steep and overhanging that winter rain never touches it. This has left the face pristine white and it's where Midnight Lightning goes, a problem acknowledged at that time as the world's greatest.

The problem was first climbed in 1978. Legend has it that one day two Valley hotshots, John Bachar and the younger Ron Kauk, were returning from the cliffs. One of the older climbers there, John 'Yabo' Yablonski, ran over to them, ranting about an amazing route he had found up the steep face of the huge Camp 4 boulder. In the 1970s, the hippy Yosemite-based climbing scene was awash with hallucinogenic drugs, and Yabo had spent that day wandering among the boulders on an LSD trip. He dragged the two climbers to the boulder and pointed out his imaginary route. The rock overhung by thirty degrees, and at twelve feet, a large roof jutted out. Above this, the angle kicked back to a slab. To the eyes of the climbers, the steep face had no holds. At that time, nothing so steep and featureless had ever been climbed, and Kauk and Bachar dismissed Yablonski's trippy ideas.

A few days later, Yablonski started trying his route. He found that there were indeed small holds on the face, just big enough for the fingertips. These were a long way apart and there were no footholds to use, so Yabo was jumping between the holds, but failing to hold onto them. When Bachar and Kauk saw this they were inspired. Together they worked on the problem continually for months until Ron Kauk finally pulled over onto the slab above the overhang. Not long later, so too did Bachar. They named it Midnight Lightning after a crucial lightning-bolt-shaped hold just below the roof. A legend was born. For years Midnight Lightning was *the* state-of-the-art boulder problem. Everyone who came to the Valley tried it and always came away empty-handed. The problem had a huge aura about it. Just before I arrived, Skip Guerin had finally done the third ascent.

After warming up, Bachar and I went to the boulder. It took three tries to work out the sequence of moves to the lightning-bolt hold. From here, another throw gets the bottom edge of the slab, just over the small overhang.

At this point, my feet were taking very little weight and the position was very strenuous. I had to try to get my foot very high so I could rock over onto the slab, but the move felt hard and committing. Below, a boulder stuck out of the ground and I could easily imagine falling off, breaking my ankles on it. I hung the lip of the slab, shaking out, trying to recover some strength. I knew that there was a small hold somewhere above, which I could use to get my weight onto the easier-angled rock above. But I couldn't find it.

True to form, Bachar stood below, arms folded, watching in silence. He knew exactly where the crucial hold was and watched me fumbling, desperate to locate it. Bachar said nothing. He would happily watch me fall off before telling me where the hold was. Eventually, after trying to commit to the move a few times, I reversed and jumped off, exhausted.

I sat disappointed on the ground.

'Good effort,' Bachar said.

A figure emerged from the trees and greeted Bachar, then nodded to me.

'Hey, how you getting on there?'

He was a muscular, tanned, dark-haired climber, and I recognized him as Ron Kauk. He had a very friendly, relaxed air about him and I told him about my attempts. He put his rock shoes on and straight off, climbed Midnight Lightning. I saw where the hold was that I hadn't found. He spotted me on my next attempts, and after a couple more tries, I pulled over onto the slab. I had done Midnight Lightning.

'That was sweet, man,' Kauk congratulated me. 'You looked good on those little holds up there. That was good to see.'

He shook my hand and said that he had to be getting off, but before leaving he added he hoped he'd see me around. We became very good friends.

Next up was The Phoenix, a desperate single-pitch crack climb, high above the valley near the Cathedral Falls area. It had earned the unprecedented grade of 5.13a. Ray Jardine had made the first ascent in 1977, sieging the route over many days. Everyone who had done it since had adopted the same style. For this reason, The Phoenix had a rather tarnished reputation among the more ethically-minded Valley climbers. I was determined to climb it on my first attempt and had trained hard with this in mind, building up stamina and crack technique. After so much preparation, when the opportunity to try these things finally comes around, the pressure is huge. After months of training and years of dreaming about it, there is only one chance to do a climb first try. One fall means failure; there are no second chances of flashing a route. I was in the bar one night after a good day's climbing, and after a few beers decided tomorrow would be the day. I had been climbing well on cracks, had a good flow going, and reasoned that if I took a rest day, what I might gain in recovery, I would lose in momentum.

The next day Skip Guerin and I drove up the Valley, parked up and abseiled to a hanging belay. Above me, a stunning one-to-two-inch crack split a big grey granite wall. I had worked hard towards this point. Now was the time to let rip.

The climb started with a technical groove leading to a rightwards traverse. I had planned to get protection at the top of the groove then down-climb for a rest, but the moves had been irreversible. I was committed. I fought out rightwards, stuffing fingers into flared jams just about good enough to take my weight, while my feet smeared desperately on the smooth rock below. I lurched into the crack proper where better jams allowed me some recovery. From here I faced another eighty feet of overhanging crack. What I had to do now was keep my cool, climb well and not blow it. Without wasting any time, I set off up the crack, every move a fight, but every movement perfect, with the pump in my forearms getting worse all the time.

Near the top the crack closes off and inclines to the right. It's too small for hands. The finishing holds are up and left, around a small overhang. I tried the move to reach them, built my feet up as high as I could, stretched out my left hand, but couldn't reach the holds. I tried again, feet even higher this time, but still couldn't reach. I felt my arms grow weaker and weaker from the effort spent climbing the last hundred and twenty feet. I was one move away from flashing The Phoenix, but time was running out. It's at moments like this that every minute of preparation matters. The difference between almost getting up something and actually getting up something, is everything. The difference between getting to the last move and actually doing the last move, could be a month of training.

I had done that month of training. I dug deep, shook the blood down into my arms, built my feet up even higher and was totally committed. I stretched out my hand. I got the hold and quickly pulled up onto easy ground. I had flashed The Phoenix. Nobody had even come close to flashing a route of this grade before, and to do it on a classic like The Phoenix was one of the greatest thrills of my climbing career. Every pull-up, every ladder session, every traverse had got me here and it had all been worth it.

Two days later, in the Valley, a short, stocky American came up to me.

'Hi, I'm Mark Hudon. I hear you did The Phoenix first try.'

Oh my God, I thought, Mark Hudon, the legend from the early Mountain magazines, and he's congratulating *me*. The Phoenix was one of the climbs that he and Max Jones had been trying in their article that had inspired me all those years ago.

'Awesome. I never thought that would be possible.'

I had done Midnight Lightning and flashed The Phoenix. I had achieved what I had wanted to do. But within days my elbows got worse. After a week, I could barely straighten my arms. The shocks that ran down them became agony. I could almost feel them falling apart. My need for painkillers rose and I found myself with days to kill in the Valley, not really sure what to do.

I started hanging out a lot with Ron Kauk. Bachar, and his wife Brenda, lived in Foresta, a town not far from Yosemite. They let Kauk and me stay there with them. We would go to Yosemite, hang out, meet people and go drinking in the valley or in town. I would go to the crag with him, just to hang out. He had that thing I really like in people, where you could have a great laugh together, spend loads of time mucking around, but when it was time to climb, the messing would stop and he would focus. Once the climbing was over, he became good fun again no matter how well or badly he felt he did. He reminded me of Kurt Albert in that respect.

Bachar had always spoken well of Ron Kauk. The most gifted, natural climber he had ever seen, he said. Kauk moved very smoothly and had great footwork. He had very strong fingers, perhaps the most important thing for a climber. He also had powerful calves and when we would later climb together, I'd be amazed at the ease with which he could stand up on tiny footholds. He was an incredible natural athlete, once appearing on a US television show called Fittest of Them All. Despite having done virtually no preparation – he showed up dressed in 1970s hippy gear of white trousers, long hair and bandana – he performed superbly against a field of top Olympic skiers, runners, canoeists and athletes from other professional sports. Had he not been deducted points when he refused to swim in a river that he considered too dangerous, he would have won. He would go on to add many of the US's hardest routes and really moved the sport on there. In 1995, he became the first American to climb 8c. On the day of his thirty seventh birthday, he redpointed Burn for You in the Frankenjura. I watched him do it and it was great to see.

After weeks of not climbing at all, I found that with enough painkillers, I could manage the odd day. It was December and I wasn't in a hurry to go back to a wet and cold British winter. I stayed in California, travelling from Yosemite to Joshua Tree, where I ran into my friends from France, Antoine, Marc and Jibé. It was good to see them again.

From there, we took a trip to a newly-discovered area called Hueco Tanks. Some of the climbers in Joshua Tree had heard about it and, along with Mike and Mari Lechlinski, and Russ the Fish, we drove an ancient Oldsmobile to Texas. Here, even though I was barely climbing, I had one of my best trips ever.

Hueco would become one of the world's major climbing areas, but in 1984, it was almost totally undiscovered. We wandered the rocky desert landscape, finding and climbing some of the best boulder problems ever. The rock was naturally very clean and the problems took no preparation. We never saw any other climbers, not even the evidence of other climbers. In fact we saw no one, only a big redneck ranger who, every time we went somewhere, would turn up carrying his rifle and smoking a cigar, and ask:

'What do you boys want here, huh?'

We climbed, wandered, wondered, and left, not recording anything. It was magical.

When I got back to Joshua Tree, John Bachar got in touch with me. Bachar was capable of some of the most frustrating and incomprehensible behaviour I have come across. At the same time, he was also capable of the most amazing displays of generosity. He had heard about my injuries.

'Jerry, I know a specialist in LA, this guy's supposed to be the best in the US. You know who he's just been treating?'

'Who?'

'Michael Jackson. You know? The kid who used to sing in The Jackson Five?'

'I know who Michael Jackson is.'

Bachar talked on about the top sports stars that the doctor had treated, but I hadn't heard of them. He then went on to say that, because he was doing well from distributing the Fire rock boots, he didn't mind paying for my treatment. I was stunned.

'These boots are looking after me well, Jerry.'

He made an appointment and the following week, I headed down to LA where I hooked up with Bachar. He had been having some problems with his shoulders and was joining me at the hospital. We arrived at a huge silver and glass multi-storey building in downtown LA and were shown to the waiting room. The doctor called me. He examined my arms, prodded the muscles and tendons. He asked where it hurt, what the pain felt like and enquired about my training history. He decided, after about fifteen minutes, that I had tendonitis in my elbows.

With heavy training, when you are always on the limit of what you can do, tendons, the thin sinewy strips of fibre that connect muscles to bones, can become damaged. The collagen fibre making up the tendon develops tiny tears and becomes rough and jagged. As these jagged fibres move, they rub against each other and cause inflammation. They develop scar tissue, making it hard for them to repair themselves properly.

'What do you suggest?'

The doctor prescribed a lengthy series of treatments in the gym and I was to start right away. These involved exercising the damaged tendons, only using the lightest of weights. This would re-align the fibres, increase blood flow and allow the tendons to heal.

Bachar came with me the first few times, doing similar exercises for his shoulders. In the gym, he pointed out some of the people there. 'That's so-and-so', he would say, 'from the Dallas Cowboys.' 'That guy plays basketball for the Lakers.' 'That guy on the treadmill got gold in the last Olympics.' He was pretty excited by this.

I stayed in LA and followed the treatment for nearly two months. In that time I lived with John's mother, in a little house out near LAX, the international airport. Bachar stayed there for a while too, but soon had to leave on a business trip, so I stayed on with his mother and brother. I didn't have too much to do. To help with the treatment, I was following a macrobiotic diet. This was based mainly on eating grains, such as brown rice, maybe a little fish, lots of vegetables and fruit, but only ones grown organically and locally. So in the morning I would get up, prepare food, go for a walk, have more food, go to the gym and do my exercises, come home, and have dinner.

In the evenings I would often hang out with Bachar's brother. He was living with his mother, trying to overcome addictions to drugs and alcohol. He was a great guy, good company and he would often bring me along to his AA meetings. Here, people would talk about themselves and their addictions and I heard some horrific tales of debauchery. It was interesting. Often too, they would have 'birthdays', celebrations of the anniversaries of the last times they drank, or took drugs. People would stand up and tell their stories:

'Hi, I'm Peter. I was a heroin user for seven years.'

So the time in LA passed, sleeping, cooking, eating, AA meetings and gym visits, desperately hoping to feel some improvement, and glad when something finally came along to give me a break from it all. I was going to be on TV.

Wide World of Sport, the ABC's flagship Saturday afternoon sports show, wanted to film Ron Kauk and me climbing The Lost Arrow in Yosemite. In the mid 1980s, the show attracted America's highest weekly viewing figures. This was the big time.

The Lost Arrow is a huge granite spire that sits beside Yosemite Falls, the highest waterfall in North America. The Falls are a massive tourist attraction, and everyone who visits them looks across to the tip of The Lost Arrow, over two thousand feet high and almost a hundred feet from the rim of the waterfall's viewing platform. It is on much the same level, but with a breathtaking chasm between the two. Kauk and I were to spend two days climbing the spire from the floor of the Valley, sleeping halfway up the route. Between shows on Friday and Saturday, ABC would switch over live and follow our progress. On the second day, our arrival on the summit would be the highlight of the programme.

Kauk and I hung out before the climb, getting to know the TV crew and preparing for the ascent. On the Friday, we set off. The route was long and, despite having a fairly low grade, turned out to be a lot harder than I was expecting. This wasn't the face climbing I was used to, with small holds and steep rock. The route was almost all enormous corners, cracks, wide cracks and chimneys. It had huge features where you would wedge your entire arm, or body, far into the depths of the crag, and wriggle and thrutch desperately upwards. The good thing was that it wasn't hurting my elbows, as I virtually never used my fingers. The bad thing was that it was absolutely terrifying, as the huge cracks would often be too wide to take any protection. On one pitch, I was leading a chimney. I was right inside it, climbing with my back pressed against one wall, my legs braced across the gap with my feet on the other. I would walk my feet a couple of steps up one wall, then, using my hands, shove my back up the other. I did this for a bit, getting higher and higher above the belay. Smooth, featureless walls swept away below, deep inside the cliff. There was no protection. My legs have always been really skinny and because they were taking all the weight, they started to become pumped. They began to shake. I looked at them, then down at the void a long way below, with my rope dropping into the darkness. It looked like death. If I fall off here, I thought, I'm in big trouble.

I felt right at my limit. The pitch had first been done in 1936 and was graded 5.8, the equivalent of HVS, a grade I had climbed as a novice. But I just couldn't do it. Praying for my life, I climbed back down to the belay.

'You're going to have to lead the chimneys,' I told Ron.

Kauk is one of those climbers who can climb anything. Put any sort of pitch in front of him, slab, crack, corner, chimney, overhang, arête and he will get up it. Kauk racked up and whistled up the chimney. I was most impressed. With a rope from above and without the fear of the protection-less climbing, I set off to follow in safety. But I still couldn't do the moves. I ended up grabbing the rope and pulled myself up hand over hand, Batman style, to the belay. I was disgusted with myself.

'No,' I said. 'I'm not having that. I'm not going to pull up the rope on a HVS, you're going to have to lower me down and I'm going to do it properly this time.'

He did. When I Batmanned up the rope for a second time, mumbling something about having to keep to the schedule, I had to admit that I wasn't very good at chimneys.

The climb went on. We did pitch after pitch and slept that night on a ledge at half height, just right of the huge waterfall. By the end of the second day, we were approaching the summit of the spire. We had suffered some hold-ups, so were a little behind schedule. Finally, Kauk led the top pitch, a very hard slab leading onto the summit. I followed, but fell off the crux move. Wanting to do it properly for the cameras, I got Kauk to lower me back to the belay and I set off again, this time successfully. I'd made it to the top. We high-fived and whooped, hamming it up for the cameras.

By now the show had over-run its schedule into the main evening news slot. They kept us running. On the summit, we had a Tyrolean traverse set up, a tensioned rope stretched between anchors on the summit of the spire over to the rim on the other side. This was our escape route. We clipped karabiners into our harnesses, attached these to the tensioned rope and then slid across the void to the TV cameras on the other side. It's a very easy thing to do, and safe, but to non-climbers it looks spectacular, probably even more so than the climbing. We arrived like two heroes on the other side.

I didn't know it at the time, and wouldn't have been particularly bothered, but we were attracting a huge audience – over thirty million viewers were tuned in. It was before cable or satellite and this programme was the biggest thing around. After it I was recognised nearly everywhere I went and tourists would buy me drinks in the Yosemite bar.

After so long in America, I now faced heading back to England. In America, despite the injury, life was good. I had spent a lot of time in Yosemite, Joshua Tree and Hueco, hanging out with friends in beautiful places, doing lots of swimming and generally having a nice time. The thought of going back to a wet English summer, hanging around in Sheffield with nothing much to do, all felt a bit depressing. My future was uncertain and for the first time ever, I had no direction.

Back in Sheffield and with nowhere else to go, I moved in with my old friends Andy Pollitt and Martin Atkinson. They were both climbing well at the time, but despite this, I made every effort to keep out of climbing altogether. I didn't follow what was going on, never asked them what they had been doing, never read a magazine. I had done the physio in America and continued to do it in Sheffield. I had done all the exercises, had eaten anything I thought might make a difference, tried everything, but still there was no improvement. Nothing. Any straightening of my arms at all and I would still get the electric shocks.

I sat around with nothing to inspire me: no trips, no projects, no direction and no motivation. After so long spent striving to achieve in climbing, I was left with no focus to my life. That was probably the biggest thing about not climbing. I no longer had any goals. As I watched my hopes of improvement diminish over time, I even lost the goal of getting better. The longer I sat there, the more I started to think of myself as an unemployable climber with no hopes or prospects and no chance of ever climbing again. It was quite a dark time.

That summer, Antoine le Menestrel and Jibé Tribout came to England.

They suffered from pretty bad weather and the only place they were able to find dry rock was at Raven Tor. Antoine soon repeated my route Revelations, which, when I had first done it the year before, had been the hardest thing around. Its bouldery nature suited him well. Jibé tried it too, but the powerful climbing was less suited to him and was having less success. With nothing much else to do at the crag, and while waiting for Jibé to succeed, Antoine led the route a few times and then soloed it.

This was a great achievement. Revelations is not a particularly big route, about sixty or seventy feet, but that's big enough and while the crux is low down, it's above a terrible landing. Above this it becomes easier, but not that easy, and the climbing is not particularly positive. All the time you're getting higher above an unfriendly landing. Fall off it anywhere and you might be lucky enough just to break both your legs.

Antoine must have been pretty pleased with himself about coming to another county and soloing its hardest route. But for me it was one of the most frustrating moments of my time spent injured. I had to admit it was a good effort, outrageous even, and there was nothing I could take away from him for doing it. But there was absolutely nothing I could do as a response to it. I couldn't go and add something harder, I couldn't go and solo something. I couldn't go back to France and do one of his hard routes. I was gutted. I had been climbing with Antoine only the year before, and had felt I was stronger than him and climbing better. Now I just had to sit and watch him do this.

I needed something to occupy my mind. My old school friend, Andrew Henry, owned a motorbike and he took me for a ride on it. It was a Yamaha TZ400, a two-stroke machine that was incredibly quick in a straight line and it really blew me away. He let me ride it and I remember pulling back on the throttle, the front wheel lifting off the ground as it took off. Wow! There had been a long tradition of climbers riding bikes. Fawcett had ridden bikes and before him, Brown and Whillans used them in the 1950s. Ben, Tim Freeman and Chris Gore all had bikes. I wanted one.

I had been well paid for the Wide World of Sport broadcast, and as a result of that, for the first time in my life, I had some spare cash. I took myself off to Manhattan Motorcycles, went in and pointed at the first bike I saw.

'I'll have that one, please.'

It was a Honda CB100, an ugly little orange single-cylinder machine, which cost £300. It was little more than a moped, and using this I learned to ride, going on to pass my test. I sold the Honda, and picked up a really nice Italian Moto Guzzi. For the first time in my life I was mobile.

Desperate to escape the endless sitting around in Sheffield, I thought about Kurt and Wolfgang. To give myself a break, I decided one afternoon that I would go out and visit them. So I gave them a ring, and within the hour, was bombing down through England. I crossed the Channel, blasted through France, and early next day, arrived in the familiar surroundings of Obertrubach. Kurt and Wolfgang welcomed me warmly and I relaxed instantly. I ended up staying with them for the next five months. It would be a great time, a time that would not only save my state of mind, but also go on to save my climbing career.

Kurt and Wolfgang always seemed to have a big and little brother relationship. They shared a house, but didn't live in each other's pockets. They would sit in silence for days and not feel any need to speak. Two good friends of Kurt's, Norbert Betz and Norbert Sander, both owned successful outdoor shops in Nuremberg. They were big shops, with separate floors for climbing, skiing and walking departments. I got part-time jobs in both these shops, working in the ski department. I would wax the skis, fit the customers' boots, get their height and weight and adjust the bindings between the boots and the skis to match their measurements. I worked a few mornings each week.

At the weekends, Norbert Sander would hire a coach and take customers and his staff into the mountains to ski. My wages just allowed me to go on these trips, and so, virtually every weekend, I would ski. Even Kurt, who was going through one of his regular non-climbing phases, got into skiing, and we had a great time together. In this way, I passed the winter. I didn't worry about my elbows at all.

One morning Norbert Sander was talking to me in his shop.

'So, Jerry, your elbows don't seem to be improving?'

I told him I was starting to lose hope for them and wasn't sure what I would do if they didn't improve.

'I was thinking last night. There is a doctor I know in Munich. Professor Feldmaier. He's the top of his field. Why don't you let me give him a call? I think he will be interested in you.'

'I suppose,' I said, and Norbert led me up to his office.

Norbert, I had noticed, seemed to be very well connected. In his conversations, and in what others had said about him, he seemed to know people in the government, and lots of top academics and business people. On the phone, he got through to the professor. It was interesting to see how relaxed he was talking to him. He laughed, then got really animated and started saying my name.

'*Englander.*' '*Kletterer.*' 'Champion.'

After some time, he hung up.

'It is so, Jerry. Professor Feldmaier will see you next week.'

'Really?'

'Of course. He says your case sounds intriguing. He has not heard of such an injury before. And I am telling him that you are a top climber, best in your field, a real world champion.'

'Oh?'

'You are, aren't you?'

'I suppose I am, yes.'

'Now, Jerry, go back to work. I don't pay you to sit around.'

I was to go to the Olympic hospital in Munich the following Wednesday. That morning, I got on my bike for the three-hour ride and thanked Norbert as I was leaving.

'Just one thing, Jerry. Professor Feldmaier, he looks… be ready.'

'For what?'

'His eyes, they are enormous and they bulge from his head. And the glasses he wears are so thick.' Norbert held his hands like crab pincers in front of his eyes, the distance between his thumb and index finger indicating two inches of glass. 'And he is very pale. And he has the biggest hands you have ever seen. Also, he is over two metres tall. And there is a hole in his head, here.'

With that, Norbert pointed to the centre of his forehead. Then screwed his face up into a Halloween face and began to laugh. Laughing too, I rode away.

The Olympic was a state-of-the-art hospital in the centre of Munich. It was enormous, with a very modern feel about it. A gorgeous receptionist sent me to the twelfth floor and a beautiful nurse told me to wait in a waiting room. After a bit, another beautiful nurse came in. Speaking perfect English, she took my details.

'Professor Feldmaier will be along soon,' she said.

Minutes later the large door opened and a man walked in. I was aghast. He must have been almost seven feet tall. His glasses looked to be an inch thick and behind them his eyes were magnified like saucers. In the centre of his forehead there was a deep indentation in his skull. His hands looked like they were wearing a huge pair of mittens. All I could think of was Jaws from the James Bond movies. I tried to conceal my horror.

'You must be Jerry Moffatt, the top climber.'

Professor Feldmaier held out one of his massive mitts to shake, and with that, his face grew wide with a warm smile.

'Now, let us see what we can do for you.'

The professor spent an hour chatting to me, asking me about the pain, my training, when it had happened. He wired my arms up to some electrodes and sent tiny shocks along them that caused spasms in my hands. He made some notes and felt the flesh and muscles around my elbow.

'You have nerve damage in your elbow, Jerry,' he finally concluded. 'Physiotherapy will not cure it and time will not heal it. You need an operation. If you wish, I can do the first one tomorrow at 3pm.'

I found myself saying yes. As I took the subway back to where I was staying, I felt deeply apprehensive. An operation seemed so drastic. What if it went wrong? One error could damage my arms forever. All the years of climbing and training put in the oversized hands of a strange-looking German doctor with a scalpel. It seemed like an incredible gamble. But what if he was right and they would never get better otherwise? What did I have to lose? That night I barely slept, asking myself these questions again and again, never coming up with an answer. In the morning, I found myself once again on the underground.

Back in the Olympic I was shown to a room and changed into a gown. I sat on the bed and a while later, a nurse came along. She took my right wrist, held it in the air to expose my armpit and produced a razor. With no water or foam, she rasped it dryly three times down my armpit, ripping all the hair out. It was agony.

I was led into a room that was adjacent to an operating theatre. The doors through had a round glass window. I went over for a look, my armpit now bleeding. Through the window, I saw the figure of Professor Feldmaier, his tall body and the hole in his head, an operating mask covering his lower face. I watched as he pulled thin rubber gloves onto his great big hands and winced at the crack as he released the elasticated cuffs. He reached down to a stainless steel tray and picked up a syringe. It was huge and had a thick, six-inch-long needle on the end of it. It looked like a knitting needle. I realised the professor was now looking at me. He raised the huge needle so that it was between my eyes and his, and as I looked straight at him, he somehow made his enormous eyes grow even larger. With a twitch, he made a small squirt of liquid come out of the needle.

Oh my God, I thought.

With that, I saw the professor's eyes crack up in laughter and he waved me in.

'Jerry.' Even through the mask I could see his warm smile. He explained a few things about the operation, how long it would take. There was a doctor there with a large camera.

'Gerhardt will be taking pictures, as this is a very interesting procedure. I have never had a case like this before and I wish to record it. You will be a good guinea pig, no?'

I didn't like the thought of being an experiment, but by now it was too late. I was in his hands. He told me to lie down on the operating table. He picked the hypodermic up in his right hand, and with his left, grabbed my right wrist once more to expose my bleeding armpit.

'Anaesthetic. This *will* hurt,' he smiled and rammed the needle deep into my armpit. It was like a poker. A red-hot poker. I felt him gouge it around.

'I must find a nerve you see. Is that it?'

'Yes,' I cried.

'No. I think not.' He carried on gouging. 'Is that it?'

'YES!'

'No.'

The photographer was taking photos of my face.

'Is this it?'

'Please, yes, yes.'

With that, the professor drained the contents of the syringe into me and withdrew the needle. He released my hand and my arm dropped to the floor. They pulled a sheet up so I couldn't see what they were doing and soon I sensed them cut my arm open.

'I can feel it,' I said, apprehensively.

'No, I do not think you can, you just imagine it.'

I had a good imagination then. In Bachar's Zen books that I had read in Joshua Tree, there was a lot of mind-over-matter stuff, the brain conquering the physical and all that. One story I had read was about someone operated on without anaesthetic, using just mental techniques to block out any pain. Right, I thought. I picked a tiny spot on the ceiling and focused my entire attention on it. This spot will become my world and I will feel nothing. I focused and focused, but could still feel the pain.

After a while Feldmaier peeked over the little screen. I could feel beads of sweat all over my head and I must have looked pretty anxious. Feldmaier's big eyes widened.

'You still feel it?'

'Yes,' I squeaked.

Another syringe of anaesthetic was emptied into my armpit and the pain went away.

The doctors worked for an hour, all the time the photographer taking pictures. Eventually it was finished.

'We are stitching you up now.'

The professor said he believed it had gone well. They cleaned me up, I got dressed and I was told to return in two weeks for the second operation.

A fortnight later I was back again. The professor had a look at my elbows, used the electrodes once more and said that things looked promising. That was good, I said. He asked if I was ready for the next operation and I said I was. Once again I put on the gown, the nurse raked my left armpit with her dry razor and I went through to the theatre where Feldmaier dug the needle in again. The photographer appeared again with his camera.

'More photos?' I asked.

'Ah yes. Last time we forget to put film in the camera. Ha, ha, ha!'

Great, I thought. I hope they're better at surgical operations than they are at photography. An hour later, once again, I left with my heavily band-aged arm.

That evening I took the subway back to where I was staying, my arm in a sling. Tubes went in and out of the bandaged elbow. It all looked very drastic. I looked at it, wondering what the outcome might be. Would I be cured? Or would my elbows be damaged beyond repair? As the train rattled through the darkness, my whole life felt very much in the balance.

NINE

Out of the Fire

Professor Feldmaier looked at me through his enormous glasses.

'I am hopeful, Jerry, very hopeful.'

Feldmaier's office in the Olympic hospital in Munich was bright, its white walls covered in medical certificates, white shelves carefully filled with textbooks and folders, and a white desk with my file on it. I was wearing a T-shirt and we both looked down at the long scars, still with their scabbed-up stitches, that ran down the outside of my elbows.

'But these are early stages still. Of course you must do rehabilitation exercises, which I have already detailed and you will come here to the hospital to do them on the days I have told you. But it is also very important that you take it easy and relax. I'm sure you can find some way of doing that.'

I had recently bought myself a Suzuki GSXR1100, the fastest production bike available at the time. It was a beautiful machine, red and black, and it went like a rocket. Since buying it, I had been riding constantly through the beautiful countryside on the outskirts of Munich, getting better, faster and more confident all the time.

I shook the professor's hand and thanked him for all his help.

'Yes, Professor, I'm sure I can find something to do.'

It was now coming into summer and the sun seemed to shine every day. On the outskirts of Munich, a long road wound steeply up a hill known as Kesselberg. The Kesselberg road was the best I have ever ridden on and there was a great biking scene there. Every evening, sixty, seventy, even a hundred bikers would gather and race up and down. The road switched back and forward for five and a half miles, hairpin running into hairpin. There was a long, sweeping bend where everyone would gather, park their bikes and sit on the hill behind in the evening sunshine to watch riders go by.

It was perfectly cambered, with a cross on the verge where a biker had been killed taking the bend. It always had flowers on it. And it was here I got my knee down for the first time.

Getting your knee down is a way of keeping more control and stability over the bike when cornering at high speed. You must get your feet up on the foot rests and slide right down on the side of the bike. You actually hook the inside of your knee over the seat and hang off that. The other knee, being so low down, is actually on the road. It's an incredible feeling and the first time you do it is a kind of rite of passage. I had been psyching for this for a while.

Modern leather suits have integral kneepads for protection, but at the time, these were still specialist equipment. I had been in touch with the makers of the Fire rock boots who sponsored me and they sent over two pads of the hardwearing boot rubber. Having taped these pads onto my suit, I was ready.

I gassed up Kesselberg, got the tyres warm and sticky and approached the bend. It was ringed with resting bikers. Approaching, I saw the bend was free, dropped the clutch, fed the power in and threw my weight over onto the right side of the bike, dropping down low. It was really stable, so I kept accelerating hard. I felt the incredible thrust of the bike under me, the ferocious scream of the engine. The road was flying past my head, so close, but I just kept accelerating smoothly through the bend.

Wow. I had got my knee down. Your first E1, the first time you catch a big wave on a surfboard. These moments are just incredible. I stormed out of the bend into the next and rode to the top of Kesselberg like a king.

I had heard that it was possible to have racetrack days on the Salzburg Ring, just across the border in Austria. I phoned the track and they said yes, this would be possible. Excited, I got on my bike and rode the four hours across the border, looking forward to pushing it out on a proper surface. I showed up at reception and said I was here for a track day.

'Sorry,' an official said. 'Today this is not possible. It has been booked out for a practice day for a couple of 250cc Grand Prix riders. Perhaps another day?'

'Come on,' I pleaded. 'I already phoned up and asked was it OK and I was told it would be. I've ridden all the way down here just for this and it's the only chance I have.'

'Well, I don't know,' he pondered. 'These guys will be riding pretty fast. How experienced are you?'

'Oh yeah, I'm really experienced. I've got lots of experience. I won't get in anyone's way.'

'Okay then, but keep an eye out for the others.'

Brilliant. I thanked him and prepared the bike – and myself. The other riders were hanging around near the starting line and by the time I was ready, they were still just gathering themselves. I revved the bike and let rip.

It was fantastic. The track was really wide, with beautiful sweeping bends. I realised at once this would let me take every turn almost flat-out. The feeling of accelerating through the bends was wild. Then I realised, too late, there was one bend I couldn't take flat-out. Approaching the pit-straight, I came to a left-hander that was way too sharp. I lost control of the back of the bike and it dropped from under me. The machine and I went flying. I came to a bouncing, skidding stop, while the bike went skidding off into a long gravel trap.

Winded, but unhurt, I stood up. I walked over to the bike and struggled to get it up upright. Some track officials came over to help me. And all this took place right in front of the Grand Prix riders. I could see them all looking at me, thinking: 'What an idiot'. I had dropped it on my first lap. Yeah, I'm experienced.

A few days later, Ben Moon came to Germany to visit me. Ben was planning a climbing trip, but he was just as hooked on fast bikes as I was, so we spent the majority of his fortnight buzzing round together on my bike. My GSXR1100 was looking a little battered since the crash at Salzburg, but it still went like hell.

We spent one weekend bombing up and down Obertrubucktal, a beautiful valley in the Frankenjura, near to some of the crags. One of us drove while the other sat on the back, and we took turns blasting up and down the hill at full speed. The idea seemed to be for the rider to scare the passenger. As Ben was driving, I watched over his shoulder as he gassed down a long straight pushing the bike faster and faster. There were open fields all around, and ahead of us, I could see a sharp ninety-degree left-hander. Ben accelerated hard towards this, through the red and white speed-warning chevrons painted on the road, to get some late-braking action. Faster and faster, then at the last moment he cranked on the brake lever. Ben had a bike in England too, but the brakes on mine were a lot better than he was used to, so the extra force he applied caused the front wheel to lock up. He lost all control of the bike. The back wheel started fishtailing from side to side across the road and he dropped it.

We both bounced along the road and finally came to a stop. I looked up to see the bike skid away down the road. It hit the ditch at the bend, bounced and landed upside-down in the hedge. We stood up and watched the back wheel spinning forlornly in the breeze.

Ben sprung to his feet and took off his helmet. He was livid with himself for dropping the bike.

'Goddammit! You stupid idiot!' he roared at himself.

He threw his helmet off towards the bike and stomped away in the opposite direction. It was pretty funny.

That was the second time the bike had crashed in a week. It was pretty new, but already looked like it had been through a war. The tank was stove in, the exhaust was crumpled, the chrome was scraped. I kept the GSXR1100 for another year, and wherever I parked it, no matter what other bikes it was near, it always attracted loads of attention. Bikers would gather round to pay their respects.

'Blimey, that's seen some action, mate,' they would say.

I stayed on in Germany, riding my bike, doing physio and partying, before eventually returning once again to Sheffield. I moved in with some climbers, carried on with rehab, and although I still wasn't climbing, felt much happier than the last time I had been there. I was having a great time riding my bike, exploring the roads of the Peak District, and it was good to be catching up with old friends again.

A housemate of mine, Steve Coates, a six-foot, blond Geordie, asked me to take him out on my bike once. I said no. I didn't want to, because whenever I did this, I always tried to show off and scare people. I also usually ended up scaring myself.

I had given Steve a ride once before. It was when I was first learning, on the back of my little Honda CB100. We were driving up Ecclesall Road, heading towards the Peak District, weaving through busy rush-hour traffic. The bike was not very powerful, so I had to slip the clutch to get it in gear when the revs were high. At the front of a queue of traffic, with the little engine whining to a high pitch, I dropped the bike into gear. Steve was sitting on the back. He had a body-builder's physique and was carrying a loaded rucksack. The revs hit the back wheel, directly under the heavy bulk of Steve and the rucksack. The wheel gave a forward jolt. The front wheel lifted right up in the air. Steve came off the back of the bike, the movement depositing him onto the road in a slight squat position. Stood in the midst of the traffic, he watched me run off after the rampant bike, my hands on the handlebars, its front wheel level with my head. The rush-hour commuters gave him a look and, as the lights turned green, they slowly moved off either side of the stranded Geordie.

'Ah, go on, Jerry, take us out for a spin,' pleaded Steve.

'Okay then,' I relented. 'Put these leathers on.' I gave Steve my spare leather suit.

'Nah, man, I don't need them, I'll be right.'

'No, Steve, put them on.'

We sped out to the Peak and I took him around some good quick bends. Coming out of one bend, I nailed it so fast that the engine hit the rev-limiter. This cuts the engine out momentarily to protect it from over-revving. But almost immediately, the power came back on again with some fierce acceleration.

This force was too much for my passenger.

I saw Steve's feet rise up by my side. They rose up and passed my body in slow motion. Steve was being turned upside-down by the acceleration. He lifted off the back of the bike, and in my mirrors, I watched him gently rotate in mid-air. He landed on his back and went skidding down the road in my wake. That was the second – and last – time Steve had a ride on my bike.

I wanted to take Ben out to show him how much better I had become. We drove out to Stoney and then on for a drive around the quiet roads of the Peak District, visiting sleepy villages. On the road between Grindleford and Calver there is a great twisting section with two crests on it. I drove through Grindleford and nailed it out of the village and up the hill. I really wanted to scare Ben and approached the first crest of the hill at top speed. I had done it myself a load of times, but with Ben's weight on the back, the front wheel was lighter and it started rising off the road. I could feel Ben on the back, his legs squeezing me in terror. I was scared myself, but I wasn't going to hold back. We came straight into the second crest and I gave it everything I had. Again, the wheel left the ground. I could hear him whimpering to slow down as the revs hit the roof. Mission accomplished.

I continued to do Feldmaier's exercises, although I still wasn't feeling any improvement. I told Ben about it, described how I felt frightened to put any weight on my fingers for fear of totally ruining them. He talked about his own recent injury, not as severe as mine, but said he knew how I felt. He told me about a physio he had visited in Wigan, north of Manchester and gave me his number. I rang the physio and he told me to come in next Tuesday. That morning, I set off on my bike.

The physio had given me a set of directions over the phone and I had written them down in pencil. They seemed pretty obscure: 'Turn right at the black house', 'There's a thing like a big W', but they led me down country lanes and past groups of buildings to a small, old-looking house sat on a patch of grass. There was a wooden sign on the door that simply said 'physiotherapist'. I knocked. Immediately a man opened it and told me to come in and sit down. He was a big man with a deep voice and looked like he might have been in the army at some point. He had tattoos and a red face, and strong, rough hands. I showed him my elbows. He looked at them, squeezed them and prodded the muscles and joints.

'What's wrong with you, laddie?' he said. 'Get on with it. There's nothing wrong with those elbows apart from the fact you're not using them. Push them. *Hammer* them. Do everything you would have done before. They're fine.'

'Oh?'

'Yes. That will be twelve pounds.'

I got my cheque book out of my leather suit.

'No, I only take cash, son.'

Luckily I had enough to cover it. I struggled into my leathers, strapped on my helmet and started my bike. On the way home I felt amazing. Could my elbows really be healed? Could it be true, finally, after all this time? It seemed unbelievable. My mind was racing with the dreams of what I could do now, thoughts that I hadn't allowed myself for almost two years. I rode home like a bullet, not able to remember feeling so good, first along the motorway, then the winding roads that led across the Peak District from Manchester to Sheffield. I was going to climb again. I was a climber again. I throttled back and watched the beautiful countryside race by my visor. My life had been given back to me.

It was the end of September 1986, almost two years since I had stopped climbing. Winter was on its way. The physio had given me a clean bill of health and told me I could train once again. I felt that if anything went wrong then it would not have been my fault, but his, and that fact seemed to take away all my worries. It was clearly what I wanted to hear. Still, there was no need to rush into hard climbing and I decided instead to spend the coming months just building my body back up, regaining core strength I had lost during my lay-off. I did long sessions of weights, always being careful not to do any damage. But I didn't mind. For the first time in ages, I had a goal again – get strong and well.

At the start, recovery was slow. Once I felt stronger, coming into spring, I started to climb once more. The first place I went to was Stoney Middleton to a traverse on Minus Ten Wall. Before I had gone to America two years earlier, I had trained by doing four laps on this traverse, followed by a set of rope ladders, footless, four more traverses and so on. On this first visit back, I couldn't do a single traverse. I could barely do the moves. I couldn't believe it. I tried some other problems that before my injury would have been warm-ups. I couldn't touch them. I had completely lost my strength. I can remember walking down to the café, throwing my motorbike helmet on a table in anger, and ranting and raging about the fact I couldn't do these problems, problems that I considered easy.

But I improved quickly. I applied myself, gently at first, building it up and up, getting my strength back. I would often go to Stoney, trying to be patient, attempting easier problems. Before, when I lived there, I had a big soloing circuit at the crag, routes that I could do regularly, ones that were difficult, but that I knew well enough to be comfortable on. One of these was Wee Doris, a notorious and pumpy E4, taking a slightly overhanging wall on polished, almost glass-like holds. One day, after I had been building up for a few weeks, I took myself to the base of the route, psyched up and soloed it. I got pumped at about forty feet, but by then I knew I could do it. I climbed on and when I stood on top of the crag, felt that I had just passed a milestone on my road to recovery.

Feeling stronger, I started to visit Raven Tor again with Ben Moon and another good climber, Ben Masterson. On my first day there we were bouldering. We warmed up and were doing some of the harder problems on the steeper part of the crag. Ben Moon showed me an unclimbed boulder problem traverse they had both spent some time trying to work out. It had good handholds, but the steepness meant that very little weight could go on the feet. Ben Moon showed me a sequence on it. Then Ben Masterson linked together a few of the moves. I had a go at what he had just done. Grabbing some of the holds, I tried to move leftwards to the next, but my bodyweight sagged to the floor. I tried another move and again I failed. I was shocked.

'Bloody hell, Ben, you made that look easy.'

Masterson turned to me.

'Well, Jerry,' he said, 'A few things have changed since you've been away.'

Oooh! Ben's words were a knife through my heart. In my head I was still the best. And here were two climbers, my old mates and now they were both burning me off. This was torture.

That was quite a shock and I realised it was time to step it up a bit. I immediately began to train hard and push myself once more. After just over a week of this, I went to Raven Tor again by myself and had another go at the traverse, this time managing to do the moves on it. I was improving quickly and applied myself harder. I have always loved boulder problem traverses. I was also one of the few people keen to do first ascents of new boulder problems, as it didn't mean so much to other climbers at the time. I could tell that this one was going to be a real classic. More than anything, I was still smarting from Ben Masterson's comment. I felt I had something to prove, most of all to myself. Over the following week, I made several visits on my own, getting better and better, and later, I did the problem. I had gone from being unable to do a single move, to doing the whole thing in just over three weeks. I had done it before both the Bens had and grabbed the first ascent of a great problem. When riding motorbikes, the 'powerband' is that range of revs within each gear where the engine delivers most power, where the machine really takes off. It was the perfect name for the problem. With my first ascent of The Powerband I felt that my climbing was once again about to take off.

But Ben Masterson was right about one thing; things had changed. During my lay-off, I had paid virtually no attention to climbing. I never read a magazine, never followed who was doing what. I now saw that things had moved on. Organised competitions had started up in Europe and America and the French were climbing really well. The cliffs of Buoux were constantly having new and incredibly difficult routes added by the world's top climbers. Everyone seemed to be travelling a lot more and the super-steep sun-soaked walls in the south of France seemed to be where they were all going. The two Bens, as well as all the other climbers I met, told me of the great routes they had tried and done there.

What's more, as these climbers enjoyed French routes, they also picked up French attitudes to climbing. Bolts had become the norm on the world's hardest climbs and doing routes on nuts was becoming a thing of the past at the top levels. Moves and difficulty were what was in vogue, not so much stunning lines or boldness. The French put bolts in wherever one was wanted. They spent as long trying a route as was needed – days, weeks, months even – to create masterpieces of the utmost difficulty. The 'redpoint' was everything, the final, successful ascent, climbing from the bottom to the top of the route, without falling off, clipping all the runners as you went. How you went about achieving this didn't matter in the least. Climbs were safe and gymnastic, and sought out the blankest, steepest bits of rock possible. No longer did climbers look for the 'lines of least resistance'. Now they looked for the most difficult. In a short period, around the mid 1980s, this French attitude swept away old British styles – in certain quarters at least – of yo-yos, minimal bolting, and seeing falling off as failing. British climbers started using the French grading system for the steeper, bolt-protected climbs in their own country. The British grades, E6, E7, seemed better suited to more traditional climbs without bolts, routes like Ulysses and Master's Wall. More and more climbers became interested exclusively in this new kind of difficulty-based, bolt-protected climbing, or sport climbing, as it became known.

I was stunned to see how well lots of people were climbing. The top climbers were training hard and they were getting good at the tactics of working routes and redpointing them. I quickly realised that if I was going to get back up to the top level, then I was going to have to play the game too. I would have to give up the old yo-yoing tactics and start redpointing. I quickly worked my way through the new, hard routes that had been added in Britain and pretty soon felt that I was back up there with the top British climbers once more. It was time to look beyond.

Buoux. Recently, two routes from the le Menestrel brothers had broken through a new grade. Their routes, Le Minimum and La Rage de Vivre, were both graded 8b+, and were probably the hardest routes in the world. As soon as I could organise a trip, I got myself down there.

Buoux was a different place from the deserted cliff where Ben and I had stayed three years before. The crags were thronged with people, German, French, Swiss, American, Austrian, Spanish as well as British. It was strange to see such widespread use of French technique. Everyone seemed to be sieging routes, people hanging on every bolt. Redpointing had obviously been embraced. At the campsite in the nearby town of Apt there was a holiday atmosphere, tents packed closely together, people renting caravans. Almost immediately, I headed for the two super-routes.

La Rage and Le Minimum represented the contrasting strengths of their creators, Antoine and Marc le Menestrel. One was a long endurance battle, the other a short power-fest. I began working on them both. Antoine's route, La Rage de Vivre, was a massive pitch – over a hundred and fifty feet of continually steep climbing, almost all on one, two and three-finger pockets. The route was actually a combination of two shorter routes. The first section was called La Rose et Le Vampire, a classic 8b. The moves on this were amazing, really technical and gymnastic, arms crossing over each other to reach the only holds, often shallow, single-joint two-finger pockets, then locking these off below the shoulder to reach the next one. Powerful moves flowed one after the other, covering steep, smooth rock with no good footholds. The end of this pitch was marked simply by good holds in the middle of the steepness and a bolt to lower off. With the new French-style routes, it no longer mattered that a climb didn't go to the top of anything. All that mattered were the moves. However, for La Rage, this was only half the battle. From here, having had a quick rest on the good hold, it was straight into another hard 8a+ route called La Secte, with seventy more feet of stamina-sapping moves. Linking these provided the ultimate in endurance climbing.

Right beside this was Marc's route, Le Minimum. This was much shorter, with a series of incredibly hard, dynamic moves. Once again, the route started by pulling a long way on small finger pockets, across rock overhanging by almost forty-five degrees. At about twenty feet, there is a small horizontal hold, just big enough to take the fingertips of two hands. At this point, with the rock sweeping away so steeply below, it is desperate to keep your feet on the rock. Still, you must lunge to get the tips of your right hand, at full stretch, into a shallow hole that's about two centimetres wide and eight millimetres deep. You couldn't even call it a pocket, just a little dished-out dimple. A heinous pull on this and you get a better hold above which quickly leads to easier climbing. This savage route was the living end and pretty much represented where power-based routes had got to, perfectly complementing its stamina-based brother next door. Neither had been repeated.

I worked the moves on both routes, building up the stamina for La Rage, as well a memory of the huge number of complex hand and foot movements that need to be executed perfectly to climb it. With Le Minimum, it was important to perfect the crux sequence, to get every movement right down to the last millimetre, get every subtle body position right. La Rage still had not been repeated, but while I was at Buoux, I saw a French climber do the second ascent of Le Minimum. Alain Ghersen was a renowned French boulderer, one of those climbers with tons of power, but not much stamina. Watching him succeed on Le Minimum was mind blowing. He was brutally powerful, just sickening to look at, and he virtually exploded up the short, savage climb. Impressive stuff.

With redpointing, trying a climb at your absolute limit, strength and fitness are obviously critical, but two factors that are not so obvious are temperature and how good your skin is. As fingerholds become smaller and more sloping, the friction between your fingers and the rock is what actually keeps you on. The less friction there is, the harder it is to hang on, and the thing that affects friction more than anything is sweat on the fingertips. This isn't drops of sweat, but microscopic moisture that can make all the difference. Hence the use of chalk, which absorbs moisture and makes holds feel better. For this reason, climbing is often best done in cold conditions, as cold as you can stand. Of course, muscles don't work well when they're cold, so the right balance must be found, but in general, the cooler the better.

Similarly, when climbing on such small holds, the entire weight of the body, as well as the extra forces developed when pulling hard, comes onto a very small area of skin on the tips of the fingers. Often your whole body-weight will be hanging from only a few millimetres of fingertip. That puts enormous strain on the skin, causing small tears in the skin. If these develop, they can tear open completely, sometimes tearing a large 'flapper', making it impossible to climb and taking days to heal. It's not simply a matter of carrying on through the pain. It's impossible to climb on a bleeding fingertip. Even if the skin doesn't tear, the harder outside layers can get worn away, revealing softer, more tender, skin below. This skin can become painful and also sweats a lot more, once again affecting crucial friction. Good strong skin is critical.

By now it was getting into late spring and the weather was starting to heat up. I was trying the routes early in the morning and in the cool of the evening. In order to save my skin, I was only having a couple of attempts each time. The battered tendons in my fingers sometimes felt vulnerable, as though I was about to be injured again. As the days wore on, this was starting to feel like a bit of a mental battle, always trying to keep at bay the thought that I was actually getting worse on the climbs the more I tried them. It was very stressful.

I worked hard to make sure I remained positive and relaxed, and to keep enjoying myself when I wasn't climbing. In the campground, I was hanging out on a rest day with Ben Moon and some other friends. We were playing hacky-sack, chatting and having fun when the lady at reception put out a call on the campsite Tannoy.

'Jerry Moffatt, *au téléphone s'il vous plaît.*'

I wandered over to the phone box. It was my dad. He spoke to me in short sentences, asked me a few questions. 'Yes,' I said. 'I understand. Yes, I'm okay. Okay. Bye.'

Hanging up the phone, I wandered back towards the circle of people playing the game. The soft ball came my way, but it just landed at my feet. I picked it up and held it in my hand.

'Who was that, Jerry? What's up?' Ben asked.

'That was my dad. It's my little brother. He's dead.'

During Toby's time at St David's, he had started to study horticulture, something he had always loved growing up. He had gone to America to study in Oregon, a dream come true for him. One evening, while having a Jacuzzi by himself, he had had a seizure and drowned in the pool. He was twenty-one.

I sat around that night, went to bed, almost in a daze. Not knowing what else to do, I went up to the crag the following day with Ben Moon and tried Le Minimum. I fell off, lowered to the ground, sat on a rock and cried. I wandered down through the trees, made my way back to the campsite, got on my bike and rode home.

The whole way my head buzzed inside my helmet. Why him? Why Toby? Toby had spent the first four years of his life in hospital, missing out on so much of his life, missing out on school, and not getting into sport. Why did so much bad luck come to him? There was nothing fair about any of this. Why not me? I was the one who had taken all the risks with my life, done all the reckless things. Why couldn't it have been me? Why hadn't I been there to look after him when he needed me? Still, to this day, if I had the choice, him or me, I would still offer myself in a heartbeat.

I got home, exhausted. The whole family was devastated. We all went over to America to collect his stuff and see where he had studied, meet his friends. Toby was cremated and his ashes scattered over the fields near our house. We had a memorial service and that was it. Toby, my kid brother, was dead.

After that, things lost their meaning for a while. Climbing, training, 8b+, it all suddenly meant very little and for weeks, running into months, I couldn't find much motivation. I would go bouldering and think about Toby. Training, I would think about Toby. Climbing, I would think about Toby. They were always the same thoughts: why? why him? This is so unfair. I'll never see him again. It was horrendous. I still ticked over, eventually doing some more climbing. I stayed in England for a while, then travelled to America and passed the summer. Thinking about it never becomes less painful, but over time, I managed to think about it less and slowly started to find my feet again. By late in the autumn, I felt ready to return to Buoux. Life had to go on.

I travelled down there with one of my best mates, Sean Myles. Sean was a fantastically talented climber, but more important, great fun to be around and an inspiring person to climb with. We hired one of the small caravans from the campsite owner and I got stuck in. Over a period of a few weeks, I worked away at La Rage and Le Minimum. Soon, I managed to redpoint La Rose, the fantastic first half of La Rage. This was the first 8b I had ever done. My previous high point had been Bidule, the 8a+ at Saussois, so it was good to feel myself move on again. Once I had succeeded on this, it was time to try the whole route and to build up the required stamina. Trying this along with Le Minimum worked well, and I found I could still try the more powerful route while feeling pumped from the longer one, and vice versa.

As the weather got cooler, conditions improved. I felt I had the moves wired. I was able to lie in bed and run through every single hand and foot move on the climbs. I felt a redpoint attempt getting close. I rested fully for two days, and over those days, felt my body grow stronger.

Sometimes you can get in the ideal frame of mind. Sometimes you wake up, having slept perfectly, the day looks great, the temperature is just right and your skin is good. These days, you just know, are the right ones and I felt sure in myself that I was ready for a redpoint. I stretched at the campsite, feeling light and strong. We drove the twenty minutes to the crag. On the walk up, the valley looked beautiful. It was autumn and the trees had turned brilliant reds and yellows. Rays of sunlight filtered through the leaves and I chatted happily with Sean on the way up. At the crag I did a couple of warm-ups and in no time, felt ready for a go at La Rage.

I looked at the huge, hundred and fifty feet of climbing above me and ran through every move in my head. I had worked the moves on the route using my eleven-millimetre rope, but now swapped this for a skinny eight and a half millimetre one. It felt like a thread. I set off nervously and just about scraped my way up the lower section, La Rose, pulling nervously to the good hold that marked the end of that route. With the good hold in my hand, I knew that the redpoint was there for the taking. I swapped hands again and again, each time shaking blood back into my forearms, all the time getting more and more confident that I could hold it together on La Secte, the upper half of the climb. When I knew I was ready, feeling almost totally recovered, I set off and simply cruised it. In no time, I was pulling up on jugs on the easy top moves. Just below the top there was a deep pocket, and inside this, Antoine had placed a trophy that he had won in a climbing competition, and as I passed, I looked at it. It really made me smile. The climb was one of the few at Buoux that went from the ground all the way to the top of the cliff and I emerged from desperate climbing into the pretty, tree-covered flatness of the top. I untied and let go of the end of the rope, watching it fall out of view. I found the descent path and ran back to the bottom. I was ecstatic and Sean was ecstatic for me. Feeling great, I decided to have a go straightaway at Le Minimum and actually got quite high before I fell off. I rested again for another day, returned, and this time made no mistakes, doing it on my first try.

Sitting on the rock under Le Minimum, feeling the warm sunshine in the cool of the late autumn day, I took it all in. This was perfect. Sean had belayed me on both routes, and I couldn't have been in better company. I had repeated two of the world's hardest routes. After all the injuries and struggles of the last two years, and after the tragedy of my brother's death, I felt I had finally got to a point where I could move on. I was back, and once again I was up there with the best in the world.

TEN

The Power and the Glory

I always enjoyed training. From the very start, swinging along wooden blocks nailed to the wall of my parents' house, to traversing along the brick wall at St David's, pull-ups in the garage on Christmas day, working out in Tom's Roof before going to America, training sessions with Bachar in Joshua Tree, doing dead-hangs in the Polytechnic gym in Sheffield, clawing backwards and forwards along Broomgrove wall on wet Sheffield afternoons, top-roping sessions at Stoney Middleton and doing ladders at Buoux, I loved it all. Other climbers had trained too. In the 1950s John Gill used gymnastics to work out for bouldering. Pete Livesey was renowned in his time for being a dedicated trainer, as was Ron Fawcett. The American, Tony Yaniro, was famous as a training fiend and was ahead of his time in many ways. And, of course, Bachar was another pioneer. Like those climbers, I dedicated myself to hard training as a way of improving myself.

I was always on the lookout for new ways of training, finding things that would let me push that extra little bit. In the winter of 1987 and 1988, I was hanging out in Germany a lot, spending time with Kurt and Wolfgang. They were still living together at Obertrubach, where I had first visited them years before. It was good to see my two friends again. When I first arrived they weren't climbing a lot, but were instead training. There was a gym we would visit called Campus. It was just a regular upmarket gym and in the daytime was full of pretty girls in thongs doing exercises with little weights. It didn't have a climbing wall, but Kurt and Wolfgang had asked permission to put up a wooden training board. They were told they could, but that it had to be kept really clean. This was to become known as the Campus Board.

The Campus Board was a flat wooden board suspended from the ceiling.

It started at about chest height, ran upwards for about eight feet and was slightly overhanging. It was covered in a series of horizontal, parallel wooden 'rungs', square rods about two centimetres deep, running about a foot apart up the board. The idea was to hang free from the rungs with your fingers and climb footless, locking off or snatching up the board in long powerful moves. When I saw it, I realised immediately that this could have a lot of potential.

I started to adapt it. I took off some of the two-centimetre holds, as there were too many of them, and put on a series of large but very sloping holds, running up the left-hand side of the board. Up the right-hand side I put a ladder of small holds, perhaps fifteen millimetres deep, but rounded-off. It was extremely difficult to hang from these. On the back, I screwed a single one-centimetre deep edge. I got stuck into working on the Campus Board. Wolfgang wasn't training that winter, so I would often go there with Kurt, and soon he became keen on it too. It was great fun.

I worked out lots of routines on it. These were mainly long reaches between distant holds, or double-dynos – super-dynamic moves where it was possible do a really quick pull-up, let go with both hands at once and latch onto a higher rung. I would do these on various sizes of holds, and over time progressed from the point where I could hardly hang on, to being able to double-dyno up and down them repeatedly, sometimes missing out rungs. This felt like great training, working the most essential aspect of climbing strength – raw power. This board would later be copied in almost every climbing gym in the world and even spawned a style of climbing. Today, 'campusing' describes a technique favoured by the very powerful, quickly snatching up overhanging rock without using feet, whether because this is a more efficient method, or perhaps because the climber lacks foot technique.

Over months of training, I felt myself improve. One essential move started with me hanging footless from the first rung, snatching up for the fifth, then pulling my body all the way through to get the eighth. One-five-eight. I eventually managed to crank out one-five-eight on the smallest holds, and by the end of my winter training on the board I could do this static, holding my body in position with one hand while I reached through to the next. Not only that, I was able to do one-arm pull-ups on the one-centimetre edge on the back of the board. That's hard, much more so than a one-finger pull-up on a piece of rope.

The following month I went to Buoux. I hadn't been doing any climbing at all in the months before, only campusing. That winter I had spent in Germany it had snowed constantly, so proper climbing was out the windows. I suspected I was quite strong, but not very fit. On the first day there, I met up with Didier Raboutou. We had a great day, and as I guessed, I was quite strong. I warmed up and climbed up and down Fissure Serge, a tough 7c+, with no problem. After that, I went over to La Rose et Le Vampire. This route, the brutal first section of La Rage de Vivre, still stopped most climbers dead with the levels of power it needed. I shot up it. The ease with which I climbed these two short power-based climbs showed I was right about my new strength levels. Didier suggested we did No Man's Land as a warm-down, a notoriously pumpy 7a+. I tried, but couldn't do it. As soon as I got pumped I fell off. Even though the moves felt easy, the length of the route beat me. So I was also right about the fitness too then. Still, I felt I was climbing like a beast and that day had felt like a perfect warm-up.

I had my eye on one particular route at Buoux. Jibé had done a new route, Le Spectre des Surmutants, the third route in France to get the magic grade of 8b+, along with La Rage and Le Minimum. It is a long endurance route following a huge barrel of grey limestone, almost forty degrees overhanging for most of its length, with a desperate, boulder-problem crux right at the very end. In the two days after that first day with Didier, I worked the moves on La Spectre. While working it, I had felt stronger and stronger all the time, with loads of explosive power. I had thought that it might take me some time to do the route, but after those two days, I felt ready. I took a rest day in preparation.

Waking up the day after, I felt great. I knew that feeling and hoped a great day was coming. I went to the crag and redpointed Le Spectre first try. Warmed up now, I on-sighted an 8a, which at the time was still pretty cutting-edge. I went down to the village for a coffee and someone said they were going to try an 8a+ of Jibé's, called La Nuit du Lézard. I had never tried it before so I went with them, worked it once quickly and redpointed it first go. Redpointing an 8b+, on-sighting an 8a and a one-session ascent of an 8a+, all in a day, all top-level achievements in their own right. My power had gone through the roof, all thanks to campus training. This really showed me how power gets you up things, and most of this power had come from my winter training on the Campus Board.

Towards the end of 1988 I decided to buy my own house in Sheffield. Looking at likely properties, there was just one feature I had in mind. Houses in Sheffield often have large cellars – it's a particular feature of the city's older housing stock – and I was looking for a house with a cellar large enough to build my own climbing wall.

For a long time I had wanted my own home-training facility. I wanted to create something exactly how I wanted it, to develop some of the training theories I had and take my climbing to the next level. Some friends had already constructed basic facilities in their own homes. Andy Pollitt had rented a house and this had a small garage outside. He got a couple of sheets of eight-by-four plywood and screwed these onto a frame to make a wooden roof. He then nailed some blocks of wood onto this for fingerholds, giving him a little bouldering wall. We would do problems, starting at the bottom and finding sequences of moves around the wooden holds, but without ever moving our feet. Although Andy's wall was small and limited, it was good, and most importantly for him, it was on his doorstep. Later, Ben Moon bolted a square of plywood to the roof of his cellar and attached some wooden holds to it. We would do footless boulder problems, swinging from hold to hold. Again, this felt good, but it was very limited. I wanted to take these ideas, combine them with some of my own and develop a really good facility, in my own home.

In the Woodseats area, I found a house with a large, dry, double cellar and bought it. As soon as I moved in, I began to build my climbing wall. I wanted to do a good job of it, to make it big and make it a good environment to train. I built a frame and bought plywood to sheet it out. In one room I made a low horizontal roof, which then angled steeply towards the roof of the cellar, to another horizontal section. The other room simply had an overhanging board, set at about forty degrees, about ten feet wide and eight feet high. I carpeted the cellar, then covered the floor in mattresses. I put in an extractor fan to remove the chalk dust and put a heavy punchbag in there, as well as a speedball, for warming up. I put in some weights, a pull-up bar and bench-press machine.

I've always believed that, of all the various areas of strength – body tension, strong arms and shoulders, powerful calves – finger strength is the most important strength for a climber to have. Fingers are your link to the rock and are most often what let you down. I was going to make my cellar good for training finger strength and this meant small holds. This was in the days before you could buy specially-made resin climbing holds, so I made them out of wood – small one-centimetre blocks, sawn-up broom handles, tiny sloping edges. I spent ages making these perfect little holds and attached them to the board. I was so excited as it progressed, desperate to climb on it, but I wasn't going to allow myself until it was finished. Finally, the last hold was screwed on. It was ready. I got my boots and chalk and sat at the bottom, fully prepared.

Desperate. I couldn't do a single move on it. Not one. I had made all the holds too small and sloping and I couldn't even get my arse off the mattress. I had to get a chisel to them, gouge out better edges and make them more positive, until eventually, I was able to climb on it. Even so, it was still extremely fingery.

I finally had my own training board and it was just the way I wanted it. I loved climbing on it. In the morning, I'd skip breakfast. I'd just hang out until lunchtime, when I would be absolutely starving. Then, with an empty stomach and feeling really light, I would go and boulder for a few hours. It was great. Often, friends would come around and we would have savage training sessions. Ben Moon, Zippy, Mark Leach, Quentin Fisher, Andy Pollitt. These were great sessions. Trying new problems, lying about playing music, doing some really hard moves. All the holds were numbered and the problems named and recorded in a book along with the name of the first ascensionist. It was great if you did a new problem that everyone had been trying.

I lived in that house for ten years and was continually committed to training on my board. Thanks to my cellar, I was able to move myself on to new levels. All through that time I was trying out new methods or theories of training. I read a lot around the subject and applied bodybuilding theories of super-sets. Super-sets are combinations of exercises designed to tire muscles out really deeply. For example, the bench press, lying on your back and pushing a weight up like an upside-down press-up, is a great exercise for chest muscles. But the movement also uses the triceps muscle, so the first exercise is a set of triceps curls, to really tire this muscle, before going straight into the bench press. Without the help of the triceps, the chest has to work a lot harder, the effort going deep into the muscle. In the same way I would do pull-ups to strengthen the latissimus dorsi muscles, or 'lats', the long muscles down the side of the torso, that are used in locking off. However, pull-ups also use the biceps muscle, so first I would do a set of curls, hammer my biceps and only then do pull-ups, so all the work was being done by my lats. Week by week I felt myself get stronger. It was time to find somewhere to apply this strength.

When I had repeated Ben's route Statement of Youth on Lower Pen Trwyn in 1984, I had noticed a slim, subtle groove slipping up through the bulging rock to the left. I could see right away that it was steeper and less featured than Statement. It was obviously a lot harder. I wondered if something that looked so hard could be climbed. In the spring of 1987, I went back for a look.

Abseiling down the line, I placed some bolts and confirmed my thoughts. It would be extremely hard, but there did look to be just about enough holds to make it climbable. It looked amazing, right up my street and I began to work on it. It took a lot of time to sort the moves out and I spent a good few days on it that year. It was extremely tough, much harder than anything else I had ever done and my attempts carried on into the following year. The next year, 1989, I felt ready again to try a redpoint. I had already spent a couple of days at the crag, linking together long sections of it to gain confidence, learning how it would feel to do sustained sequences of really hard moves. Late on the third day, I had another redpoint attempt, getting through the crux to the last hard move before falling off. It had gone well. Encouraged, I decided I would have a rest day and go back after that to finish it.

I was still riding bikes a lot, so for my rest day, I decided to take my Suzuki RGV250 down to Cadwell Park in Lincolnshire and have a track day. I loaded it into a van and drove down. I took the Suzuki out on the track, but the tyres didn't feel too great when they warmed up. Going round a right-hand bend, the back wheel lost its grip, skidded out, then suddenly re-gripped, sending me over the handlebars at over 80 mph. I broke my wrist, ribs and bones in my feet. I was out of action for months and my project slipped away for another year.

May 1990. After another season spent training in the cellar, I came out feeling as strong as ever and made my way to Wales again to try the project. But on my first day, I was barely able to do any moves. I was shocked. This was how it had felt in 1987. Had I really lost three year's strength? On the second day, however, I did the moves much more easily and I thought I might be close. I was excited. I had almost forgotten how amazing the route was.

Steep limestone, the best rock for sport climbing, is common all over Europe, but in Britain it is much more rare. For this reason, it is hard to find cutting-edge unclimbed lines in this country. In some countries in Europe, there was a tradition of chipping top-level climbs, adding a hold to a blank section or chipping away a good hold that made the climbing too easy. In this way it was possible to create the perfect route that suited a first ascensionist's strengths and weakness. I can see why someone might do that, but I never liked the idea myself, and in Britain it was seldom done. In Britain, where the rock set the challenge, potential new routes that would be a perfect test for a climber's strength were like gold dust.

The Pen Trwyn route was perfect. It really was the most incredible climb, power-endurance all the way. The first fifteen feet up a vertical wall are quite straightforward. Then it explodes outwards and it's hard all the way for the next forty feet. Every move is extremely difficult. You can't stop, you can't shake out. You can't even chalk up. Clipping the rope into the runners is a move as hard as any, as the positions you must hold are so strenuous. A lot of the moves are slapping between undercuts, with very few positive holds. The whole time my body was absolutely tense and flexed just to keep it in contact with the rock. The crux is high on the route and involves a long dyno off an undercut to a sloping fingerhold. Above that, more long reaches off small edges lead to the top. With moves of this difficulty, there is no way you could do them if you were pumped.

After that second day of working it in 1990, I knew success was close. I decided to have a rest day, then redpoint it the day after. On my rest day, and following the idea of 'active rest', I set up a top-rope on the classic E5, Axle Attack. I did this about eight times, cruising, shaking out, enjoying myself. It was after seven o'clock, on a lovely cool evening. Climbing the route, I felt great, except for a few nerves about the redpoint that was coming up the following day. I thought about how good I was feeling and how well I was moving. Then it all felt right. Why not try it now? With nothing to lose, I scrambled down to the boulder beach below.

Conditions were ideal, the crag dry and cool. There was only one other team there. First I climbed the route resting on each bolt to get a feel for it again, lowered off and prepared myself mentally. I knew I had to do everything, every single move, perfectly. One fumble would end in failure. Grabbing a hold anywhere other than in the perfect position, placing a foot half an inch from where it's meant to be, any hesitation and you're off. But I had every movement wired into my brain like a programme. I knew not to deviate in any way from what I had to do. I stepped onto the rock and fired it first try. To watch, the ascent might have looked easy, but it felt like one of the performances of my life.

I gave it 8c, the first route of that grade in Britain, and it really is rock solid at that level. Later I would do more hard new routes, at Raven Tor and other limestone crags in the Peak District and further north in Yorkshire. None of them ever matched this route, not just in terms of difficulty, but for how it felt. It had something special, the line, the moves, the position and what it meant to me personally. Ben Moon later said it was the best limestone route he had ever done – high praise indeed. He also said it was probably harder than some 8c+s he did in France the following year.

When my brother Toby had gone to America to study horticulture, we sometimes wrote to each other. Toby described how he had developed a liking for a particular species of tree, a Liquid Ambar. He told my parents that when he returned to Britain, he was going to plant one in the garden. He never got the chance, so that's what I called the route: Liquid Ambar. The best new route I ever did, a tribute to Toby.

Around the time I was trying Liquid Ambar, a few of us were also trying an open project at Raven Tor. It was something Andy Pollitt had bolted and, figuring it was too hard for him, said he didn't mind who tried it. In contrast to Liquid Ambar, this route was very short, almost more like a long boulder problem and there were a couple of moves on it that were the living end. At the time, we weren't sure whether the moves were even possible and it became a goal to see if anyone could do them. I did them first, but with doing Liquid Ambar, training for competitions and other things, it was actually Ben who redpointed the project. He named it Hubble and gave it the then-unprecedented grade of 8c+.

Over the years, Ben and I have always been great friends, have trained together and travelled together. But we were still rivals. I wanted to climb harder than him and he wanted to climb harder than me. We both wanted to be the best. It was motivating and definitely made us push ourselves. I would have loved to do the first ascent of Hubble, a short power route at the top level to sit beside Liquid Ambar, a state-of-the-art endurance route. But I was happy for Ben to have done it too and he had certainly earned it. For me, he was the best redpoint climber in the world at that time.

Campus boards and home training boards were very important developments in climbing and ushered in a big step forward in climbers' training and strength in the late 1980s and 1990s. Soon people everywhere had a cellar board. Sheffield is full of them. People around the world have them, from London to Alaska to Australia, and this means that no matter where you live, you can train, provided you are motivated enough. And those two routes, Liquid Ambar and Hubble, were two direct results of the gains Ben and I had made over a couple of winters of training in my cellar. Hubble also saw an even bigger leap in standards due to home training, when it had its second ascent.

In 1991, a young Scottish climber called Malcolm Smith built a replica of the moves on Hubble in his bedroom at his parents' house near Edinburgh. At the time he was a good climber, but nowhere near the best. The hardest thing he had done was a 7c+. Over one winter he trained hard on his board, using some great techniques he had learned from others and worked out for himself. After his winter training, he came to Raven Tor and redpointed Hubble, making the second ascent. It was an incredible achievement, going from 7c+ to 8c+ over a winter. And not only that, he seemed a lot stronger than we were. On Hubble, where Ben and I had been slapping and snatching, Malcolm was reaching powerfully between holds, locking each one off. He was so strong, simply from training in his bedroom.

Watching Malcolm trying Hubble was impressive. He was like a robot. He was, in effect, stronger than the route. Despite this, it still took him some time to do it, illustrating another fact about redpointing. People with little experience of redpointing hard routes often think that climbing in this way is a formality, that if you spend long enough at a climb, you will get up anything. This isn't true. Redpointing is as stressful as any other kind of climbing. You have to put so much in to each attempt, that you cannot have many tries at a climb. It is possible for an ascent to stretch out and take over your life, so that you become trapped by it, and if you develop a negative frame of mind towards it, then it can be very hard to succeed. As this was one of Malcolm's first hard routes, he had still to learn the mental techniques of redpointing, which is why it took him a little longer than his strength would have suggested. He soon picked them up and went on to succeed on lots of hard climbs.

But the mental side is often the crux. My ability to claw my way up things whatever it takes has always been my strong point. So often, before a route, I find myself thinking: 'Here I am, I'm about to try this route and I can only just about do the individual moves, but you know what? It's just like me to scrape my way up this and pull it out of the bag.'

Then, when I do, I think: 'That was just like me to do that.'

It was never that I found things easy. I would fight like crazy, almost falling off every move, feet slipping, pumped stupid, fingers uncurling, skin bleeding, all the way to the end. But I have always believed I could do it and that's the hardest thing. People can train and work and get stronger, and lots of people do, but to arrive at that level of self-belief is much harder. And I worked on that for twenty years.

I saw the same thing in the American climber, Lynn Hill. During my time in competitions, she was someone who impressed me a lot. I would watch Lynn climb, thinking, my God, I can't look. She misread sequences. She would get the holds with the wrong hand and then have to do awkward crossovers. She'd get it wrong, but none of that ever slowed her down. She would look to be pumped into oblivion, but she never faltered. She always moved up and she won loads of competitions. Lynn wanted it – and that brought out the animal in her.

For me, first ascents were the thing that motivated me most and that motivation gave me the edge. People would show me something they were trying and I would often get it before them, like The Powerband at Raven Tor. There are problems all over the place called Jerry's Wall or Jerry's Arête, often someone else's lines that they showed me. In the Llanberis Pass one day, I was climbing with Johnny Dawes. He had been working on a traverse on a boulder he had found on the steep hillside opposite the Cromlech. It was a classic problem, with fantastic, hard moves on sloping holds. We tried it for a while and eventually I managed to scrape my way along the problem. In the afternoon, he showed me another unclimbed classic on a long steep boulder right beside the road on the other side of the Pass. The moves were tough, but soon I managed it, just about. I don't think Johnny felt he was giving away the first ascents of classic boulder problems, because at the time, most people didn't think like that. But I did and I wanted to do them, and now there they are, The Barrel Traverse and Jerry's Roof. I gave these problems names, but they have been forgotten, as at the time, no one ever wrote up boulder problems in guidebooks and the record was only kept in the minds of locals. Names are often forgotten. Of all the Jerry's Traverses, Jerry's Roofs, Jerry's Walls and Jerry's Arêtes, I never named any of them after myself. It's just the name they have grown to have. I only ever called one problem after myself, Jerry's Slab, to the left of Joe's Slab at Froggatt. Ironically, that name has never been used.

The 1980s was a fantastic decade for climbing and saw a huge leap in the levels that people were climbing. Sport climbing, increased bouldering, training facilities, competitions, dedication and perhaps high unemployment, all came together to mean that climbers were training more and training better, and this transferred onto the routes that people were doing. At the beginning of the decade, the hardest climbs in Europe were probably 7b or 7b+ at most. This rose steadily to 8a some time around 1982, then the le Menestrels' routes at Buoux introduced the 8b+ grade. Ben Moon did much to push standards higher again, first with his route Agincourt at Buoux, and then with Hubble, the first 8c+. Levels were rising all the time. This surge culminated in 1991, when a route was climbed that would set the standard for sport climbing for the next decade.

Wolfgang Güllich was an amazing climber. When I first met him in 1983, the hardest climb he had done was Heisse Finger, at about 7b+. Two years later, he added a route to Mount Arapiles in Australia called Punks in the Gym, which got the Australian grade of 32, somewhere in the 8b/8b+ range. I repeated it sometime later, and while it wasn't as hard as Marc and Antoine's Buoux routes from around the same time, it would still have been one of the world's hardest climbs at the time. Punks represented a huge improvement for Wolfgang. Later, in 1987, he did a route called Wall Street, maybe the first 8c in the world. He had become motivated, trained hard and had a vision of where climbing could go and where he could take it. He became a real specialist in redpointing, working hard on something to produce routes that were at his absolute limit and didn't climb on-sight or boulder so much.

I spent time with him in 1991 and he told me he was trying a new climb, and although he made no mention of its difficulty, I could see it was pushing him. He was dieting. In the morning he would have some muesli and lots of coffee. He would eat nothing again until evening, when he would have a fillet steak and a small salad. With hardly any carbohydrates at all, he was incredibly ripped. The skin around his stomach was like the skin on the back of your hand.

At the same time he was taking training to a new level. The route he was trying was beautiful, absolutely stunning. It was on one of the typical little white limestone towers in the leafy forests of the Frankenjura and followed a very overhanging arête, almost like the prow of a ship. The holds were mostly single-finger pockets, and these were widely spaced. The climb involved jumping from holds and, at full stretch, stabbing the tip of the middle finger into another shallow pocket and locking the entire bodyweight onto that, and doing the same again. To train for it, Wolfgang had been working out on the Campus Board by climbing only on the middle finger of each hand. He could do one-five-eight with just single fingertips hooked over small edges. It was incredible.

He eventually did the climb, naming it Action Direct, and gave it the German grade of XI-/XI. This translated as 9a, the hardest route in the world at the time. It was a world-famous event and everyone knew it was incredibly hard. Action Direct was a result of the incredible training that Wolfgang had put in and it showed how far things could go with dedication. It's a benchmark 9a to this day. Even now, if a climber does it, it's big news. Action Direct represented how far climbing had progressed in the previous decade. Ten years before, the level had barely been 8a. In the nearly two decades since Action Direct, the top level has only moved on a couple of grades to 9b or so.

In 1992 I was due to attend a trade show in Germany. As I would be passing near Obertrubach, I thought I'd stop by and catch up with my friends. I rang up to see who would be home. Norbert Sander answered the phone:

'Bad news, Jerry, Wolfgang has been in a car accident and it's serious.'

He had been doing a radio interview in Munich, and driving back early in the morning, somehow lost concentration and went off the road. A simple error. By the time I got there, they had switched off the life-support machine. Wolfgang was dead. Not long before I had attended his wedding. It was such a great event, full of joy and it was wonderful to see Wolfgang so happy. Now, so soon after, I was at his funeral. Wolfgang had always been a special friend to me, so it was a great honour when Norbert asked me to give the funeral address to the hundreds who came to pay their respects. It was one of the hardest things I have ever had to do.

This is what I said:

'I feel very honoured to be able to say something at a time like this about such a great man. It doesn't seem possible that Wolfgang has lost his life. His physical features, huge muscles and strong character made him seem almost immortal. We all knew Wolfgang in one way or another. He was mild-mannered, a gentle giant, focused and with direction, polite to everybody, treating all men and women as equals. He was never big headed and almost embarrassed when people spoke of his achievements. He was proud of what he had done, but never in a boastful way. I'm amazed at what he achieved in the 31 years he was alive.

'I think it's not important how good a climber he was at this time. I know for me he was one of the greatest climbers the world has ever known. His new routes will be enjoyed by thousands of climbers over the years and the difficult ones by few. These are more things we have to remember him by.

'What was so inspiring about Wolfgang was his attitude towards the way he lived his life. He wasted no time, saw his goals and went about getting them in an honest and fair way. He was a gentleman, was generous with his money (about which he cared little) and his compliments to others.

'Today must be a positive day. We are gathered here to celebrate Wolfgang's life, to think of the good times and give thanks that in our lives we were able to meet such an inspiring man. We live only for a short time on this earth, we don't ever know how long. I shall try to follow Wolfgang's example, live my life to the full and try to better myself. He had no regrets. So, Wolfie, you have left us to start a new life, we know not where. We're proud to have known you and will never forget you. We send our love and thanks for showing us how to lead a good life.'

ELEVEN

Playing the Game

In the years following my injury, from 1985 to 1986, I kept away from climbing almost altogether. During that time, the sport as I knew it changed in many ways. The French style of climbing, with its redpointing and bolts, became the style of the day. People were training more than ever, and harder and harder routes were appearing all the time. But perhaps the biggest change that occurred was the appearance of organised climbing competitions. When I began to recover and got back into climbing again, there was only one thing people were talking about – competitions, competitions, competitions.

I had heard a little about climbing competitions before. My friends Wolfgang Güllich and Kurt Albert had gone to a few in the old East Germany late in the 1970s, but from the way they talked about them, it seemed they were just excuses for drinking sessions, and the actual competition side was not taken too seriously. Russia had also been hosting some events, but these were speed-climbing competitions, based on how fast you could race up a wall. This was a peculiarly Russian thing and had very little in common with the difficulty-based competitions that have taken off since then.

I first became aware of these new competitions in 1985. During my injury lay-off, hanging out in Yosemite with Ron Kauk, the organisers of an upcoming climbing competition contacted me. This was the first event of a kind we would later come to know well. The Italian town of Bardonecchia, a little skiing resort in the Alps, was planning to host an event in May of that year and the organisers were hoping to make a big splash. They wanted all the top climbers in the world to be there and asked me to attend. I explained that was impossible because of my injured elbows. They said they were still keen to at least have me there. I didn't know what to make of it, but they offered to fly me over. I decided to go, seeing it as a chance to catch up with old friends.

I arrived in the village, checked into my hotel and went out to look around. In years to come, when competitions became well established, they would take place on huge artificial structures – metal frameworks covered in plywood sheeting, covered in holds created from resin bolted onto the surface. The Bardonecchia competition, however, was to take place on natural rock. However, since competing on an existing route would give an unfair advantage to locals or anyone who had climbed it before, route-setters used hammers, drills, chisels and glue to create special competition routes on the rock where none had existed before. Chipping holds often happened in Europe. Perhaps it was because Europeans had so much good rock that they seemed to treat it as being less precious. In Britain, where there was a very strong tradition of respecting the rock, chipping was a mortal sin, even on the scrappiest, ugliest quarries. To my British eyes, the lines of chips and glue that ran up the competition faces looked ugly and very unappealing to climb on.

It was great to catch up with Wolfgang, but I could tell that he was nervous about the competition and that his heart wasn't in it. Normally Wolfgang was teetotal, but the night before the competition, there was a reception with free wine and he got really drunk, swilling down glass after glass of wine. We went on to a bar and partied till four in the morning.

The next day I wasn't feeling too good.

The way the competition was run was far from perfect. There was no isolation zone, so climbers got to stand around and see others try the routes. Obviously, whoever went first had a great disadvantage, as all the other climbers could see how they got on and how they did the moves. Wolfgang came out with an awful hangover and climbed poorly. I watched him clunking up the route. He came to a sudden stop, hung around for a bit and then fell off. Other good climbers, who I thought would do well, didn't fare much better than Wolfgang. Stefan Glowacz, a German, climbed really well and won it. I hadn't heard of Stefan before, but he would go on to become one of the great champions of climbing competitions.

Afterwards, Wolfgang was disgusted with himself. He was a good sport, always prepared to have a go at new things, but that first experience of competitions really put him off. In many ways, Wolfgang's experience put me off competitions too. All I could see was bureaucracy, climbers being told how long to climb for, waiting around and red tape. They seemed to have none of the things I wanted from climbing, hanging out with friends and having fun, doing new routes, doing the hardest climbs, the freedom. There was the sense that businessmen were running everything. At the end of the day, somebody had lost and somebody had won. All these things you get into climbing to avoid. I didn't want any part of competitions.

Later, in 1987, thanks to the operations in Munich and all the physio I was doing, I was feeling as strong as ever. I was mad for it again and couldn't wait to get back on the rock. When I did, I was surprised to see that, suddenly, everyone had become keen on competitions. When I went to Buoux in the spring of 1987, it seemed everyone was saying how great they were, how much they liked them, and that I should take part.

I still wasn't keen. Since Bardonecchia I had heard more unpleasant stories about these competitions. The first events were notorious for bad organisation. I had heard tales of climbers waiting in the isolation zone, usually some draughty schoolroom or village hall, from early in the morning until late at night. It sounded like torture. They seemed to take place on some badly chipped outdoor route, and as far as I could tell, everyone I knew who had tried them had found the experience miserable. It was all very strange. Some of my friends would enter a competition in Europe, get really excited about it, train, go off and compete, then return swearing that they would never do another one. Weeks later they would be raving about how great they were and in no time they would have entered another.

'Why don't you come along, Jerry? You'd love it.'

Gradually I came around to the idea that I was going to have to start doing them. This was against my better judgement in many ways, but I could see that they were becoming established as an important side of climbing. Not so much in Britain, but in Europe and America, magazines were very excited about comps. They were attracting coverage and money, and advertisers and sponsors seemed to be very keen on them. At the time, I was a fully professional climber. It was how I made my living.

'Climbing competitions are going to be the next big thing,' people were saying. 'TV is going to get involved.'

On top of that, the winners of these competitions were beginning to be called the best climbers. The logic was that if climbers competed against each other, then the winner must surely be the best. Would comps take over from new routing or on-sighting as the way top climbers were measured? Eventually, it became obvious that I could no longer afford to avoid them. I was going to have to get stuck in. By the summer of 1987, I was fully fit once again. The time was right.

My first competition was in late 1987, in Troubat in the French Pyrenees. Ben Moon, Ben Masterson and I would drive down through France, get some climbing in along the way, and compete at Troubat. We would then drive over to Arco, in Italy, where there was another competition two weeks later. We would do the competition there, and do some more climbing on the way home. At that time, although climbers from other countries would have their expenses covered by their national bodies, in the

UK, we still had to pay our way. This could make going to competitions an expensive gamble, as a trip to Europe could easily cost £300. If we got some climbing in, at least the trip would be more worthwhile.

Despite this, we did harbour secret ambitions. Ben Moon had already competed in Arco the previous year, and had performed well. Not many had heard of him then, so when he came second to Patrick Edlinger, beating lots of good climbers, he really surprised people. With our quiet hopes of success, we got in some last-minute training, and looked forward to setting off. Then disaster struck.

We were to head down in Ben Moon's Volkswagen Scirocco, but just a couple of days before departure, Ben was driving down past Froggatt in the Peak District, going flat out, as usual. Going round a right-hander, he lost the back end. The car skidded up a bank, bounced off a wall, back down the bank again, rolled three times, and came to a stop. Somehow he got out of this unscathed, but the Scirocco was a write off.

We no longer had a car. Even though cash was tight, I decided I would have to buy one, the cheapest, most economical car I could get. Someone told me to get a Citroën Dyane, the old French classic, with the funny gear stick in the middle of the dash. I was told it would do 50 miles to the gallon. I bought a paper, and found a Dyane for £140. The next day we left for Europe.

The Citroën was great. It even had a fold-down roof, and on a hot, summer day we squeezed everything in, left Sheffield, and pootled out to the motorway. Joining the M1, we settled in the inside lane. The car didn't have a radio, so we took a portable ghetto blaster. Ben Masterson put in a Wham cassette and pressed play. With my foot pressed firmly on the floor, shaking our heads to the music, singing along, we soon reached speeds of fifty miles per hour. It took about four and a half hours just to get to London. Everything was overtaking us – grannies, wide loads, mobile libraries, everything – but we were having a great time, psyched, and looking forward to a great trip, and wondering to ourselves if we would win the competition. After what felt like weeks, we crossed the Channel into France, and headed south.

We'd planned to stop off at Saussois to break the journey. After a marathon driving session in the scorching French heat, we got there. It was incredibly hot, like a desert, and too hot to climb so we decided we would just press on to Troubat. This was miles away, right down in the French Pyrenees, but we just thought we'd get it over with. As we weren't going much above 50, we decided that there was no point in taking the motorway. The tolls would add up to quite a lot of money, and we seemed to be annoying a lot of French drivers with the speed we were doing. We decided that the Citroën might like it better if we went cross-country, along smaller roads and through little villages, avoiding motorways altogether.

The car rattled southwards, slowly, but cheaply, through the beautiful French countryside. As we were passing through one small town, we came to a crossroads. The traffic light was red, and as we approached, I put my foot on the brake. Instead of stopping, the Dyane floated, very gently, through the crossroads. Luckily nothing else was coming. At the far side I blinked, and wondered whether it had really happened. I put my foot on the brake again, and this time it worked. Ben looked up, and asked what was going on. I said that I thought the brakes didn't work, but now they were okay again, and that maybe I'd imagined it. Half an hour later, going through another town, the same thing happened again. This time I was sure. I pulled over.

We got out, not sure what to do. Someone told us there was a garage just around the corner. It was really nothing more than a barn, with half-dismantled cars lying about. We called hello, and a small Frenchman came out, dressed in dirty blue overalls, wearing a black beret and smoking a cigarette. We told him what had happened in the best French we could, and he told us to bring the car round.

Slowly, we drove to the barn, and the Frenchman had a look under the bonnet. While we sat around on bales of hay in the sunshine, he spent an hour tinkering with various bits. He took the wheels off, put the wheels back on again, and then told us it was fixed. He held up a rusted fitting to show us what was wrong. We said thank you, and asked how much we owed him. No, he said, he wouldn't take a penny for the work he had done. He pointed at the car, then said 'Français. Français,' patting himself proudly on the chest. Thanking him again, we got in the car and drove off. I slammed the brakes on, and the Citroën drifted to a stop. It was fixed.

We hit the road again, and turned George Michael back on. In the heat, we continued south, and every now and again I'd check the brakes. In the fields, farmers were burning stubble, and there was smoke all around.

'What's that smell, Jerry?' Ben Moon said, after a while.

'Don't worry Ben, it's these farmers.'

'No, it's not that. I'm sure I can smell burning rubber, and my feet are getting hot. Pull over.'

We pulled over, turned off the engine, and got out of the car. Ben was right. I could see a little wisp of black smoke coming from under the bonnet. I reached back into the car and popped the catch, then went round to the front and lifted the bonnet up. A ball of flame whooshed out. The engine was ablaze. It was a fireball.

Panicked, we all fled and hopped over a wall to hide from the inevitable explosion. On the other side of the wall with our eyes closed and our hands over our ears, we realised all our climbing gear was still in the car. If the car went up we would lose everything. Heroically, we hopped back over the wall, and reaching into the back of the car, began hurling our gear over the wall. It was all very frantic.

Then, all by itself, the car started up again.

The heat of the fire had caused the engine and plugs to warm up, and the expansion had begun pumping fuel once more into the system. The car burst into life, and started bunny-hopping along the verge all by itself, the roof down, the bonnet up, an inferno issuing from the engine. Some of the farmers stopped to watch. I thought I was dreaming. We were now jogging alongside the car as it hopped along, salvaging ropes and shoes and tents. I didn't know what else to do.

A lorry pulled in just behind us, and the driver hopped out. We called to him to help. He walked over to the Citroën, reached through the driver's window, and pulled the car out of gear. This, at least, stopped the car from bunny-hopping, but it was still blazing. He then went back to the lorry to grab a fire extinguisher, and aimed it at the engine.

Pffftt.

A little whiff of air came out. It was empty. He threw the extinguisher over the wall, reached into the burning engine and started pulling out leads to try to stop it. One of these was the fuel line. He put his thumb over the top of it, but petrol was still squirting out, just missing the burning engine. He turned round and pressed the tubes into Ben Moon's hands. At this, I hopped back over the wall. I took one more peek to see Ben still standing there, fuel line in his hand, engine blazing, the lorry driver pulling leads out from the engine. More cars began to stop and eventually someone located a working extinguisher, and they put the fire out.

The Citroën was badly damaged, but luckily we had insurance, and later that day took delivery of a brand new Opel Corsa. We were soon speeding down the motorways in comfort, arriving at Troubat the day before the competition.

The competition was to take place on a steep limestone cliff on the outskirts of the town. Competitions could come in various formats, including on-sight, but this one was a redpoint event. This meant spending half an hour the day before the final trying the route and rehearsing the moves. Then, on the day, you would try to redpoint it. Trying the route in rehearsal, it didn't feel too hard, probably about 7c or 7c+. I had already on-sighted this grade, so I was able to do the moves relatively easily. It actually felt very straightforward, and miles below the standard I was capable of redpointing. I was careful not to overdo it so I wouldn't tire myself, but just enough so as to feel confident. I could do well here, I thought to myself.

The following day I got up early, and made my way to the venue with the two Bens. We were led to an isolation zone where the competitors would wait their turn to climb. I did some warming up, then wandered over and sat down on some gym mats.

As the climb had felt so easy the day before, I decided that all I had to do was to stay relaxed. If I did that, all would be well. So that's what I did. I stretched out on the mat and told myself I hadn't a care in the world. This would be easy. I didn't go over the moves in my head, I didn't think about strategies, I didn't get myself psyched, all things I would do for every other route I had ever done before. Instead, I lay on the mat, unfolded a brochure for the competition, covered my eyes with it, and fell asleep.

Eventually someone woke me up and said I was to climb in twenty minutes. I snoozed for a little longer then got up and did a little stretching.

'God, I feel so relaxed,' I thought to myself. 'I've hardly even thought about the competition.'

An official came to me a little bit later.

'You may go now,' he said.

I had been relaxing in a little room a hundred metres from the climb. I stepped out into the sunshine, and strolled casually along to the cliff. The crowd was silent, and everyone was looking at me. Over the loudspeaker system, I heard a foreign voice call out my name and say 'Great Britain'. Suddenly I was stood underneath the climb. An official walked up to me:

'Two minutes.'

This was the time we were allowed to look over the route and reacquaint ourselves with the moves and get focused. I looked at the route. My mind was blank. I found myself staring at it, thinking, what am I supposed to do? I tried to remember what I had done the day before, where had I gone, what moves had I done. Which were the good holds? How had it felt? Nothing. I couldn't remember a single thing.

The two minutes went by. The official came over again and barked: 'Climb!'

Whatever relaxation I had found in the isolation zone had disappeared. I felt incredibly nervous. I hurriedly tied onto the rope, approached the wall and started to climb. I grabbed holds, anything I could reach, and pulled. My hands and feet were all over the place, and I was squeezing the life out of every hold I reached. Even as I climbed, all I could think of was how badly I was doing. I soon felt my forearms getting pumped. Eventually, after about forty feet of this, my foot slipped off a big hold, and my tired forearms gave out. I was off.

I lowered down to the ground feeling shocked. I untied, and walked away from the wall in a daze. What had gone wrong? I should have just walked up this climb. So how come I had found it so hard? In the end I had come sixth, which wasn't that bad, but I was still disappointed. I felt I had fallen so far short of what I expected of myself. The two Bens had similar experiences, and had both fallen off even lower than I had. Competitions were clearly harder than I thought they would be. Driving over to Arco I felt much more apprehensive than I had before Troubat.

The Arco competition was in two parts, an on-sight and a redpoint, the winner being whoever did best overall. The order of climbing was set by a lottery, and by chance, I was picked out of a hat to climb first in the on-sight round. This meant climbing at nine in the morning. Even at that hour, the summer heat was ferocious, with the climb in full sunshine. I hid under an umbrella, sweating, waiting for my turn. When it came, I stepped into the glare, and tried the route. The hot limestone felt slippery under my sweating fingers, and, not very far up, I greased off. Twenty minutes later, the route went into shade for the rest of the day, making it far easier. I hadn't done very well.

The next event was the redpoint event. Just as in Troubat, we had a chance to work the moves the day before. Once again, the route was in the full sun, and the moves felt desperate. There was one move I couldn't do even while working it, a big rock-over near the top, at the end of a long, fingery, rightwards traverse.

The following day, as the redpoint approached, I felt dejected. If I couldn't manage moves sitting on the rope for rests between attempts, then there was very little chance of doing it at the top of a route, pumped from the climbing below. I felt I had no chance. I made my way to the isolation zone, and did some warming up.

I recognised many of the other competitors, and began to feel intimidated. Patrick Edlinger, from France, was there. He was a great competitor, a good on-sight climber, and had a good style for competitions, slow and controlled. The le Menestrel brothers, Marc and Antoine, were there, so were Jibé Tribout and Ron Kauk. Stefan Glowacz, very professional, very strong and controlled. Didier Raboutou, one of the best competition climbers at the time. Earlier, as he worked the route, I had watched him do the move, the move that I couldn't touch, three times on the trot. I was gobsmacked. Didier would grab the holds, and press them down to his waist like a machine.

I had a real sense of tension and apprehension in isolation. I looked around at the others. There's a guy who's just done some new route, that guy's just done a really hard boulder problem, this guy's just done an amazing on-sight, and all I could think is how am I going to beat all those great climbers? Soon I was thinking: 'Forget it, you're not.'

My time came to climb and I went out to try the redpoint. This time, however, it was later in the day, and the route had gone into shade. The moves felt so much easier than when I had worked them the day before. I got to the traverse without too much trouble, and followed this rightwards.

Jerry and Ron Kauk climbing Midnight Lightning
(V9) in Yosemite, in 1984. The 'lightning bolt'
can be seen level with Jerry's right foot.

Raw emotion after climbing Le Minimum (F8b+) at Buoux in 1987, belayed by good friend Sean Myles.

Soloing Flying Buttress Direct (E1) at Stanage.

Complete focus while visualising the moves before climbing at a competition in Germany.

Winning the World Cup event at Leeds in 1989. "My only regret is that Jerry stopped competing in '90. He was very ambitious and loyal competitor (which is rare in climbing comp.). Come on Jerry, come back to make us cry like at Leeds '89." *Three-time World Champion François Legrand in an article for Grimper Magazine in 1994.*

Jerry nipping out for a pint of milk in the Peak.

Jerry and Ben, dedicated to training in the cellar.

Jerry climbing Liquid Ambar (F8c+)
at Lower Pen Trwyn in 1990.

The late Wolfgang Güllich training on the
original board at the Campus Gym in Germany.

The boulder problem Superman (Font 8a+) at Cressbrook in the Peak District.

Jerry making the crux move of The Dominator (Font 8b), Yosemite in 1993. "The Dominator was the standard by which everything else was measured, it opened my eyes to how cool bouldering is and the level of difficulty that can be achieved in just several moves." – *Chris Sharma*

Small holds and big moves on Evolution (F8c+) at Raven Tor.

Malcolm Smith making the second ascent
of The Ace (Font 8b) at Stanage.

Johnny Dawes taking the train to Hampi, India.

Jerry soloing Big Guts (E1) in Hampi, India, while
Johnny seeks out new lines to climb.

The monkeys show the climbers
how it's done in Hampi.

Jerry flashing Super Imujin (5.12d) at
Ogawayama, Japan.
"Led first try. Hard to flash as gear was hard to

Jerry climbing above the Emi Koussi volcano in Chad.

The remains of war. A soldier's hand and tank in Chad.

Jerry bouldering on one of artist Jean Verame's coloured rocks in Chad.

Repeating Nutsa (Font 8a+) in South Africa. Jerry also climbed 'Ard eh? (Font 8a+) on the same trip – his final first ascent.

Jerry climbing Nelson's Column in 1995, with Johnny Dawes and Simon Nadin. The stunt was for Survival to publicise the plight of Canada's Innu people.

A self-portrait shot for French magazine Grimper in 1992. The theme was top climbers and what was important to them – Jerry bucked the trend of other European climbers who had posed with training equipment and dietary supplements, and instead opted for a more humorous approach.

Surfing warm water in Banyak, Indonesia, 2008.

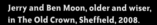

Sharon with Lily (aged 5) and Barnaby (aged 3) at Cloggy, over 20 years after Jerry left his mark on the crag.

Jerry and Ben Moon, older and wiser, in The Old Crown, Sheffield, 2008.

Sharon, Barnaby (4), Jerry and Lily (6). Sheffield, December 2008.

At the end was the desperate rockover, which I hadn't been able to get close to previously. I shook my arms out, chalked up, and prepared for the move.

'I might get this,' I said to myself.

There was a rule in competitions at the time, whereby whoever touched the highest point of the wall won. But this meant competitors, when faced with a move they didn't think they could do, would simply jump, and try to touch the wall, without actually trying the move. I had seen people do this, but it had always seemed like cheating to me. Yet just for a moment, under the rock-over, I hesitated, and the thought of doing it crossed my mind. I immediately decided not to, but I had lost momentum. I tried the move above – and very nearly did it – but came off.

As it turned out, I did quite well, and drew with Didier Raboutou for first place. He had looked unstoppable the day before, but on the day of the competition, fell off the move in exactly the same position as me.

Despite this, my poor performance in the on-sight round meant I hadn't done well overall. I was unhappy with my performance, and found the whole experience very stressful. I wanted to quit competitions altogether, but as soon as I thought that, I thought, no. I needed to master this new challenge. I knew I'd have to win a climbing competition before I could drop them. Things had gone badly, but once I'd started, I couldn't stop. I had to prove it to myself, to everyone else, that I could win them. Even though I didn't much like them, there was no way I could let it rest.

My next competition was in Grenoble. The event took place on an indoor wall, on a plywood-covered metal framework, and I liked the look of the route. It was steep, with leaning sections and roofs, which suited my strengths. I knew, all the same, that I would need a better approach. Having decided that my super-relaxed approach from Troubat wasn't going to work, I decided this time I would get myself revved up and climb quickly. My name was called. I hurried out of the isolation zone, tied on, and raced at the route, climbing aggressively, almost like a speed climber. I flew up the first section to an overhang. Unfortunately, I was climbing in such a rush that I hadn't seen it. I whacked the top of my head into the overhang. I felt the whole structure boom and vibrate from the force. My body did the same. Stunned, I wobbled up about another three moves, and fell off. I felt like a simpleton.

So far, things weren't going very well.

The following year I got invited to a comp in France, in Aix-les-Bains. I seriously wanted to win this one, and had an extra motivation. Two weeks before, the engine of my motorbike had seized. The Aix-les-Bains comp had a first prize of £2000. If I win, I told myself, then I'm going to buy myself a new motorbike.

I got psyched, and trained like mad. All I could think about was the new bike. I was living in Germany at the time, training really hard and climbing lots, and more importantly, on-sighting well. I had a German friend, Uli, who said he would come with me to France for the competition. I'd take two days to drive down, stay nice and relaxed, prepare well, and win.

The first day's drive went okay, and we got to a hotel. I parked the car for the evening and we went out for a meal. Uli started chatting up a waitress, and later in the evening, they hooked up and started getting drunk together. Wanting to be well rested, and to let them get on with it, I said good night and went off to bed. Lying there, waiting for Uli to come back, I couldn't get to sleep. Expecting to be woken up when he returned meant I just couldn't drop off. At about two o'clock, I heard the door creak open, and Uli tiptoe into the room. Then I heard giggling. He'd brought the girl with him. They got into the bed next to mine.

'Uli,' I said, 'I'm trying to sleep. I've got a competition tomorrow.'

Uli apologised, and asked to borrow my car keys. I gave them to him, without really thinking. They left, and I sighed in relief. I heard the car doors close, then a few moments later, to my astonishment, heard the sound of an engine start, followed by a loud rev and the squeal of tyres. They roared off into the night. 'Oh God,' I thought. Not my Peugeot, not my 205, please, no. It was all a little unreal, and I lay awake all night worrying about my car. A little before six I heard the car come back, and Uli, still sniggering, came into the room and crept into bed. Within five minutes he was snoring loudly.

In the morning I was exhausted and Uli was hung over, and very apologetic. Luckily we had left ourselves plenty of time, so we took it gently for the second part of the journey. We drove down to Aix-les-Bains, a beautiful university town in Provence, with loads of time to spare. We relaxed in the town, had some nice food and then decided to go register for the event. When we went to look for the venue, we couldn't find it. We tried the tourist office and they hadn't heard of it.

We phoned the organisers, only to find out the competition was actually in Seynes, another six hours further south. We'd gone to the wrong place, and had to be in the right place in four hours. We screamed down the motorway, and just made it, exhausted, and stressed out of our minds. So much for being relaxed.

All I could think about was the bike. I had my eye on a Yamaha 250 TZR, a fast, lightweight, two-stroke racing bike. This motivation gave me a different outlook. Some of the best climbers hadn't shown up for this comp. But that didn't matter. I wasn't there to prove anything. The competition went well for me. The final route was an on-sight climb, up a vertical, fingery wall. I liked it, fought hard and fell off the final move. That was enough to win my first international climbing competition. I got the cash, travelled back to Germany and bought my bike.

Back home, with my new toy and a trophy on the mantelpiece, I realised I could win these things. Coming first in Seynes was great, but what I really wanted to do was win one of the big ones, with all the best climbers there. At that time, the best were Stefan Glowacz and Didier Raboutou. Didier, especially, was phenomenal at competitions. He climbed statically, never slapped, and moved in a very methodical way. This was a style of climbing that worked well in competitions. He used his feet well, and seldom made mistakes. He was cool and I liked to watch him climb. Once he reached a hold, he would latch onto it, and pull like a robot. He was also a nice guy, very quiet, and kept himself to himself. I had a lot of respect for him.

Stefan was similar in many ways, being quiet and fairly introverted. He too was a really good competitor. He liked competitions, and had a naturally gifted mind for them, which meant that he could perform to his best in situations climbers like Wolfgang found so hard. He climbed well, but could also try hard, which was critical. He could think fast, and had incredible stamina.

Both Didier and Stefan were very much endurance climbers. On-sighting was their thing, and they could hang on forever. Neither of them bouldered or redpointed much, so they weren't particularly powerful. At the time, endurance was what counted in the comps. Good routes were ones without a definite crux. If a crux was too hard, then all the climbers tended to fall off there, making it awkward to declare a winner. With long, grinding stamina routes, ones that tested your ability to hang on, and to keep making that next move, climbers fell off where their strength failed, and these always gave better results. Didier and Stefan were the best because they could just keep going.

They were different from me in one other respect. Competitions for them were the most important thing, it was what they cared about most. They trained for them, climbed indoors a lot in order to get good, and wanted to win. For me, new routes were the most important things. Doing hard first ascents of the best lines on rock was what mattered most.

In 1989 two of the biggest competitions in Europe, the ones with the biggest prize money, the ones that everyone wanted to win, were Bercy in France, and Munich. At the time, I was living in Germany, and Munich was all anyone could talk about. Clearly, it would be great to win this competition.

I was climbing well beforehand, consistently on-sighting 8a, and feeling positive. As the competition approached, I cranked up my training even more, and, a couple of weeks before the event, went on a low-carb, water-reduction diet. This involved eating few carbohydrates, loads of vegetables and nothing with any sodium in it at all. Without these minerals, the body can release a lot of its water. I took some mineral tablets to keep cramp away.

It's a hard diet to stay on, because it's difficult to get enough calories from eating vegetables, and you experience severe hunger practically all the time. It's at times like this that motivation needs to kick in. The week before the comp I dropped from 64.5kg down to 61.5kg. At that weight, I felt super strong. I was ready.

Jibé, Didier, Stefan, Edlinger – all the people I had to beat were there. In the qualifications I didn't climb well. The route was weird, off-balance and slippery. My footwork was poor, and I climbed stiffly. I over-gripped, pumped out, and fell off. The route was only 7b+. I hadn't fallen off a route of that grade for three years. But despite this, I managed to get through to the semi-final.

The next day, I sat in isolation, and felt all over the place. I was disappointed in myself for my performance the day before, and now I had to go out and climb again. I hoped I would climb better this time, but in the pit of my stomach was worrying that I wouldn't. My turn came around. I came out of isolation for the semi-final, and looked the route over. It had a slab going up to a big overhang. I remember seeing it, and thinking to myself, please, *please*, let me climb well. Thankfully, I did. I got to the overhang and cranked through it. It was a good route for me, and I got higher than anyone else. The others all fell off at various points near the bottom of the overhang. This was only the semi-final, but after this round I felt confident. It was the first time I had beaten all the best climbers. This was a massive psychological breakthrough.

The top ten climbers all went through to the final, which turned out to be a horrible climb. From the first moment I saw it, I knew I wouldn't like it. It had awkward moves on tiny little sloping holds. It was the sort of route that you would just slip off with no warning, even if you weren't pumped, and a lot of climbers did. I was moving up an arête at about twelve feet, looking at the next moves. Just as I was about to take a hold with my right hand, my left foot slipped and I fell. Lowering down, I untied and went straight to the isolation zone. Being Germany, they had laid out an amazing spread of food and beer. I poured a beer and downed it in one.

I had put so much work into this. I was as strong as I'd ever been, I was on-sighting my best on rock, I was lighter than ever, I was desperate to win – so what had gone wrong? Why were things always going wrong?

That night, once again, I lay in bed in turmoil. I never wanted to do another competition ever again. I knew from experience that I would feel terrible now for weeks to come. I always did. I had never become frustrated like this over routes on rock. Yet these competitions were taking over my life. I was putting in so much time and effort, missing out on first ascents and great times with friends, and they just kept spitting me out and making me depressed.

But if I never do another one, I thought, then I've failed. I knew all these climbers. I had climbed a lot with Didier, Stefan and Jibé. I knew how good they were. And I knew I had it in me to do well. I had done harder on-sights than any of them on rock, had done harder boulder problems, and harder redpoints. I was the best, but the frustration of not being able to perform in comps was really getting to me.

I wanted desperately to win, but I just couldn't take the agony of failure any more.

TWELVE

Winning in Mind

Coming back to England I was devastated. I had put so much into the Munich competition, had done well in the qualifying rounds, but in the final I climbed like an idiot, and blew it. I knew from experience how depressing this was going to feel, dreading the long grim period that followed all my poor performances in competitions. I had wanted to win so badly at Munich that now, in the face of this failure, I had to try hard to find the motivation to carry on competing.

Yet I felt I couldn't just give up. How could I think of myself as a top climber if I had failed at competitions? Ten or fifteen years later, competitions would be something that a large number of climbers chose to avoid, but in the late-1980s, all the top climbers were competing: the boulderers, the on-sighters, the redpointers, everyone. I didn't feel I could just turn my back on them. To do that would definitely have been to fail, to leave a gap in my climbing career. It was crunch time again.

In the summer of 1989, Britain would host its first ever World Cup climbing competition in the Yorkshire city of Leeds. A big competition on home ground was a chance to show British climbers what competitions were all about. It felt like such a great opportunity. If I could win, it would be massive. But pressure was starting to build, and I wondered if I could put myself through the mental turmoil. Could I go through all the preparation again, and fail? Again?

I couldn't help thinking back to Munich. I had been so fit, so strong and light. I had trained hard and was climbing so well. I had fallen off a route that was miles below my usual standard, yet physically I knew I had been in incredible shape. So if it wasn't my body that let me down, then it must have been my mind. Somehow my mental approach was stopping me from winning. If I was to have a chance at Leeds, I knew I was going to have to sort myself out mentally.

In the week after getting back to England, I was in Leicester visiting my family. My mum asked how the competitions were going, and I told her about the difficulties I had been experiencing. I told her about my conclusions about the mental side of it all. I thought she was just asking to show interest, and that she probably wouldn't understand, but some days later she gave me a call to tell me something she had seen in the local paper.

She'd read an article in the Leicester Mercury about a female archer who lived in the area. The archer had talked about losing badly in her events until she was given a particular book on sports psychology. She read the book, and pretty soon began to win.

'This book was the closest thing to cheating I could imagine,' the archer said.

My mum knew a reporter for the Mercury, and through her, got the number of the archer. The archer told my mum the name of the book, and she sent off for it. A few days later the book, and a box set of cassette tapes, arrived from America. With Leeds coming up, and not knowing what was worse, not entering or the inevitable failure, I grabbed at the chance to change things, and drove straight down to Leicester to pick up the book and cassettes.

Lanny Bassham had been a medal-winning rifle shooter at the 1972 Munich Olympic Games. His mental failure in the final meant that he won the silver, not the gold. He talked to the gold medal winners in the US Olympic squad to discover what it was that made winners. He studied them closely, and came to the conclusion that what separates winners from the rest of the pack is the way they think. He found that virtually all winning is done by a tiny percentage of people who think like winners. He combined his findings in a book, *With Winning in Mind*, aimed at training people's psychologies for competition. Using these mental techniques, he went on to win gold at the 1976 Montreal Olympics.

Straightaway I tucked into the book. It talked about common mistakes, and the more I read, the more I thought, that's me, that's what I do. Bad habits and attitudes. Lack of belief. Talking myself down. Not being in the correct frame of mind to win. I reflected on the Munich competition. When I had gone out there for the final, I didn't have any particular strategy. I didn't know what I should be thinking. All I remember is seeing the route, and saying to myself, I don't like the look of that.

My skills had been there, I had trained hard, done lots of on-sighting, and was really fit. I had been on a great diet, and had been super-light. I concentrated hard, and really applied myself. The problem was that my confidence wasn't there, what the book called my 'self-image', the way I view myself. When I thought about it, I didn't see myself winning the competitions I entered. I wanted to win. It would be great to win. But I found myself thinking, well, if he falls off, or if he messes up, then I'm in with a chance. That's one way of winning. The other way is not to think about anyone else's failures, to think only about yourself, to take the competition by the scruff of the neck and go out to win it. That's the only way to succeed at something with consistency.

It was obvious I didn't have a clue about the psychological side of competitions. Realising this, the reason for my performances became clear. This book offered a means of changing that. There were five weeks to go before the competition in Leeds, and from the moment I had Bassham's book, I dedicated myself to it, learning, understanding and applying all its principles, believing in it totally, and setting out to change myself into a winner. It had to work. It just had to.

'Self-image is the total of your habits and attitudes. And the great thing about your self-image, is that it can be changed.'

I had to change my self-image. I had to believe I would win Leeds.

'The mind can only concentrate on one thing at a time. If you are picturing something positive in your mind, it is impossible, at the same time, to picture something negative. And, if you have a negative thought, you cannot, at the same time, think positively.'

That is a basic principle of the book.

The subconscious mind is what controls skills and movement. From one thought, a thought like 'catch a ball' for example, the body knows what it is doing, and carries out many actions, all led by the subconscious. Yet what's going on in the subconscious is informed by what the conscious mind is thinking. So if your mind is thinking one positive thought, then the subconscious will act that out. Think negative thoughts, and you will probably fail.

An example. You're playing darts. If you're looking at a dartboard, you don't think about swinging your arm at a certain angle and certain speed, then release the dart at a certain point. If you need the twenty, you think about hitting the twenty. You just throw it, and the details are done by the subconscious. But if you are thinking: 'I hope I don't hit the one', then your subconscious is confused, and can easily start thinking more about the one. Chances are the one is where the dart is going to end up. What you must do is think only positive thoughts about the twenty, so the mind has no room to start thinking about the one.

Applying Bassham's principles to my situation, I realised I had to take my mind off possible failures: my foot's going to slip off that hold; it feels greasy; my fingers can't hold on; I don't feel good today; I've got a stomach ache; I didn't sleep well last night; it's too early in the morning; it's too late at night. There really are a million excuses for not doing well. You've got to block them out of your mind and think, 'I'm on it today.'

I thought about Munich, how disappointed I had been when I saw the route, thinking it didn't suit me. I remembered how I had pleaded with myself to do well. I realised how stressed I was in earlier competitions because I was climbing early in the morning, or in the sun, or too soon after an earlier round. All these thoughts were destroying my chances. I had to learn to control this, to learn to like every kind of route – slabs, corners, overhangs, vertical walls, traverses – and to believe that they all suited me.

'The more we think about, talk about, or write about something happening, the more we improve the probability of that thing happening.'

The book stressed the need to *want* to win, to reinforce this in yourself, then believe that you really *were* going to win. To do this, it advocated the writing of lists, so I wrote down every reason I could think of why I wanted to win at Leeds, and then made a list of all the reasons I *was* going to win. I wanted to do it to help my career; I wanted the prize money, and when I got it I would buy a new Peugeot 205 GTI; all my peers were going to be competing in this competition and they were the ones I wanted to beat; I wanted my friends and family to see me win; I wanted to show the British climbing public how I climbed, and I wanted to show them how good competitions could be. There had been so much awful negativity in the British climbing press about competitions that I wanted to show the positive side. The list of reasons why I wanted to win more than anyone else grew. So too did the list of reasons why I would: my boots are better than everyone else's; I have a better diet; the temperature will suit me; I won't have travelled far; I'm stronger than everyone else; I'm better than everyone else; I have the book.

I still have my diary from this time. At the bottom of every page, for each day, I have written: 'I am the best competition climber in the world. I always succeed. I always flash 8a. My footwork is precise and efficient. I move on rock fast and gracefully. I have plenty of time to work out moves, because my recovery is so good. I can de-pump anywhere. I am the strongest, fittest climber in the world.'

This wasn't arrogance or big-headedness, as I kept it completely to myself. This is what the book referred to as Directive Affirmation. Tell yourself that you are good at something, and you will believe it. These things

I wrote down weren't what I was. They were what I wanted to become. I wanted these things to be true about me. For example, I knew I might sometimes rush at things, pulling hard, going into situations without thinking them out thoroughly. This sometimes meant I made hasty decisions, sometimes the wrong ones. The statement about my footwork and grace meant that if I believed this was how I climbed, my anxiety about rushing would be reduced. Likewise, if you believe that before any move you can relax and get some strength back, then you will be more relaxed, have time to think and recover.

I had to be totally prepared for anything that might happen in a competition, and remove any possible anxiety from that. I made lists of things that might go wrong and knock my concentration, and my response to them. What if, say, my chalk bag string came undone, and I dropped my chalk? Then I would think of all the boulder problems and redpoints that I have done without dipping into my chalk bag, to see that I didn't need chalk to climb. What if one of the plastic holds came loose, and spun when I was using it? I thought of all the times on a route I snapped a hold off, and how I just fought back into control and carried on to the top. What if I arrived at the route and there was a delay, maybe the rope wasn't ready, and the crowd was watching? No problem, it would simply be an opportunity to observe the route and work it out some more. I once saw Edlinger, before a competition, tightening his shoelace for a last time before setting off. He snapped his lace. What if that happened to me? It wouldn't stop me. I'd climbed hard routes where my shoes were two sizes too big or on the wrong feet. A snapped lace wouldn't make anywhere near that difference. Nothing was going to faze me.

I have always liked peace and quiet when I am climbing, but in competitions you don't have control over that. You must walk out in front of a huge audience that is shouting and clapping. So in the comfort of my own house in Sheffield, I practised my entry into the competition hall. I would walk into the front room as if it were the hall. I would stop, and wave to the crowd. Everyone cheers, and I give a smile. Someone I know shouts something at me, and I acknowledge him. I walk across to the TV, where there is a bit of rope. I pick up the rope, and tie it into my harness. Now I look at the route, and visualise myself climbing it, twice. The first time I watch myself climb it, imagine seeing myself move my hands and feet, crossing over, locking off, snatching and clipping. The second time, I try to feel what it's like actually climbing it, how the footholds might feel, where I am getting pumped, where I am feeling sketchy. Not trying to imagine cruising it, but really feeling the pump and the difficulties. Having done this, I get a nod from an official, and go over to the route. I climb. I get to the top, turn around and give the crowd a victory wave. I rehearsed this so I knew exactly what I was going to do.

Practising all this at home, I felt I was removing any possible surprises from the situation. Everything was planned. There wasn't a single situation where there was room for the slightest negative thought to slip in anywhere.

To make sure my physical strength was a match for my growing mental strength, I trained like a monster. At that time I was working out almost exclusively at a bouldering crag called Cressbrook, a little overhanging wall of limestone in a very quiet dale in the Peak District. I would drive out to Stoney Middleton, warm up on Minus Ten Wall, and go from there to Cressbrook. There was a series of very hard problems there, and I worked on a circuit that linked them all together. This was the same principle that I had used to train for my first American trip, when I had linked endless problems on Tom's Roof at Stoney, to make mammoth stamina circuits. The Cressbrook circuits took this idea to a new level, as the individual problems that I would link together were so much harder. I climbed a problem called Jericho Road, and reversed it, did a traverse called Moffatrocity, then reversed that. I climbed down to a foothold at the bottom of Jericho Road, did a low-level traverse, then climbed back up to rejoin Moffatrocity, and climbed that again.

This link-up was the living end. Moffatrocity had a particularly nasty hold on it at the start, an evil, long and very sloping hold where it was just possible to get the fingers of two hands on. Each time I got to it, I tried to shake out to recover some strength. At the start I could barely hold on. Over the course of a few of weeks, as I got fitter, I was able to hang on a little longer until, eventually, I was able to hang there long enough to recover strength. This was to prove to myself that I actually could de-pump anywhere, as I had been writing in my diary. If I can de-pump on that hold, I told myself, then I can de-pump on anything.

I would hang there, shaking, psyching up for the next circuit, and each time I would think to myself, 'This one's for you, Didier,' and blast off again. 'This one's for you, Patrick.' 'This one's for you, Stefan.' These were the kings of competitions at the time, and my respect for their abilities really squeezed every ounce of effort out of me.

Time passed, and as the event got closer, I got stronger, fitter and more convinced I was going to win. On the morning of the event, I woke up, and drove to Stoney to warm up. I was in a fantastic mood. I went to Minus Ten, and the sunlight was filtering through the trees and lighting up the crag. It looked great. I did my regular problems, feeling strong and light. I was moving well and enjoying it. I thought to myself: 'Isn't this great? Here I am warming up at this scruffy old crag by myself. The sun is shining, and later on I'm going to a World Cup climbing competition. What could possibly be better?' Then I drove to Leeds.

Everyone was there – Stefan, Didier, Jibé, Patrick, Marc le Menestrel – all hanging around in the isolation zone. Slowly they filtered out to compete in the first round. I felt very ready for this, and knew it would not be hard, just there to knock out the bulk of competitors. I prepared myself mentally, and when I climbed, it went well, and I topped out on the route, as did a few other climbers. I was comfortably through to the final. I went back to the isolation zone.

I waited again, and eventually my name was called, and I went out for the final route. It followed a long steep section, then a traverse, which had thrown off a lot of competitors. I felt strong there thanks to all my travers-ing, and comfortably cranked through. Above this there was a bulge. From a poor hold, I had to make a long move up to a sloping hold. The way to do this was by an aggressive lunge. But for some reason I hesitated before doing the move. I just touched the next hold, but failed to hold it properly, and fell. I lowered down, cursing myself for my hesitation.

Fortunately no one got past that move. However, two other climbers had reached the same point. There was to be a super-final between myself, Simon Nadin, another British climber, and my old rival, Didier Raboutou. It was back to the isolation zone for the three of us while the organisers put the route together. Here, I collected myself, realised that I had been given another chance, and determined this time I wouldn't blow it.

I sat in the isolation zone listening to a Walkman, staring ahead, feeling relaxed. I felt great. I probably looked like I was listening to some music or something to try to stay relaxed, but I wasn't. I was listening to one of Lanny Bassham's cassettes. I was listening to the story of an Olympic pistol shooter. The shooter won the gold medal in one Olympics, but after that was involved in an accident and had his right hand amputated. So he learned to shoot with his left hand, went to the next Olympics and won another gold medal.

I was psyched. My mind was just surging with incredible thoughts of certainty and confidence. I am going to take this competition by the scruff of the neck, and there is no way I am going to be beaten. Winning this com-petition means more to me than anything else in the world. No one wants it more and no one deserves it more. I am stronger than everyone else, I am fitter than everyone else, and I am better than everyone else. It is my destiny to win this competition, and I will win it.

Didier was sat beside me. There was no one else I would rather have been competing against in the final. I turned to him and we smiled.

'I'm winning this one today,' I told him. He smiled back.

First Simon left, then Didier. I sat alone in isolation, feeling a tremen-dous pressure, the last to climb. From outside I could hear the applause, encouragement, and gasps as my rivals climbed. From all this noise, I could tell that they had both done well, but had not got to the top of the climb. If I wanted to be sure of winning, then I would have to get to the top. I felt excited that I was going to go out and try to flash the route in front of this crowd. An official came in. Time to climb.

I walked out and the crowd erupted. I gave a wave. I walked to the route, and tied on. Then I stood back and looked at the climb, exactly as I had practised. It was steep, overhanging about fifteen feet over sixty feet in height, with big bouldery-looking bulges on small holds. It looked perfect for me, just my style. Looking at the route, I visualised myself fighting up the climb, all the way to the top. I then imagined being myself fighting to the top. I felt nervous, adrenaline coursing through me. But that was exactly how I had prepared myself to feel. This was how the book had told me to expect to feel. Time to climb, an official told me. I stepped forward, and began.

Right from the start I climbed with focus, reaching holds well, moving upwards with determination. Despite this, I still nearly fell off a move low down. It didn't knock my concentration. I just kept moving upwards, eventually getting to a hold below a massive bulge. A long way above, there was a good hold. I shook out and composed myself. I saw immediately that the move would require a massive jump. After the hesitation in the last round, I had decided that this time there would be no mistakes. Eyeing up the good hold, I sucked in on the holds I had, wound myself up, focused, and let rip with everything I had.

My right hand just about got the good hold. I held it. The instant it did, my feet came off their footholds, and my left hand slipped off its handhold. I swung from one hand on the good hold, got both hands onto it, and placed my feet back on the wall. The crowd went crazy. From their reaction, it was obvious that Simon and Didier must both have fallen off before this move. I had won. But I paid this no attention. My only thought was to get to the top of the route. I locked my feet back into position, and fought upwards towards the top. I have seen this competition on television since, and I looked comfortable on the final section. I wasn't. I was pumped out of my box, my arms screaming. The last move was to clip the rope through a karabiner at the belay, and if this had been an inch further away, I wouldn't have been able to do it. Barely, barely, I clipped the rope into the belay.

It was wild. My first thought was only that I had flashed the route. When I heard the crowd go mad, I allowed myself to know that I had won. From there it was just a bit of a blur. I lowered off, there was lots of applause, and I was interviewed. Afterwards I was ecstatic. I had won. I had put all that work in, and it had paid off. I had beaten a field of all the best climbers, and had won a fantastic competition in front of a home crowd. I had succeeded at last, and everything was worth it. The book had worked.

Leeds was one of the highlights of my climbing career. The competition was broadcast on TV, and the magazines were full of my victory. I felt I had finally mastered competitions. I had a formula, and it worked. It marked the beginning of a successful competition career for me.

After Leeds, and throughout 1989, I went on to win at Cologne and Madonna in Italy, and came second at Lyon, La Riba, and Bardonecchia. A World Cup circuit was held, where a champion would be decided over a series of events spread around the world. But to do well in the World Cup meant travelling to lots of out-of-the-way events in uninteresting places for small prize money. It seemed like a waste of time.

I became involved in a new organisation called ASCI, the Association of Sports Climbers International, that tried to make sure the climbers had some say in competitions. It selected the ten most important events of a particular year, ones that the whole field entered, ones with the biggest prize money, and awarded points according to how climbers did in these. It awarded points for your best five results of the last ten comps. This then produces an ASCI ranking, and if a masters' event came along, often invitation-only big-prize events, then the organisers had to select our top climbers. At the end of 1989, I was at the top of the rankings.

In 1990 I carried on competing. A regularly held event was coming up in Bercy in Paris, with a prize of £5000. To get fit I had to do a lot of sport climbing, and France was still the place for that. I travelled to Buoux, lived in a caravan, and worked at it. The weather wasn't very good, and it was a real struggle to climb every day, but I kept at it despite the rain. In the campsite, I listened to the French Fun Radio station. It carried an advertisement for the Bercy competition. Every time it played, the names of my main rivals blared out of the radio: the names of : 'Jacky Godoffe... Marc le Menestrel... Jibé Tribout... Stefan Glowacz... ' Huh? No mention of me? I'm the one who's stuck down here in this caravan, training hard, putting in the time. Right, I thought. I know who's going to win this competition. It came down to Jibé and me in the final. He put up a hell of a fight. In the end I beat him, but only by the skin of my teeth.

From Bercy I headed to Briançon. Here, I was last out of isolation. All the other climbers had gone and no one had yet managed to get past a desperate move into a groove at half-height, and it looked like there was going to be a draw. I managed to get past the hard move, and climbed the route all the way to the top to win the competition.

Later, as we were leaving, Jibé came up to me in the corridor. He looked disgusted with himself. Like everyone else, he had fallen off the move into the groove. He stopped right in front of me, looked me in the eye, and said:

'Yes, Jerry, it is true. For the moment, you are the best.'

Then he walked off. I'll never forget it. For Jibé, of all people, to come and say that felt like getting a knighthood. I could see that he was really annoyed at himself for not winning, but he still made himself come up to me and say that. I realised that people must be saying I'm the best. I was absolutely elated.

The latest big competition was in Saint Jean de Maurienne, between Grenoble and Chamonix. It was to have five disciplines – on-sight rock, on-sight artificial, redpoint, bouldering and speed climbing spread over five days. It also offered big prizes: £500 prize for each event, and £3,000 for the overall winner. With all those disciplines, whoever won at Maurienne had to be the best overall. I trained like a dog, and was hungry to win.

Maurienne was tough. I came joint first in the on-sight rock competition, but performed less well in the speed-climbing event. I was more hopeful about my chances in bouldering, one of my strong points. However a misunderstanding about the rules, where I was deducted points for only hanging the finishing jug with one hand and not both, meant I lost out and only came third. I was lagging in the overall competition. There were only two events left – on-sight indoor and redpoint indoor – and I would have to win them both to win overall. On the last two days, I competed at midnight, at the end of a five-day competition, both nights. I managed to win the redpoint competition. It was all down to the on-sight. It was me against a young French climber called François Legrand. We were both to compete at the same time, on two identical routes separated by a curtain, a real duel.

We sat in isolation and chatted. I really liked François; he was a great competitor. He told me that it was his ambition to beat me in competitions. François had been competing for a while, but hadn't really cracked them. I could see he was one of the best around, but at the time he still seemed young, and perhaps hadn't quite got his self-belief yet. Later, the following year he got his head around competing, and started winning, and then just won and won and won, but at the time of Maurienne, it frustrated him.

'And you know, Jerry, I always climb very well in qualifiers, but in the final, always do badly.'

I was glad to hear that, and I knew from the book and from my own experiences that as soon as he thought he would climb well in the finals, he would be dangerous. However, that night, at midnight, we went out and I managed to get a little higher up the route than François, and I won the event and the entire competition.

It had felt like a war. It had been an incredibly tough competition, both physically and mentally, and I was wiped out. But from there it was straight onto a train to Barcelona for another event. I got there, and straight away I felt as if I didn't care. Despite that, I won the first day, but on the night before the final, I was in a nightclub at two in the morning. Next day, I came second in the redpoint round. I no longer cared.

How do you keep the hunger? How do you keep the motivation to win again and again, to put yourself through all that? If you're starting out, it is easy. You want to be the best; you want to win. But then what? You want to win again; you want to remain the best. But that's not such a great goal. Even Tiger Woods has a goal. He wants to beat Jack Nicklaus, to become the greatest golfer of all time. Nicklaus won eighteen major golf titles, and Tiger Woods wants to beat that. But even he, once he has done that, what then? I was definitely losing the hunger. And in competitions, it's always the guy that wants it most that gets it.

The book I had read had produced incredible results. I told no one about it, or about how I had achieved my success. It all took place behind closed doors. My training, too, was mostly done in secret, as I never wanted anyone to know what I was up to, or how good I was. I was becoming an introvert, distancing myself from my friends, and it didn't suit me. Success came at a price.

My last competition was at Arco in Italy. I got there, but for me the thrill had gone out of comps. The first day was an on-sight round. I'll just go up and fall, I thought. Only half trying, I found myself twenty feet from the top, and, deciding that as I had come this far I may as well carry on, I topped out. François was the only other competitor to do so. On the next round, the redpoint, I walked out and knew I didn't want to be there. I fell off midway, and still came fifth. As I left the hall, I thought to myself:

'That's it. No more competitions for me.'

And that was that. I never did another competition. But I had got the better of them. I sometimes think that I would gladly swap some of those victories for a first ascent, but I also know that I would have missed out on a really important part of my career. Even if people soon forgot who won, for me, it was really important. At that time, in the late 1980s, it was where the game was. Most of the top climbers did competitions, and those that didn't were those that couldn't. I had proven to everyone that I could. At the end of the 1980s, the French climbing magazine, Vertical, sought votes from all the best climbers to see who they thought who was the most influential climber of the decade. I was considered the most influential male, with Lynn Hill being the top female. No doubt this was down to the hard redpoints and on-sights I had done, the boulder problems I had added, the fact that I travelled the globe in search of the hardest routes, but I believe that if it hadn't been for my competition victories, then I wouldn't have had that acknowledgement. It was great to get that, especially in a French magazine.

'I am the best competition climber in the world. I always succeed.

I always flash 8a. My footwork is precise and efficient. I move on rock fast and gracefully. I have plenty of time to work out moves, because my recovery is so good. I can de-pump anywhere. I am the strongest, fittest climber in the world.'

That message reinforced itself at the bottom of each day in my diary for nearly two years. Then one day, on 16 September, 1990, it just stopped. I no longer had the energy to keep it all up. I wanted to get myself back again. I wanted to see my friends. I wanted to climb for myself. I wanted to do first ascents. Most of all I wanted to have fun.

THIRTEEN

Travels with a Monkey

My decision to stop competing was a great relief. I was suddenly released from the endless schedule of intense training, mental stress, isolation, climbing indoors, rivals, losing and winning. It had taken over my life a bit too much for a bit too long and I revelled in my new-found sense of freedom. What I most wanted to do was have a really fun trip with some great friends.

Not long after I was in Llanberis with Johnny Dawes, and we found ourselves in Pete's Eats café talking with one of the locals, Paul Pritchard. Paul was a very bold and talented climber, and also a real adventurer, often going on expeditions to out-of-the-way places. He had some photos with him and was telling Johnny and me about a trip he had recently been on to India. He had visited an area called Hampi, east of Goa, and showed us some of his pictures. Hampi was the old capital of the Vijayanagara kingdom in the fifteenth century, a kingdom that covered most of the bottom half of India. After the kings left it became a place of pilgrimage for Hindus. Paul's photos showed somewhere that looked a little bit like Joshua Tree, only with lots of beautiful old temples. Like Joshua Tree, the landscape was strewn with huge golden granite boulders.

'They're awesome,' Paul said. 'Perfect boulders everywhere and no one has ever climbed on them.'

He told us he had done a few of the problems there and the rock was as good as it looked. It did look amazing. I had always wanted to go to India, so I suggested to Johnny that we went. He agreed. A couple of days later I was talking to Kurt Albert on the phone and told him about our plans. Kurt, always up for a fun-sounding trip, said he would come too.

We began to make plans. It looked perfect and it was quite easy to get to for somewhere that seemed so exotic. Hampi was a long but straightforward bus ride from Goa, the popular Indian holiday resort, and there were frequent flights there from England. It looked uncomplicated.

'No, we can't do that,' Johnny said. 'We can't just fly to a holiday resort then get a bus. What's the point? This is India and we must experience it fully.'

Johnny Dawes is a unique character and has his own way of doing things. We've been friends for a long time, so I can sometimes forget how unusual he is, but my wife often reminds me. The first time she met Johnny was in the Peak District. Sharon and I were driving towards Sheffield and saw a squat figure with black hair and shabby woollen clothes, hitching. It was Johnny. We gave him a lift. He hopped in the back seat, full of energy. He immediately stuck his head between the front seats, almost in front of us and started chattering at high speed. He told us he had been zooming around the Peak in his Peugeot 205. He had been driving much too fast, and, going round a bend, had hit and killed a sheep. Distraught at his actions, he parked the car near Millstone Edge and took off across the moors, casting away his clothes as he went. Naked, he ran through the heather waving his hands in the air in order to appease nature for what he had done. He was feeling better now and, having gathered up his clothes, was making his way back to collect his car.

'Oh, who are you?'

'This is Sharon, Johnny.'

'Oh hello Sharon, very pleased to meet you. I'm Johnny.'

'Hello Johnny.'

'There's a party on at the Riverside Bar in Sheffield tonight,' he said excitedly. 'Are you coming? Perhaps I'll see you there, Sharon.'

'I think so, Johnny.'

Later that night, we went to the party. As we walked in, we saw Johnny. He was standing just inside the entrance door, from where a flight of about eight steps ran down to the main bar. Johnny wasn't looking at us. Instead, we could see he was eyeing up a girl from behind. She was standing at the top of the steps. Suddenly Johnny give the girl a hard shove from behind, propelling her body over the steps. I still find this hard to believe, but as she was in the air, Johnny jumped down the flight of steps, got to the bottom, turned around and caught her. He put her feet back on the ground, beaming with pride at his trick.

'You STUPID little… ' she began, calling Johnny every name under the sun, while flailing him with her arms. 'You could have killed me.'

Johnny, all the time, smiling.

'We can't fly to Goa,' Johnny said. 'We need to suffer a bit more to get the authentic experience. We will fly to Mumbai and travel overland by train. It will be the most amazing thing you have ever done, Jerry. I swear.'

The train clunked along for days at never more than 45mph. Mumbai, for-merly known as Bombay, was more than three hundred miles north of Goa, but for some reason we had agreed to Johnny's plan. Three hundred miles in India is like three thousand in North America. The flat land moved by slowly. I was hot and hungry – too familiar with horror stories about food poisoning to eat anything. We chatted and looked out the window. After a while I started to doze. The train would occasionally gather speed, but spent ages slowing down, especially coming into a station. Approaching one halt, I was fast asleep, my head leant against the window. Seeing this, Johnny and Kurt jumped off the slow-moving train, ran around to the window and, jogging alongside, started punching the window, waking me up.

'Jerry, Jerry, get up, the train's leaving, quick!'

I started to come around and saw the two of them running alongside the train.

'We forgot about you Jerry, hurry!'

'They've left me,' I thought, still dozy. 'I'm all alone in the middle of India and they've left me.' Panicking, I started gathering my stuff, while they slapped the window and roared at me – 'Quick! Quick!'

The train slowed to a stop, and through the window, I watched them both erupt in laughter. We had tea at the station, then got back on for the endless train ride.

'Why didn't we fly, Johnny?' I asked, but looking back now, I'll never forget that journey.

'Let's go up on the roof, everyone,' Johnny said on the second day. 'That's what you do in India.'

Johnny said that travelling on the roof of a train was a big Indian tradi-tion, as you see more and it's cooler. I wasn't sure, but Kurt and I followed him to the door between the carriages and got onto a metal platform on the outside of the train. Johnny scrambled up a ladder and crawled onto the roof. I got to the top of the ladder and suddenly the train didn't seem to be going slowly any more. I nipped back to the carriage to get my harness and camera out of my bags and clipped onto the top of the ladder. By now Johnny had moved along the roof of the carriage and was a few feet away, grinning.

'Stand up, Johnny,' I said, waving my camera.

Slowly, timidly, Johnny rose to his feet. The rushing air from the train's movement felt like a very strong wind, and the carriages were rolling and rocking from the clickety rails. He was now on his feet and moving a little more confidently. He came back to Kurt and me.

'Come on you two,' he called.

'No way, Johnny, it's too dangerous.'

'No it's not,' he said. 'And I'll prove it. I'm going to run all the way down the train and then I'm going to run all the way back.'

With that, he bolted off towards the engine. At the gaps between carriages, he would leap over the void, time and time again, until he was at the front of the train. All the windows had Indians looking out to see what the noise on the roof was. At the front, Johnny had now turned around and was running and leaping towards us, his manic laughter filling the air.

We finally arrived in Hospet, the closest station to Hampi, on New Year's Eve and booked into a hotel. That night, during the celebrations, we felt like royalty, with Indians patting us on the back, shaking our hands and asking which country we came from. The following day, we got two motorised rickshaws to Hampi, Kurt and me in one, Johnny in the other. The whole journey we could hear Johnny trying to get his driver to race us, or encouraging him to get the rickshaw up on two wheels.

'Well if you don't want to, let me try,' I heard him say.

Hampi was stunning, a golden, rocky landscape of low, rolling hills, with a big river meandering through it. There were lots of paddy fields, filled with bright green shoots and banana trees and elephant grass grew everywhere. There seemed to be endless temples, many of them carved out of the solid granite boulders and very decorative. Just like in Paul's pictures, there were boulders of all sizes scattered everywhere. There were square white houses, alone, or in small groups. Relaxed-looking Indians milled around, working in the fields or laughing by the river. It was scorching hot.

We took a small room in a backpackers' hostel and collapsed in the shade. Later, feeling rested, we went to a restaurant for some rice and lentils. I hungrily ate a couple of platefuls. We were sitting by a wall and I heard a rustling on the other side. I looked over to see a man squatting beside a bowl, washing cooking pots. The bowl was filled with the dirtiest looking water, dark brown and thick. The man looked up at us and smiled a toothless grin.

'Oh God,' I thought. 'I'm definitely going to get sick here.'

We would wake at dawn each day to the sounds of people performing morning pujas at the large temple in the centre of the village. The cool of early morning was the best time to climb, so we immediately headed off in search of unclimbed rock. This was great fun, exploring the boulders, getting excited about possibilities, doing problems. The rock, unlike the glacially polished granite of Yosemite, was wind-sculpted, making everything very rounded. Some boulders had no holds on them at all. We would try problems on one boulder then move on to the next. There were thousands of them. It was amazing to think that virtually no one had ever climbed them before. It was like my first trip to Hueco Tanks.

Because of the religious significance of Hampi, there were a lot of holy men, or sadhus, hanging around. They were tall, super-skinny, with extremely long, matted hair and dressed in loincloths. They prayed a lot and meditated, I think, but from what I could see, they also smoked an enormous quantity of marijuana. All day long.

On the second morning, we were all trying an arête on a nice big boulder and a sadhu stopped to watch us. He must never have seen anything like it before and stood, silently, smiling, for about an hour, then attracted our attention. We said hello and he ushered us into a temple, where he was more than generous with his hospitality.

We lay there, laughing a lot and after a bit he got a game out. It had a board and some coloured balls. He arranged the balls on the board, then moved some, but I didn't know what to do. Still, I moved some balls and he seemed happy. He moved some more. Johnny seemed to know what he was doing and moved some around, but the sadhu replaced them again and waved his finger to say no. More balls were moved and Johnny, who now seemed to have mastered it, took over. A long time seemed to pass and then suddenly the sadhu indicated the game was over. We all stood up and slapped each other in congratulation. Afterwards I asked Johnny how the game worked, but he told me at no point did he understand what was happening. I felt peckish, so we wandered back for some food.

I was always paranoid about getting sick. On the first few days I took it easy, only eating little bits of well-cooked food, avoiding any uncooked vegetables, anything with ice, to try to get my system used to the diet. Johnny had been to India a few years before. He had become very ill, and his horror stories of stomach cramps were what made me most afraid of getting sick. However this time, he seemed to be tucking in to everything with gusto.

'I can't believe I'm not getting ill,' he said. 'I can eat anything I want. I must have developed a powerful immunity last time I was here.'

He seemed to be happy eating anything – fruit, salads, milkshakes, ice water. On the third day, he exploded from both ends, and spent days curled up in bed. I watched him with pity laid out, groaning, dribbling, weakened, too weak even to be angry.

That was a real shame, because the food was amazing. It was mostly curries, but nothing like the curries I was used to in England. There would be lots of little pots of chutney and sauces and pickles. The flavours were unbelievable. We had garlic chicken, cooked with about ten bulbs of garlic, yet the flavour was not overwhelming, just delicious. I only became ill once, so for a few days ate only western food again, egg and chips mainly, until I recovered. Kurt didn't get ill the whole time and became quite adventurous with his diet, his efficient German immune system able to cope with anything. Funnily enough, six months later, Kurt came to visit Johnny and me in Sheffield. We took him out to our local Indian restaurant on Abbeydale Road. It annihilated him and for two days he was pole-axed with sickness.

While Kurt might have been strong enough for whatever diseases India could throw at him, the big German was no match for a proper Sheffield curry.

More than anything, we wanted to see the monkeys. When Paul Pritchard first told us about Hampi, the thing that really got us hooked were his stories about the monkeys. He described watching them climbing on the rocks, doing some of the hardest moves he had ever seen.

'The monkeys will blow your mind,' Paul told us. 'I watched one of them do a third-generation dyno to get a banana skin.' A third-generation dyno was the sort of thing Johnny would talk about. I wasn't sure what it was, but it sounded pretty far out. I never did find out what one was.

Amongst the gods celebrated at the temples in Hampi, Hanuman, the monkey god, is one of the most important. Hampi is believed to be his birthplace. Hanuman was able to fly and led an army of fighting monkeys. There are lots of carvings on the temple walls of this half-human, half-monkey figure.

It wasn't until the fourth day that we finally saw the monkeys. We were trying a traverse when we saw a parade of little figures come down a ridge of rocks right beside us. They stopped, watched us for a while, before carrying on down to a temple. It was good to see them.

Two days later we were bouldering near the river and spotted the monkeys again. We were trying a traverse on good holds across a totally blank wall. We wondered if the monkeys would be able to do it. Kurt had a banana in his bag and balanced it on a good hold in the middle of the traverse. We sat back to see what would happen.

One monkey approached, skipped up to the bottom of the wall and looked at the moves to get to the banana. It looked like it was about to try, but then it stopped and looked in our direction. We were staring at it and I could almost see it become shy. It ran off, but soon reappeared at the top of the boulder. The boulder was about fifteen feet high, with the traverse, and the banana, at chest-height. The monkey leaned over and looked down at the banana. There was about ten feet of vertical, featureless granite between them. Down it went, head-first, like the face was the easiest slab in the world. It got to the hold, sat down, peeled the banana, and ate it coolly. Finished, it threw the skin to the ground and scurried back up the wall.

We ran over. There was barely a hold on the whole face.

Another day we set up a top-rope above a larger wall and spent a while doing a tough 7b+ crack. Some monkeys came along. We hatched a plan to tie a bunch of bananas onto the top-rope and use it to lure a monkey up the problem. One soon came along, showing some interest, and we inched the bunch upwards. The monkey started jamming up the crack in pursuit of the bunch, then moved out onto the 'blank' face, abandoning the crack altogether. This was incredible. We were taking up the bunch fairly quickly, keeping them out of its reach. Then, getting to a hold, the monkey crouched down, sprung upwards, leaping what must have been twice its body-length, and caught the bananas.

We discovered a boulder on top of a hill, where the monkeys all slept and went one evening for a look. It was about thirty feet high, had a vertical face, a slabby face and an overhanging face. The monkeys climbed all over this boulder, so we observed them and their various approaches. It was obvious that there were different levels of difficulty involved in getting up the different faces and the monkeys were trying all the different problems. On the vertical side there was a hold about ten feet up, above a bad landing. On a boulder across from this, about six feet away, a few of the bigger monkeys were gathered. One by one they would come to the edge of the boulder and look across at the distant hold. Nervously they would look at the drop, before making an enormous spring across the void to catch the hold and top out. Meanwhile, the baby monkeys were trying a smaller wall on the opposite side. They would climb up a steep section on invisible holds. At a certain point, they stopped, looked up, looked down, looked up and looked down. Commitment time. Some would press on boldly to the top, while others would bottle out, scampering around the base, clearly disappointed in themselves. Others would try but fall off hard moves and bounce and twist acrobatically downwards, negotiating dangerous boulders, before coming to a safe stop on the flat rock below. They would then scurry back around to the top of the block the easy way, to look down at their problems.

Most days we went out climbing we would attract big crowds of onlookers. They all had a lot of free time, or at least the men did, as the women seemed to do all the work, so they loved to have something interesting to look at. One day we were trying an arête near the river. I did it, and then so did Kurt. Johnny was just getting back into climbing again after his illness and was still weak. He was struggling on the problem and getting short-tempered at his lack of success. Two Indian men were watching him. After a while, one of them came up and, pointing to a piece of rock, suggested Johnny put his foot there. Johnny said he wouldn't. The man suggested it again.

'Who do they think they are, telling me where to put my foot?' he snapped. The men smiled politely. They were only trying to be helpful, but Johnny's competitive side was obviously feeling touchy because of our success.

'It's because I'm short, isn't it? They didn't try to tell you where to put your foot did they Jerry?'

Johnny continued to try the problem, being careful not to put his foot where the bystander had suggested. Eventually he got up it.

We wanted to climb on the other side of the river one day and found the man who ran the ferry, a wicker basket covered in pitch, who took us across. On the other bank we found a beautiful boulder and did a couple of problems, and, as usual, a crowd gathered. Kurt tried a steep, strenuous wall on biggish holds but got pumped and fell off. As he stood on the ground, one of the Indians walked over. He was small and thin, dressed in light clothes. He stood beside the German's vast bulk, looked at Kurt's bulging blood-filled biceps, reached up and gave them a squeeze.

'Very big guts,' he said.

The man was joined by a friend and they both expressed an interest in trying the problem. The first man was fairly fit looking. We gave him a push at the start so he could grab better holds above and he was soon standing on top. His friend tried, but being less agile, struggled. Soon, Kurt, Johnny and I were all shoving him from below but it wasn't until the first man dropped him his scarf that he was able to get on top. Cheers and clapping. Only then did they realise they couldn't get back down. A small girl was ordered off and half an hour later she returned with a ladder.

In this way we climbed and relaxed at Hampi for two weeks. When I came to pay the bill for my accommodation, I was stunned to find that it came to about £35, but was even more stunned to learn the bill was for all three of us. We'd been living like kings. Once again, we set off on the overland train to Mumbai. I moaned to Johnny about the long journey. But I enjoyed it again, in its own way.

It was great to be able to do the first ascents of great problems and to have so much virgin rock to go at. It was the perfect antidote to the stress and rigours of competition. Today Hampi is a popular destination for climbers. The monkeys are still there, probably climbing harder than ever.

Travelling was a way of life for me. I was always on the move or staying in foreign countries with friends. For about two decades, I only ever spent about three months each year in England. The rest of the time I would either be in Germany, France or America, or travelling to some further-flung destination. This would be on a pure climbing trip, or more often, combining climbing with business or a lecture tour. As I had always climbed a lot in other countries and made great efforts to publicise myself in their magazines, I was well known internationally. This often led to invites from various climbing federations throughout the world to come and give talks and show my pictures.

One of my favourite trips was to Japan. Just before I went to America in 1984, the Japanese federation paid for Chris Gore and me to visit and do some climbing. It was a horrendous journey, two back-to-back eight-hour flights via Alaska, before we finally arrived in Tokyo, frazzled. We couldn't find our contacts, so it took us about three hours to reach the house where we were staying. We walked in to find a crowd of Japanese climbers there. They all cheered.

'We have a party in your honour,' they shouted.

We were knackered and wanted only to sleep, but had to spend hours chatting. In the morning we were up at first light and set off to the cliffs, six hours through constant traffic jams. I felt terrible from jetlag and lack of sleep. When we arrived, it was raining heavily and the cliffs were soaked. Thank God, I thought. Saved.

'No,' they cried. 'There will be one dry climb.'

We stumbled through wet foliage to the base of an overhung, dry crack. Luckily it was only HVS, but we had to do it. As I climbed, I looked down to see about fifty men stood around at the base of the climb, each one holding an umbrella, watching me. It was surreal.

The Japanese are beautiful people, and their culture and hospitality are incredible. We stayed in a stunning old hotel in the mountains. It had beds on the floor and paper-curtain walls. We were given kimonos and ate traditional breakfasts of raw fish and fermented soya beans. On the second day they asked me if I wished to have a bath. I said no, I had already taken a shower. They asked again and I said no. They explained that taking a bath was nothing to do with having a wash, but was an important social event among the men.

Chris and I were led into a beautiful bathroom. It had decorative taps and benches around the edge, where we were told to wash ourselves. In the middle was a huge bath, fifteen-foot square, filled with crystal-clear water. All the men came in, washed themselves under the taps and got in the bath. I put my toe in. The water was excruciatingly hot. Slowly I eased myself in, suffering the heat, until I was submerged. We floated about chatting and laughing for over an hour. It was bliss.

They told us that Ron Fawcett had been a guest a year or two before. It happened that he ended up in the bath first, and, not having had the significance of the ritual explained to him yet, took it as an ordinary bath. He got out a bar of soap and had a scrub. When the rest of the Japanese came in they found the surface of the water covered in a film of suds. It came as quite a surprise to them.

We travelled to a few cities where the locals showed us round. In the daytime, we would be taken to their local crags to try their climbs. Japan's hardest route was Super Imjin, which had taken their top climber some time to do. I was super-fit, in training to do The Phoenix, and managed to flash it. I got the front cover of the Japanese climbing magazine and left with some great memories.

It all sounds like fun, and it was, but like anything you are doing professionally, there was always an element of work about it. You are always alert, making sure you are nice to your hosts. And they always wanted to be having a party.

Closer to home, I went on a lecture tour of Poland. I don't know why, but I often seemed to do slideshows just as I was coming back from a long flight. Poland was no different and I had to go there immediately after a trip to America. Still exhausted and jet-lagged, I arrived in Warsaw and was whisked off to a bar. I hadn't had anything to eat in the airport and was starving, but I was promised there would be good food where we were going. When I arrived, there was a rowdy throng waiting. Everyone cheered me, but all I could see was vodka.

'Food,' I kept saying. 'Food.'

'Yes,' a man said, and pressed a huge glass of vodka into my hand. 'But first, we drink.'

Thinking that the quicker I got this over with the better, I downed the glass in one. The crowd cheered. A deathly shudder went down my body as the spirit found its mark. Shaking my head to try to clear the pain, I tried to push past the man to see where there might be some food. He put his hand out, stopping me.

'We have a saying here in Poland. We say that you must have a drink for both legs.'

He pressed another, even larger glass of vodka into my hand and once again, the crowd cheered. I never got any food. For the rest of the week, every night was vodka night, as I travelled from town to town doing slideshows.

Sponsors like things such as competition victories or hard first ascents, as it gets coverage, and it's a chance for them to have their products seen. They also like it if the climbers they sponsor go on interesting trips to exotic locations, as this is just as good for getting exposure. For me, in the years after I gave up competitions, going on such exploratory trips was a good way of satisfying sponsors' wishes, and it was a lot easier than beating François Legrand.

One of my main sponsors was a German outdoor gear manufacturer called VauDe. They also sponsored people beyond the climbing world, including a general adventurer and explorer called Bruno Baumann.

Baumann had spent some time applying for permission to explore an area in the north of the African state of Chad called Tibesti, a little-known Saharan wilderness. Tibesti had not been explored much, and Chad itself had become largely unknown. Libya's Colonel Gaddafi had launched attacks on the north of Chad in the 1970s, greedy for the plutonium that was abundant there. The Chadean army had routed Gaddafi's troops, but since then it had closed its borders to the outside world. Few people had entered or left Chad for twenty years. Baumann had finally got permission and was planning a trip. This was to be covered in magazines, and perhaps on television. VauDe thought that having me along to do a bit of climbing could give the trip another angle. It sounded interesting.

A team was gathered, included Heinz Zak, a top German climbing photographer, who I knew well, two other photographers, a documentary filmmaker and a couple of adventurer friends of Baumann's. Mercedes also sponsored the expedition, supplying two four-wheel-drive jeeps. The Germans travelled overland to Chad in these and were waiting for me in the country's capital, N'Djamena, when I flew in on the one flight that entered Chad each week. I landed and went to the hotel where I met Baumann and his team.

We were briefed on the expedition and told of the possible dangers ahead. It was still pretty wild and most of the country was lawless. We were given an armed guard, warned about minefields and unexploded bombs and sent on our way. Less than five miles from the capital the roads diminished into rough tracks, then into desert. Twenty miles from the capital, it felt very remote. It was going to be a long journey.

We drove out of a sandstorm on the second day and came across a village. This was really just a collection of five or six huts, woven together into a small unit. Two women stood outside a doorway and looked at us, their eyes red-raw from constant exposure to the desert sand. Some hens scurried about. All I could see was the Sahara desert. Not the sand dunes of legend, which were less common, just a bare, grey gravel-covered wasteland. As far as I could see, there was nothing. Not a tree, nor a lake, nor a blade of grass. How did these people survive, I wondered. What do they have? We left them some spare sunglasses we had brought along. They seemed grateful.

We drove on. And on. Days went by. All there was to see was just a flat expanse of grey gravel. There were no hills – no features whatsoever – just more flat gravel. It was like being on the ocean. You could fall asleep with your foot on the accelerator and snooze for several hours and not be in any danger of hitting anything. Eventually, from miles away, we saw a rock protruding from the desert. Hours later we reached it. It was a block of red sandstone. We all got out, excited about seeing something. Petroglyphs carved around the base showed giraffes and elephants. It was amazing to think that, at some time in human history, this wasteland actually supported life. The change in the environment was mind-blowing. We drove on.

We camped in the desert. Every morning we would get up at five, take the tents down, get on the road and drive all day. I snoozed, or just looked out the window.

I found it very relaxing, but some of the Germans were getting on each other's nerves. At least four of them considered themselves to be the leader of the expedition. In my jeep, there were two who had different opinions on the air conditioning. One always wanted it off – 'Ach, this air makes my throat so dry. Turn it off' – but the other wanted it back on again – 'The heat in here is unbearable. Turn it on.' The control switch was constantly in use. Another was obsessive about food. Every night for dinner we ate pasta, onions and tomato puree. The German had his own precise idea of how onions should be chopped, and if I ever deviated from his wishes, he would instantly correct me.

Slowly we moved north towards the Tibesti region, eventually arriving at Bardaï, the largest town in the region. I was glad to arrive because there was something there I really wanted to see. In 1988 the French artist Jean Verame lugged three tons of red, white and blue paint into a remote rocky valley in northern Chad, and spent months painting a collection of boulders. Painting boulders was his thing, and he was famous for it. His painted valley was very close to Bardaï, so Heinz and I went for a look. It was an amazing sight. Some of these coloured boulders are thirty feet high and forty feet across. After so long sat in the back of the jeep, I was desperate to get some climbing in. There were bolts on the top of pillars from the painting work, so, using these, we set up a belay and I top-roped an overhanging blue wall. It was great climbing, about 7c, and I decided to lead it. I wasn't totally sure of the rock quality, but the thick blue paint made it look quite solid. I did it once more, pulled the rope down, tied on and set off. I reached up for the first holds. They crumbled under my weight, depositing both the crumbs and me back on the desert floor. Maybe I wouldn't lead it after all.

One of the objectives of the trip was to visit a village of Yebbi-Bou, home of the Tubu tribe, fearsome warriors living in the north of the country. The Tubu are a minority Muslim tribe, aggressively distrustful of non-Muslims in particular and any stranger in general. These villagers had no reason to visit the next village and didn't particularly want anyone else to visit them. It was said that the first white man to visit them in the 1960s was immediately thrown into a cage and kept there for over three years. The Tubu weren't noted for their hospitality.

After two weeks of travelling, we approached their village. There was a military camp on the outskirts, so we set up our tents there. It was reassuring to be near the soldiers, after hearing stories of the Tubu. We were warned that rule of law didn't stretch this far north. The military were tolerated, but when it came to justice, each village had its headman, and what he said was law. The security we felt from the soldiers was slightly offset by the fact that they never ever put their weapons down, usually keeping their finger on the trigger. They would subconsciously swing their weapons in your direction if they were talking or listening to you. I made sure not to say too much. We spent the night at the camp then in the morning drove into Yebbi-Bou.

The village was gobsmacking. There were lots of wicker huts, mostly woven together in groups. And that was it. There was nothing else. There were no shops or cafés, of course. There were only dwellings. There was nothing made of plastic. There was no rubbish blowing up the street. Only the dwellings. I'd never seen anything like it. Beyond the village was a shallow valley with a small stream. A few crops were growing on the banks and there were a couple of black cows. Women were working at the crops, doing something with the animals or carrying water up to the village. Women seemed to do all the work in the village, while the men stood at the top of the village and looked at us.

They really did look like warriors. Their skin was very black, their faces deeply gouged with decorative scars. They looked at us, but all I could see in their eyes was their hatred for me. They were fearsome. Our driver warned us not to take their picture. I asked him why not. He turned to me again:

'Don't take their picture,' he repeated, shaking his head.

With that, one of the Germans went off and organised a spot of filming. He wanted to film the Tubu warriors cooking and doing other domestic chores. He found a willing tribesman who would allow the German to film his family inside his home for a price. It was arranged. Heinz and I went off photographing the landscape and old huts and things, while the others went off to film.

They all went into the hut, got the cameras set up and filmed as a veiled woman milled some corn. It was all going okay until our driver, for some reason, flicked away the woman's veil, revealing her face. She screamed. The man of the house, a skinny teenager, stood up and started protesting. 'Out! Out!' he shouted.

The German film crew resisted, pointing out that they had paid for a certain amount of time to film and they must get a refund. The teenager got angrier and the driver was now looking fairly scared.

'We must go now,' he insisted.

'But ze refund!' complained the Germans.

'Out. Now.'

The driver ushered everyone onto the trucks and called to us to come too. Heinz and I came along. As I neared the trucks, I could see there was a commotion, and approaching, saw the tribesman. He was wearing a long trench coat, and pulled it aside to reveal a Kalashnikov rifle. He pulled it up, but a group of women surrounded him and tried to calm him down. We got into the truck and sped off toward our camp. There was a crack, and a bullet went through the door of the jeep and into the engine. It all suddenly started to seem very threatening. I was sitting opposite one of the Germans. I had never seen anyone shake the way he was shaking, his face a clammy grey colour.

Baumann suggested we headed south again. There were no complaints.

After more days of driving, we began to see evidence of the war with Libya – destroyed tanks and other military vehicles. We stopped at a village that had been taken over by the Libyans during their occupation to make an airstrip. They had put down a metal runway and laid a minefield to protect it. This had never been cleared, simply roped off to keep people out. The roped-off area around the village must have been three miles in circumference and about a hundred metres deep. It was enormous. A fifty-metre-wide strip had been cleared through it to give access to the village. That was the only way in or out. Inside the roped-off area I could see ruined tanks and unexploded bombs. I saw a human ribcage. I saw a pick-up truck with a helmeted skeleton sat at the driver's seat.

We left the village and drove on. A few miles on, the grey desert landscape was strewn with barbed wire and white shards of what looked like seashells. We saw some ruined tanks and got out to look them over. One of the Germans pulled out a rib, still hung with sinews, mummified in the dry wind. Heinz saw a hand sticking from the sand, its skin still intact. Looking at my feet I realised that the white shards I had dismissed as seashells were actually thousands of pieces of human bone. I saw eye sockets, fingers. Small pieces of human beings scattered like litter. I was looking at it, but could hardly take it all in.

An adjacent field was scattered with dead soldiers from the Libyan army. Again the skin had hardened over the corpses. Men were curled in foetal positions, limbs lying feet apart. There were holes in their heads and grim looks of horror on their faces. It was a snapshot of an apocalyptic event. I stopped and tried to imagine what it must have been like at the moment it was all happening. I could barely imagine the horror. I really don't want to go to war. Stunned, we eventually got back into the vehicles, and sat mostly in silence for the rest of the journey back to N'Djamena. Forty-eight hours later I flew home.

I've seen some amazing things in my life, but I will never forget what I saw that day in Chad.

FOURTEEN

The Money Game

In my younger days, when I was totally focused on climbing, I told my dad that the last thing I wanted was money. He often reminds me of that. I was living on £1 a day, eating the cheapest food, sleeping in caves and shelters. I felt that having money would complicate things, get in the way and disturb my focus. Money wouldn't have added anything to my life. All my friends were at Stoney, living the same life as I did. If I'd had £20 a day to live on, there would have been nothing to do with it.

Even though I had very little, it was a great time, perfect for that stage of my life. But as you get older, things change, you get more responsibilities and, sooner or later, most people will need to earn some money.

I've heard it said that I never had a proper job and that I never did a real day's work in my life, but that isn't true. When I was sixteen, after we had finished our exams, there were still a few weeks of term left. We had to stay in school, but there was no schoolwork to do. I had a friend, James, whose dad owned a fish and chip shop in Llandudno. I was desperate to buy my own climbing gear, so asked James to ask his dad for a job in the shop. He said yes.

I was put in the back room. I would get sacks of potatoes and tip them into a machine that peeled them. Then I'd empty the peeled potatoes into a water-filled plastic dustbin and pour in a bottle of chemicals to stop the peeled potatoes from going brown. This was horrible stuff and I remember running out of the room with my eyes streaming from the fumes. When they were needed, I'd pour the potatoes into the chipper. As well as that, I made batter for the fish and mixed together a strange yellow powder with boiling water to make curry sauce. This was the same curry sauce I would live on later while staying at Tremadog with Andy Pollitt.

One day, I was put behind the counter, while James' dad went out for a while. I waited apprehensively as my first ever customer looked at the menu. They asked for some chips, some fish and some sausages. I immediately forgot how much of each they wanted and felt my face flush with embarrassment. I got some of each and heaped them all together on some newspaper. I hadn't even been shown how to wrap them up, so just scrunched the paper together and put the package on the counter. As I let it go, the package unravelled. The customer looked at me. I looked at the till, at all the numbers and finally said: 'Two pounds fifty please'. The next customer got the same treatment, only this time the price was fifty pence. A little later, James's dad came back and could tell from the mood of the customers that things weren't going well. I was sent back into the peeling room. My career serving the public ended there and then.

I worked at the chippy for three weeks, at fifty pence an hour. At the end of those three weeks, I had saved fifteen pounds. I went to Joe Brown's climbing shop in Capel Curig and bought my first rack, a set of nuts made by Inter Alp, two massive hexes, some karabiners and some nylon webbing slings. I now had my own set of climbing gear and it felt fantastic.

Just by chance, one of the shop assistants mentioned that Pete Livesey had been in the shop the week before and had bought some nuts. I thought this was strange. Pete Livesey was one of the most famous climbers around, yet he still had to go into shops and buy his own climbing gear. I was surprised he didn't get it for free.

Those three weeks in the chip shop in Llandudno was the last normal work I would ever do. Luckily, the climbing lifestyle was a very cheap way to live. When I stayed in Tremadog with Andy Pollitt, we were living on a budget of 70p a day. Later, living in Stoney and signing on the dole, £15 a week easily covered everything, so much so that I actually saved a little money.

Saving was something taught to me by my dad. He was an accountant and astute in financial matters. Whenever we were given any money, at birthdays for example, my dad would take us to the bank to deposit it. This was a great habit to get into as a youngster and it helped me a lot in later life, from scraping by on little money, all the way up to doing business deals with large amounts of cash. My dad's early lessons were critical to my life, not only in business matters but also in how I was able to live on what I had.

My parents were always supportive, but giving me my airfare for my first trip to America in 1983 was the only time they directly funded my climbing. However, one of the most special things they did, one of the most important things they gave me, was that they trusted me and let me get on with what I wanted to do. I never thought about it much at the time, but never once did they suggest that I was wasting my time. Never once did they suggest it was time to stop mucking around and get a proper career. They saw I was enjoying climbing, that I worked really hard at it and they saw how much it gave me. They both had successful careers. My older brother Simon worked and studied for years to become a chartered accountant, going on to become head of international finance for British Gas. It must have been very alien to them to see me pour all my energy into climbing when all it would ever give me was a mention in guidebooks and front covers of magazines. They must have worried about me and what I would do in the future, but they never once tried to stop me from doing what I wanted. If they had, it would have made it very difficult for me to carry on. It took me a long time to appreciate that and I'm very grateful for it.

Despite my surprise at hearing that Livesey bought his own gear, everyone knew that you could never make a living from being a climber. Despite the fact I wanted to be a 'professional', I knew no one would ever give me any real money to go climbing. Professionalism, for me, just meant applying myself fully, doing what I was doing to the best of my ability and fully committing myself to climbing. Never in my wildest dreams did I think that I could one day survive on what I earned from climbing. I climbed because I loved it and loved doing it well. It was always just for its own sake. You didn't want money; you wanted the hardest routes. You didn't want an expensive car; you wanted to sleep at Stoney with your mates.

When we saw successful climbers, we never saw or thought about them in terms of money. What we did see, when we were young and impressionable, were people like Fawcett and Livesey, who seemed to go on amazing climbing trips all the time. There were often photographs of them in exotic climbing venues. They travelled. They seemed to have a great lifestyle. That was what I aspired to, the chance to climb and travel and see the world. So the money I saved, almost always, went on climbing trips. As soon as I decided I wanted to be a professional climber, I realised that the more experience and recognition I got, the better it was for my career. As such, I saw any money I spent on climbing trips as an investment in my own future. I never had any issues about spending money on trips.

In my youth all I had wanted to do was just to get by. I didn't really think about the future that much, I just presumed that I would move into one of those jobs that climbers got. I would work in a climbing shop, become a sales rep, or teach climbing as an outdoor instructor. I always felt that I could fall back on one of those things, which took the pressure off in my days when I had no money.

In 1983 I came back from America with my new pair of Fire rock shoes. I did Ulysses and Master's Wall in them and they created a massive stir in

Britain. Everybody was talking about these special boots and everybody wanted a pair. Yet, for about a year, I was the only person in Europe who had them. Bachar was still sorting out a deal to distribute them in the US. In Europe, while it was possible to find some shoes that looked the same, they didn't have the magical Fire rubber. The shoes were like gold dust.

Wild Country was one of the largest climbing equipment manufacturers in Britain at the time. It was responsible for Friends, the spring-loaded camming devices that had revolutionised crack protection. Friends were invented by an American, Ray Jardine, but he was unable to find an American manufacturer to produce his designs. Mark Vallance, the entrepreneur who founded Wild Country, immediately saw their worth and struck a deal with Jardine. Soon Valance was manufacturing the devices in his Derbyshire factory and distributing them around the world. Wild Country also made a harness called the Black Belt, and would soon produce Rocks, a development of basic nuts that would become the standard around the world. Mark realised that if he could arrange distribution of Fires throughout the UK, he would be onto a winner. We arranged a meeting at Stoney café.

I was already linked with the shoes in climbers' eyes because of the ascents I had done in them – Master's and Ulysses in particular – and I already had a worldwide reputation. Mark suggested that if I would agree to represent Fires in Britain, he would import and distribute them and I would get a percentage of sales. He was going to approach the boot's manufacturers in Spain, Boreal, and if he had my support it would strengthen his case. I agreed and we shook hands. Then, almost secretly, Mark took something out of his pocket. It was a length of purple-coloured webbing, a quickdraw, used between two karabiners when clipping the rope to a runner. At the time, quickdraws were usually six inches long.

'Try this out and let me know how you get on. It's eight inches long.'

He gave me a secretive wink, placed it on the table and left. I looked at the quickdraw. Eight inches of webbing, which probably cost a penny to make. But it was my quickdraw. This is it, I thought. This is my first ever piece of free gear.

I'm a sponsored climber.

Mark got the contract to distribute Fires and I got two and a half percent commission on British sales. I also built a very good relationship with Boreal and over the years worked closely with them developing their shoes. Wild Country and Boreal were both terrific sponsors. Mark carried on sponsoring me for years. Even through my years of injury, when I thought I'd never climb again, he stuck with me, always believing I would come back, even when I didn't think I would. There aren't many sponsors who would do that and it's something I really appreciated. He was always up front and eventually, when he had to drop me, he explained why. It was very amicable.

Boreal used me to sell their shoes in America, Germany and France, as well as in the UK. It was a family business run by Jesus Garcia, and good to work with, being a fun, forward-looking company and very loyal. I ended up going over to the Boreal factory in Spain a lot, developing new products and seeing what could be done to push climbing shoe design forwards.

At the time everyone climbed in boots, with the upper coming up and covering the ankle. EBs, Fires and all the other new boots that followed them were like this. I met up with Bachar, now also working with Boreal, and we started to develop the shoe, without the extended upper. We tried out lots of different shapes, adjusting toe point, the lacing system, the colours, eventually coming up with the first real climbing shoe. I thought up the name, the Ace.

Jacky Godoffe, a top Fontainebleau boulderer, had been working on another revolutionary design, an extremely light and thin, soft-soled slipper. The Ace and other shoe designs that followed it, were heavy and solid with lots of foot support. Slippers swapped a lot of that support for sensitivity. Jacky had done a lot of work on the design, and when I tried one on, it seemed fantastic, unlike any other shoe anyone had ever made. It was very sensitive and its snugness and flexibility let it mould very well for smearing. It had no laces, just broad elastic across the top that kept it tight on the foot. We did some more work on it, redesigning the front a little, and finished it off. At the time, I had a Kawasaki GPZ600 Ninja, so I called the shoe the Ninja. It was Boreal's bestselling shoe for years.

I had the idea of swapping the elastic for laces to give more foot support, to produce a lace-up slipper, and together with Bachar and Jesus Garcia, began to test some prototypes. With climbing shoes, tiny adjustments in things like rubber thickness, toe shape or width can make a massive difference to performance. I continually sent the prototypes back to the factory with new suggestions, all the time looking for what I considered to be the perfect climbing shoe.

When I won Leeds in 1989, I was wearing a prototype pair of these shoes. They ended up being released, but with a stiffer sole than I had used, and called the Sprint. But the shoe never became popular being too stiff for most people's taste. Eventually, we worked together on the original, softer-soled version and in 1990, Boreal released the Laser. The Laser, a soft lace-up slipper, black with pink nylon reinforcement on the uppers, was fantastic, and reigned for many years. I was very proud of it, and, knowing that I would find it hard to improve on, stopped being so involved in rock shoe design after that.

Over the years I did well out of sponsorship and got lots of good deals. They gave me a great lifestyle, even though, at the same time, hardly anyone else in Britain could survive on sponsorship. I was probably getting twice what the next best-paid climber was getting. There might have been some resentment among other climbers about this, especially if they had just added a hard new route or had done well in a competition. However, I quickly realised that it wasn't just a matter of how hard you climbed. You had to sell yourself. It was business, and in that respect, the same professionalism that I brought to my climbing helped me in my business.

I worked hard to fulfil all my obligations to my sponsors. If I ever went anywhere or did a good ascent, I made sure I wrote an article about it for the magazines. This wasn't something I enjoyed, or something I found easy, but I did it. I would always arrange with a photographer to get pictures. This was a big change for me, because in the early days, when the cool thing was to be underground, the last thing anyone wanted was someone taking your picture, or any kind of publicity. All through my early climbing years, in Tremadog, Stoney, America, France or Germany, if there are any pictures of me climbing, then they just happened to have been taken by the belayer or another climber. But with sponsorship, that had to change. You had to get the picture.

At the start I hated doing it, messing around all day on a route, holding positions, repeating moves over and over again, with people looking at you like you're an idiot. In fact, I hated it so much, I decided to learn about photography myself. I got some good kit, read lots of books on the subject, and every time I was with a photographer, I would ask lots of questions. In this way I came to understand photography and what photographers were after. Knowing this helped me appreciate what they were trying to do. In that way I was able to help, making the job a lot easier and more pleasant.

On top of this, I made sure that if I promised a magazine or sponsor an article or some pictures by a certain date, they got them on time. The trust that this built up always made the relationship easier. I also made sure to introduce myself to the editors of all the magazines when I got the chance, not just in Britain, but America and Europe. Then, any time I did an article, I sent a copy off to all the other editors too. It also helped that I travelled and climbed a lot in other countries, and had done hard new routes outside Britain. In that way, I made myself known internationally, making me worth a lot more to my sponsors.

The other commitment I made, which hardly any other British climbers did, was to go to all the trade shows in Britain, Germany or America. These were international meeting places for manufacturers, where the latest products were unveiled. I didn't particularly enjoy spending three days indoors under horrible lighting, making small talk to business people, introducing myself, shaking hands, continually talking about myself and what I had done, and asking them all about their products. But I did it. However, going out in the evening with bosses of companies eating nice food and getting drunk was more to my liking.

These shows were critical. This was how I got sponsored: by networking, being someone the marketing people actually knew, being friendly to people. They were hard work, but in reality they took up about ten days in any year, so it wasn't much to ask. It also helped that I am by nature very chatty and a bit of a performer, so I found it a lot easier than many climbers would.

While I wasn't overjoyed about writing articles, photo shoots or trade shows, the one side of it I really did like were the actual meetings. At these meetings I would have to go in, meet with the heads of a company, and convince them to sponsor me. Convince them to give me large amounts of money so that I could travel the world and go climbing and have a great time. These meetings, which would probably last about an hour, would determine how I would survive for the next year.

To prepare, I would spend time thinking of and writing down all the reasons why this company simply had to sponsor me. I would do this and convince myself that I was actually worth all the money I was about to ask for. I had to believe I was worth it before I could convince anyone else I was. I'll represent your brand, I'll get so many front covers, I will win competitions in your gear, I will work in product development, I will mention you in lectures, I will appear in your brochure, I will have pictures of me doing the hardest routes using your products. And in return I want *this* amount of money.

I almost always got it.

One time I didn't was during negotiations with a German clothing company. I wanted a certain amount of money; they were offering less. I tried to explain that my competition victories would be good for them, but at the time, I hadn't yet won many, so they weren't convinced. As a compromise, I said I would take the lower amount, if they would give me a £1,000 bonus for every competition I won. In the end, it cost them a fortune and the following year, they paid what I wanted.

I also got some sponsors outside climbing. The Swiss watch manufacturers, Swatch, paid me to open the new-year sales at Harrods department store in London. It was a stunt. On the morning of the gig, I joined the queue with everyone else, then broke free from the crowd, ran to the front of the queue, scrambled onto a platform, and then, clipping into a top-rope, climbed up the front of the building.

This led to another stunt on the nearby Nelson's Column, in London's Trafalgar Square. Johnny Dawes, Simon Nadin and I had been approached by a group called Survival, to bring attention to a threat to Innu hunting grounds in northern Canada. The column is across the road from the

Canadian High Commission. At around 6 a.m., the three of us ran across the square, got onto one of the lions, then scrambled up onto the bottom of the column. From here you can clip into a bolt and climb an overhang to the base of the column proper, towering a hundred and fifty feet above us. A lightning conductor runs the height of the structure, attached by rusty old screws, placed over a hundred years before. The idea was to thread slings behind the conductor as protection. I took one look at them and decided to let Johnny lead the climb, as he was fearless. At the top, he dropped ropes down for the two of us. Simon climbed the rope to get pictures, while I attempted to climb the column, just by pinching the decorative flutings with my hands. I got to within thirty feet of the top, but having done the same move over and over for a hundred feet, was pumped into oblivion. Still, I was feeling pretty pleased with myself and looked down to see the crowds watching. Except that of all the people in the square below, only a handful of tourists were looking up in my direction. They were more bemused than impressed. God, I thought, I'm free-climbing Nelson's Column and that's all the interest I'm getting. What do you have to do for attention these days?

Then, just off to the left, I saw a commotion. A large crowd had gathered in a circle, and at its centre, a scantily clad blonde with long legs was having her picture taken holding various shoes. As she held up each pair, flashguns went off and the crowd gave a round of applause.

Back on Nelson's Column we unrolled our banner: *Save the Innu*. We looked down at our little crowd of spectators. Simon had brought a thermos flask and some sandwiches, and we sat and enjoyed the view for a while, before abseiling back to the ground. Here, the police took our names and addresses and cautioned us. Then we were free to go.

In the spring of 1989, I went to Belgium to talk about a sponsorship deal with a company there. Belgium had quite a few keen climbers, but very little rock. Because of this, a couple of indoor climbing walls had been built, which were very advanced for the time. An old friend, Arnold T'Kint, worked at one of these walls called Alpin. I was keen to see both the wall and Arnold, so I also arranged to meet up with him and check the wall out.

I was very impressed. It was housed in a large warehouse, whose walls were covered in the shaped metal and plywood-covered structures like those used for competitions. The walls were tall, up to forty feet high and bolted, so customers could actually lead the routes. They were covered with coloured bolt-on resin holds, and by following lines of different colours, routes of different grades were possible. In Britain, at the time, there were indoor climbing walls, but they weren't nearly as good as this. They were often flat, vertical concrete walls with holes chipped out, or sometimes stones or small flakes of rock cemented in for holds. You traversed and made up your own problems. I could see the Belgian idea was a great one, with lots of potential. At the time, I had one of the first generation of handheld video cameras, which I'd picked up in Japan, and made a record of everything I saw.

Back in Britain, I started thinking about building an indoor climbing centre myself. If need be, I could work in it too, which could give me some security, and it would provide climbers with great training facilities. I would need backing. I approached Mark Vallance with the idea and showed him my video. He thought it looked great and suggested we approached Dick Turnbull. Dick ran an outdoor shop called Outside in the Peak District village of Hathersage. The idea was that if we ran the wall, Outside would have a shop there and would make their money by selling equipment to the customers. It was all agreed and we began looking for potential premises.

At the same time, another Sheffield climber, Paul Reeve, had much the same idea. He had heard on the grapevine that I was looking at building a wall too. He approached me one day and told me he had found a potential building. He wanted to know if I would come into a deal with him. He thought my reputation and experience would help him make a better wall. I said I was interested and he took me to a building in the old industrial area of Sheffield. It had once been a steel foundry and now lay deserted. It was basically a huge empty box of a building, and as soon as I saw it, I knew it was perfect.

I told Paul about my dealings with Mark Vallance. I thought that finance would be a problem for just the two of us, so convinced Paul to allow Outside and Wild Country to get involved. Without their backing it would have been prohibitively expensive and too big a risk. At the time, there was no wall anything like we were planning in the UK, and although every city now has one, we didn't know if people would use it. I didn't want to risk losing my house over it, so in the end, Paul and I put in 24.5 percent of the investment and Wild Country put in 51 percent. Work started. Lots of leading walls were built, a bouldering wall, a shop, a café. We named it the Foundry.

On the first day of trading, the weather was on our side. Rain was lashing down. Perfect weather for the great indoors. And yet we only had two visitors. I spent the whole day with my head in my hands. What had I done? Of course people aren't going to climb indoors. What was I *thinking*? All that first week, a pathetic dribble of customers came through the doors. But after that, slowly at first, then rapidly increasing, more and more people began to come. It became a famous destination. In the first year alone, we had 90,000 visitors. People from America and Canada would come to visit it. Since then, it has continued to do well, bringing in a very steady income. Eventually, Wild Country and Outside wanted out, so now Paul and I own the Foundry fifty-fifty. It's still one of the best walls around and provides work for a great group of people.

During my mid and late thirties, I started thinking longer term about how I was going to survive. I could see an end to my climbing career and knew I would need to diversify somehow – move beyond the sport to find a way of making a living. I was in a good position to do this. I had made some money from the Foundry and had cash tied up in shares, so I had some security and breathing space. And I had a lot of free time to put into a project. Also around the same time, I was starting a family and financial security became much more important. This changed my outlook a lot. It was no longer good enough for me just to get by. I was going to have to provide for others.

I had a good friend in Sheffield called Paul Watson. Paul was an ex-professional cyclist and had been the British road race champion in 1985. He had also competed in the Tour de France. Much like me, Paul had left sport and had looked around for a way to make some money. He bought property in Milton Keynes and rented out rooms to professionals. They were in a good area and the rents they attracted easily covered the mortgage. He told me about some other houses for sale there and suggested that I check them out. I liked the idea. I cashed in my shares and bought a house in Milton Keynes. It rented out well, and soon I bought another two, taking money out of the first house. Not long after, property prices rose dramatically and my houses were worth a lot of money. I felt very lucky. This was in the early 2000s and house prices continued to rocket for a few years, some doubling in value in the space of five years.

My experience of business has made me think that the way you actually make money is by sitting around chatting with people over a cup of coffee. People tell you ideas. Opportunities come your way. I had learned all this from my experiences in climbing. If opportunities and good ideas come along at the right time, you grab them if you can.

Another friend, Ashley, a property developer, told me about a pub he knew of, The Old Crown, coming up for sale in Sheffield. It was in a bad state and would be in need of renovation, so Ashley suggested he would finance it and I, with all that spare time, would oversee the renovation. We could then rent out the pub to a landlord and run the upstairs as flats. I agreed and we bought it.

I realised that the sooner I got the pub project finished, the sooner I could start renting it out and making some money. Once that was done, I would again have time to climb, play golf and get my life back. I immediately set to work. Almost seven days a week, I was there, overseeing builders, filling skips, running to hardware shops, decorating, anything I could do.

Seven months later, it was finished. We rented the pub and also rented out the upstairs flats.

About a year later, Ashley needed to raise some capital, so I bought him out. I now own the pub myself and have converted the flats into bed and breakfast. My wife Sharon takes the bookings, the pub cooks breakfast and a cleaner comes in to change the bedding and tidy up. It's a great feeling when you look at the booking sheet and all eight rooms are taken. The B&B has been a fantastic source of income and now that it's up and running, needs little further investment.

The Foundry is located on one side of a courtyard. In 2002 the other building that faced onto the courtyard came up for sale and I suggested to Paul Reeve we buy it. I wasn't sure what to do with it, but if nothing else, it seemed like a good idea to have complete control of the courtyard. He wasn't sure, but I liked the idea of owning it and after we both changed our minds a few times, I convinced him it would be a good idea. We bought the building.

Now we had it, we weren't sure what to do with it. I once had an architect down there and he asked if I had thought about putting in a planning application for apartments. A planning application goes to the local council and seeks permission to develop a building into flats. If it is granted, it vastly increases the value of the property. I got advice from experts and they thought it was a hopeful case. However, the process is expensive, involving lots of tests and needing designs drawn up, and is a huge investment on what is ultimately a risk. Paul, by this stage, was starting to find it too big a commitment, as he had lots of other projects going on. I took it on myself and bought Paul out. It was a very expensive and stressful process, lasting almost six months, but finally the day came and the council approved my application. This was fantastic news. I decided just to sell the building, rather than taking the risk of developing it myself and after a few agonising false starts, a year later, it was sold. Financially, it was a huge success.

After the sale went through, I couldn't help myself from going to the bank and asking for my balance. The assistant told me.

'No,' I said, 'Would you print it off, please, I want to look at it.'

I took the slip of paper home and pinned it to the wall. I looked at it for a few days, thinking I should do something with it, but it was too much to know what to do with. In the end, I decided on a top of the range watch, a Breitling Super Avenger, encrusted with eighty diamonds. I wore it out, but everyone thought it was a fake, so I sold it back to the dealer.

I don't kid myself. I know that I have made a few good deals and that they have gone right for me. The Foundry has done well, the pub is going well and the warehouse deal was a success. But I am not under the illusion that I am a natural businessman, or that I will keep on making big deals. Those went well, but I was careful with them, despite risking a lot sometimes and I grafted hard to make them work. They had seemed like good ideas, with good returns, and at the time, I had been lucky enough to be in a position to take advantage of them.

Today, I am financially secure and am happy with how things are. The B&B largely provides for the family, and if my children need something, they can have it. If someone phones me up today and asks if I want to go and play a round of golf this afternoon, I can go if I want to. If the forecast says there'll be great surf in Whitby tomorrow, then I'm going to Whitby tomorrow. Maybe some time in the future I will get into something else, but right now, I couldn't ask for more than that.

FIFTEEN

Power Struggle

Bouldering has always been a big part of my climbing and my approach to it has gone through many stages. In my early days, I bouldered outside on the school wall as a way to climb when I couldn't get to the cliffs. It developed into a way of training fitness, or gaining certain strengths for doing longer climbs. Later, it became a discipline in its own right, where I could look for the hardest possible moves, unencumbered by ropes or the need for belayers. Finally, towards the end of my career I enjoyed it just for the pure pleasure of it.

Bouldering, originally climbs on boulders rather than proper cliffs, is any climbing done in that style, without a rope and free from danger, where you may fall off repeatedly while working out a sequence of moves, be that at the base of a cliff, on a wooden board in your cellar, a concrete bridge or plastic indoor wall. The first bouldering I ever did was at St David's College. There was a wall around the outside of the school, about twelve feet high, and my friends and I would climb on this whenever we could.

This was bouldering, but it wasn't bouldering. It was bouldering, because we would get our wash bags full of talc, tie on our headbands and work out moves to the top of the wall. We would traverse back and forward, and get pumped. But at the same time, it wasn't bouldering, because we never had it in our heads that we were bouldering. As far as we were concerned these were mini-routes. We climbed on the wall because we were obsessed by climbing and we weren't allowed to go to a crag. We gave our problems names and graded them VS or HVS.

In my last year at school, when I was kept back to repeat some exams and only had four subjects, I had a free period at the start of every day. By then, I had decided I wanted to be a professional climber and took it more seriously. I decided to treat climbing like one of my subjects, so in my school timetable, I wrote in 'climbing' as the first lesson of each day. At nine o'clock every morning I went out, no matter what the weather, hopping over the wall where no one would see me. Then I'd traverse for thirty minutes.

This training was a way of getting fitter for routes. Routes, long leads or bold solos, were what climbing was all about back then. Until the late 1980s hardly anyone bouldered in Britain, and when they did, it was more just to mess around at the bottom of the crag to pass some time or to warm up. Never did we, or anyone else, think of bouldering as an end in itself, or think a boulder problem to have any real worth. They weren't recorded and there was seldom anything about bouldering in magazines.

After reading *Master of Rock*, a book all about John Gill's bouldering, I was inspired to boulder myself. It was at that time that Mel Griffiths first showed me his boulder problems at the overhanging wall at Carreg Hylldrem. I realised how little strength I had, especially considering how well I was climbing, and decided that bouldering was how I would develop this strength. I worked hard at Hylldrem and over the course of the summer, saw my power and strength improve until I could do the hardest problems there.

That was when I was only seventeen, still young. I was lucky enough to develop this strength and attitude so early. But climbing was still all about routes and I saw bouldering purely as a way of getting better at them. Later, when I left Tremadog and went to Stoney, I found that there were boulder problems at the base of the crags, and that some problems actually had names. I would sometimes see climbers bouldering, and one of them, a local Sheffield climber called Mark Stokes, said he preferred bouldering to doing routes. This was an attitude you almost never came across in Britain. Bouldering wasn't really climbing. But slowly I started bouldering and enjoyed it more and more. Then, in the winter of my first year of living at Stoney, a climber called Pete Kirton showed up. Kirton was to have a big influence on my attitude towards bouldering.

Pete started climbing in the quiet county of Northumberland in the northeast corner of England. In Northumberland there are lots of sandstone outcrops. The rock is fantastic, but the cliffs tend not to be very high. Because of this, climbers often don't use ropes, preferring instead to solo routes. In essence, these routes are long boulder problems. Pete Kirton was one of those extremely rare climbers at the time, someone who was a boulderer first and foremost. Apart from his upbringing in Northumberland, there were two things that set him out as a boulderer. First, he didn't have a particularly good head and would get nervous on routes. Second, he was very strong, with incredibly strong fingers. Legend had it that when he was younger, only climbing VS, he was able to hang one-handed off the edge of wood around the top of a door frame, even though it was only an inch or so wide. He was once demonstrating this to some climbers. He reached a hand up to the door frame, gripped and lifted his feet off the ground. The sheer force actually broke a bone in his finger.

I climbed a lot with Kirton over the winter of 1980 to 1981. Our time together was hugely motivating for both of us, as well as brilliant fun. His climbing was really advanced at the time, and he showed me some of his dyno problems. Dynos, or dynamic moves, involve springing upwards, using the force from your legs and arms, to catch a hold far above. When you dyno, your whole body can part company with the rock. Watching Kirton doing his dynos, springing between holds that were sometimes six feet apart, I was amazed.

In Stoney there is a really basic problem, dynoing between good handholds. Kirton showed it to me. He grabbed the handholds and hung down straight-armed from these, crouching low on the footholds. Then he exploded upwards, pulling in quickly with his arms and pushing off his legs. He sprung up and snatched good holds above. I tried, but couldn't make any impression on it at all. I was moving too statically, getting no speed or power into the move. I couldn't co-ordinate the push from my legs with the pull from my arms. But I stuck at it and finally did the move. It felt great. For the next two weeks, all I did were dynos, learning how to co-ordinate my arms and legs, releasing the move, catching and holding the hold above. After that fortnight I began to get the idea.

I had a great time with Pete, bouldering at Stoney and at other limestone crags like Rubicon and Raven Tor. We used to have competitions to see who could do the most boulder problems that the other couldn't do.

'How many have you got?'

'I've got four, what about you?'

'I've only got two.'

In the winter before I went to America for the first time, I visited the Polytechnic gym a lot in Sheffield and would spend long periods of time hanging from wooden blocks with one hand to strengthen my fingers for Psycho. Kirton was a master at this kind of strength; I once watched him hang for nearly twenty seconds. The next best anyone else had done was eight seconds. I got better and better at this, timing my hangs, and eventually managed twenty-one seconds. In the spring, Kirton visited Sheffield for the first time in a while and I met him in the gym. I immediately challenged him to a dead-hanging competition.

'Come on, Pete, check this out.'

I had been there for a while and was well warmed up. I told Andy Pollitt to get his stopwatch ready. I stripped off to my shorts, removed my shoes, chalked up and hung off the hold. Go! I hung, focused, thought to myself:

'Relax, breathe well, focus.' The seconds ticked by. Eventually my fingers gave out and I dropped off.

'Twenty-three seconds Jerry.'

'Twenty-three seconds, Pete, what about that?'

I punched the air in triumph. I beat my best time by two seconds and was over the moon.

'Go on Pete, get warmed up and beat that.'

But Pete didn't warm up. He was dressed in one of those old tweed coats and without even removing it, without chalking up or preparing at all, he locked his fingers onto the block and hung free. He looked around, looked at me, at Andy and at the watch. Thirty seconds soon passed and he casually put his feet on the ground.

'Bloody hell, Pete, that was amazing. I reckon you could have done even more. Why did you let go?'

'Got bored, youth.'

He later admitted to me he'd been doing some secret training and had already warmed up before I saw him.

My trip to America in 1983 really changed my attitude to bouldering. The days I spent in Colorado after doing Genesis and Psycho, wandering the hillsides of Flagstaff or Horsetooth reservoir with Gill's *Master of Rock*, doing the second ascents of problems that I had read about for years, were some of my best times. I loved it all – the problems, the moves, the history. For the first time, boulder problems gave me the feeling that I got from routes, that sense of reward, the sense that they were worth it. From that point on I enjoyed bouldering more and more.

After getting back from America, Pete Kirton suggested a trip to the Lake District, one of the most historic climbing areas in England, famous for its high mountain crags. Until then I had never climbed there, so agreed to go along. Pete was a member of the Northumbrian Mountaineering Club and the club owned a hut at Bowderstone Crag. The crag is named after the Bowderstone, a boulder that sits on the slopes below the cliff. Our plan was to stay in the hut, repeat the hardest routes in the Lakes, then add some harder ones of our own. This wasn't quite how it happened.

The Bowderstone itself is huge. It must be twenty feet high and thirty feet long, shaped like a massive diamond, with a small point sticking into the ground. There is a ladder leading to the top for tourists. Famously, you can go to the bottom where it narrows, and if one person stands on each side, they can reach through a hole at the narrow base and shake hands. Because of the diamond shape, it has overhanging faces all around the base, and these are covered in little holds. It must be the best single boulder in the country, and when I first saw it, it blew me away.

'My God Pete, this looks amazing, what are the problems here?'

He told me that only a few of the obvious easy ones had been done. I couldn't believe it, as some of the lines on the steep faces looked brilliant. He had already spent some time here and had named a lot of the problems, but still hadn't succeeded on many. As soon as he said that, all plans to do routes went out the window and we spent most of the next two weeks bouldering.

The sun shone every day. We would get up, or, rather, I would get up, and start making breakfast. Pete was really slow moving and it took forever to get him moving. In America I had thought Skip Guerin was laid back, but Pete was something else. He really took some shifting. Once he was up, he would take a chair, sit outside in the sun and I would bring him the first of several cups of tea. Then I would pack both our bags and we'd go bouldering. I would make lunch too. In the evenings we would sit round the hut with a bottle of Southern Comfort whiskey. Pete loved it, although I only ever managed to swallow a little.

Pete had already named the problems he had conceived with great, futuristic names – Inaudible Vaudeville, Impropa Opera, Picnic Sarcastic, Slapstick – and showed me the moves. Standing on the ground he acted out enormous reaches between poor holds up very overhanging rock. When he first showed them to me, I thought he was dreaming.

'This will never go, Pete.'

But slowly we would piece the moves together. Usually, Pete would demonstrate the moves and I would struggle. Then Pete would try the problem and I would manage some of the moves. Finally, Pete would fall off high on the problem and then I would do it. In this way I got almost all the first ascents and Pete would usually repeat them next try. This never happened in a bad, competitive way; we just wanted the problems climbed.

Tourists would often come along and watch for a moment. They would say things like 'Why don't you use the ladder?' In fact, I think they all said that and we would just laugh along because they were only being friendly.

There was one particular problem we were both trying, which became Inaudible Vaudeville. It involved getting an awful, pinchy two-finger pocket and using it to jump miles to a flat hold. It felt like the hardest move either of us had ever tried. One time I tried it, gave it everything I had and launched for the flat hold. I got it. The upward force threw my body backwards in a wild swing and I tried with everything I had to keep my hand in contact with the hold. At the very apex of the swing, my body almost horizontal and face down, I came to a momentary stop. For an instant I felt time stand still. Questions hung in the still air. Will I hold the hold or won't I? In that space, in that moment, I heard the voice of a surprised tourist:

'Ooh, he looks like a monkey!'

I was there, every muscle flexed, every tendon in my body popping, face red, busting a gut, my body and mind screaming, thinking this is a move at the very limit of human ability. But to the tourist? I looked like a monkey. I held the hold, pulled back into contact with the rock and finished the problem, the hardest problem I had done up to that point. A monkey.

That was my first pure bouldering trip. We did one new route on the crag above, but apart from that it was just bouldering. Thanks to my change of attitude, a guilt that I might once have felt, the guilt of neglecting routes, had gone. I really felt I had achieved something.

Closer to Sheffield, some climbers had started exploring a crag called Cressbrook and added some problems. The first time I saw it, I fell in love with the place. It was a limestone dale with a long wall of smooth limestone, about fifteen feet high. Over a summer, some friends and I developed the crag a lot further adding problems like Jericho Road, Moffatrocity and the Hulk, all pretty hard.

That was in 1988, and the following year, Ben Moon started going there a lot. He started trying a sit-down start to my problem, the Hulk. Sit-down starts are where, instead of just starting with whatever holds you can reach while standing, you sit on the ground and get your feet off the floor before pulling onto the rock. They are a way of adding length and difficulty to boulder problems, without adding any more height or risk, and they can often be the hardest part. Ben was doing well on this. It looked like a fantastic, hard piece of climbing. However, I was injured. A tendon problem in my finger meant I couldn't push it too hard, so I couldn't join in. I was jealous.

As it happened, by the next year, 1989, Ben still hadn't done it. I had recovered, and now he was injured. I managed to do the problem and called it Superman. This was probably the hardest problem in Britain, but at the time, nobody was that interested, apart from those of us who climbed there. Bouldering just wasn't news.

These days, that's all changed. If you go to the crags, half the people are bouldering. I'm not sure what happened, or how to explain this development. Things came along that influenced people. Around 1992, the first bouldering guidebooks were produced. In 1994, Ben Moon made a film called One Summer, showing bouldering on Minus Ten, Cressbrook and some gritstone crags. Not long after, bouldering mats came along. Even with bouldering, when you are not very far up, a fall can still hurt, especially after a few falls, or you can twist an ankle on uneven ground. Bouldering mats are nylon-covered squares of reinforced foam that make falling off a lot less dicey. The first time I saw a mat was in America and I thought it was cheating. You won't catch me using one of those, I thought. But they changed bouldering, hugely reducing the numbers of bad falls.

I love Yosemite. For the climbing, the friendships I have shared and for the fantastic times I enjoyed there, it holds a special place in my heart.

There's something special about the boulders in Yosemite, and Midnight Lightning really sets the standard. Not only is the climbing superb, it's right in the centre of the world's most popular climbing destination. Everybody comes to Yosemite and everybody stays in Camp 4. There won't have been a climber who didn't go over and try to pull on, or at least feel, the first holds. And even from that, they will get a sense of what it would mean to climb it. That makes it a world-class problem.

In the 1990s, I went on several trips to Yosemite. This was at a time when I'd really begun to love bouldering, and during these trips I managed to add a few cutting-edge problems of my own to the fantastic Camp 4 boulders, first Stick It and The Force, and later The Dominator. These problems were as good and as hard as any in the world at the time, and are among my greatest and proudest achievements.

In the spring of 1991, tired of the demands of competitions, I arranged with Kurt Albert to go to Yosemite for a bouldering trip and to catch up with Ron Kauk. That's as good as it gets. It was great to be back in the Valley again with two great friends and over the following month, Kurt, Kauk and I would boulder almost every day.

Ever since the days when he first did Midnight Lightning, Kauk had really pushed the standards of bouldering in America, and since my last visit, had done another top-notch problem in the Valley, Thriller. I repeated it and it really was a thriller, with hard moves up a beautiful, slightly overhanging wall, with your feet an ankle-breaking ten feet off the ground.

Kauk pointed me out an unclimbed problem to the left of Thriller and straight away I began to try it. The moves were fantastic, with powerful surges off small sidepulls and undercuts to a committing final slap. It was a noted unclimbed line among Valley locals and had seen some attention in the past. One of the holds, a small flake, flexed a little under bodyweight. If it had broken off, it would have ruined the problem. So, about a year before, a local climber called Mark Chapman had poured a tiny bit of glue down behind the flake to reinforce it. It was subtly done. If you looked behind it you would see the glue, but otherwise it was invisible.

The problem, like Thriller, was high and hard all the way. We had a short ladder, so I would lean this against the wall and step off onto the problem to try the upper section. The landing was very rocky, and since this was in the days before bouldering pads, I spent some time burying wooden pallets to flatten out the ground. I soon started to get the moves sorted. When we tried it we would bring a cassette player along. At the time, we were listening to Michael Jackson's album Thriller. There was one song in particular I would listen to while I looked at the problem, visualising the moves before an attempt. It started off:

'The Force. It's got a lot of power.'

It was a great line. Later, when I did the problem, I called it The Force.

At the same time, I discovered – and began working – another line that would become Stick It. I had seen a single fingerhold over a pristine bulge of granite on a boulder near the campground. It looked like a nice hold and I thought if I could get to it, it would be a great line to the top of the boulder. The rock below didn't have any holds, only vague features, so I had to see if I could hold these features and support my weight. I got Kurt to help me. He was six foot two of solid German muscle, so he would pick me up and hold me onto the rock while I figured out the positions.

'Up a bit, up a bit, left a bit. Right! Now let me go!'

With that, Kurt would release me and I would struggle to keep my body in contact with the rock for a moment before falling off. I tried the moves below the fingerhold. Nothing. Perhaps further right? Nothing. Right again? In this way, I worked right along the boulder, trying various ways of getting to this hold. Eventually, I found a position on two opposing sidepulls that I could hang on for a millisecond. Above that there was an awful pinch hold that could support me for a moment. And that was it. The positions worked. Now all I had to do was to find a way of moving through them, but I knew I could do that.

I worked on the moves on both these problems and soon had them both figured out, ready to climb. After two rest days, the weather turned cool. Perfect. I went to the boulders and did a problem to warm up. That was all I needed. I felt so good – strong, light and moving well. I went straight to Stick It and climbed it first go. After so much preparation, the actual ascent took less than six seconds of pure explosive movement. It is a superb problem, which barely exists. If you looked at it without chalk marks on the holds, you wouldn't be able to see it. You would walk past and think there was nothing there. It was a true creation, based purely on a vision. If I hadn't seen it and started trying it, it might never have been done. The creative process that brings problems like this into existence is fantastic.

From there, it was over to The Force. It was just the same. I got straight on it, climbed it first go, perfectly. It was done. These were two of my best problems to date, both done within half an hour of each other. Sometimes things work out perfectly.

Later that year, my old friend John Bachar went to The Force, got a crow bar and levered off the formerly loose flake that Mark Chapman had reinforced. He claimed the glue was unethical, and for that, he destroyed the problem. Left behind, in place of a tiny hold that gave a desperate move, there was a large flat ledge which allowed an easy reach high into the problem. The Force was changed utterly, nowhere near the problem it once was. Originally Bachar denied it, but Mark Chapman had seen him at the boulders, so he admitted it later. I was angry, frustrated and disappointed. The glue was invisible and made no difference, serving only to protect the problem. Bachar had been going through a bad time back then. The nature of climbing, always so precious to him, was changing. In Yosemite and other crags, the use of bolts was becoming widespread, threatening the traditional values of boldness and commitment that he had always championed and excelled at. He became entrenched, began to lose friendships and, perhaps, perspective.

Not long after the incident with The Force, things turned nasty. In the parking lot of Camp 4, an argument flared between Bachar and Chapman over the bolting of routes. It started getting aggressive. Suddenly, Bachar sprung up in fighting pose.

'So, you wanna hit me? Hit me! You wanna hit me? Go on.'

He squared up to Chapman and adopted a martial arts self-defence pose, Bruce Lee style.

'I don't want to hit you John,' Chapman protested.

'Go on. You think you can? Hit me.'

Bachar was hopping around lightly on his feet, preparing for violence. Then Chapman, who was a big guy, threw his heavy right arm. I think Bachar, who had always read a lot of Kung Fu and other martial arts books, thought he would get out of the way, but the big arm whacked him in the neck and down he went. After that, Bachar left Yosemite and seldom returned. It was all a bit of a shame for John.

In 1993 I went back to Yosemite again with a crackpot plan, hatched with Kurt. El Capitan is the most incredible rock face in the Valley, perhaps the world. It is three thousand feet high, explodes out of the ground right beside the road, and is pretty much vertical or overhanging all the way. The central line on it is a vertical ridge where the angle of the left half and the right half change slightly. This line was climbed in 1958, taking many days of effort spread over a couple of years, by Warren Harding to give The Nose, perhaps the most famous rock climb in the world. It relied for most of its length on aid, Harding having hammered thousands of pegs into cracks and flakes, including, at one point, the legs of a stove, to get to the summit. Over the years, as people free-climbed more, fitness increased and protection became better, the amount of aid was reduced. In 1993 Kurt and I decided we would go and try to free The Nose once and for all, and produce the world's greatest free-climb. Our sponsors gave us thousands of feet of rope and a ton of gear.

We arrived in Yosemite and scoped out the massive route with binoculars. It looked incredible, but while having a wander through the boulders the first evening, I noticed something much more interesting. To the right of Stick It, there is a single pinch hold on a largely featureless ten-foot overhang of orange granite. There was always some chalk on the pinch, but it seemed like a joke, as the overhang had no other good holds. Playing on the pinch, I once again got Kurt to hoist me onto the rock. At full stretch, there was a tiny fingerhold, and, if Kurt let me go, I could hold myself there for almost a millisecond. Higher, he held me on to another position and once again I could hang on for a moment. And that's it, I thought. This will go. Suddenly, the thought of three thousand feet of El Capitan seemed unimportant in comparison with these ten feet of rock, with the promise of three moves at the very limit.

It was a super-short problem, which is how I like them. Bouldering is generally a test of power, first and foremost. If you have a long, fifteen-move boulder problem, you can work on it, become more efficient, do the moves better and you will do the problem if you stick at it. With a power problem, three moves, two moves, or, better still, only one, the question is simple: do you have you the power, or don't you? If you haven't, it's goodbye. You won't do the problem. Either give up, or go and spend two years getting stronger and try it again.

I became obsessed with this problem and over the next few days began to figure out the moves. I told Kurt our plans for The Nose would have to wait. He seemed happy enough about this. However, my timing wasn't great. It was getting into May and the weather was beginning to warm up, making conditions bad. But I knew I could do it. The first move was the hardest and I hadn't managed it yet. From there, if I was pushed on, I could do the next moves to the top. It all came down to this one move. The pressure was mounting.

I had to believe I would get the chance. I went on a strict diet for about a week. Salads only. As a pure power problem, I didn't need any stamina, so didn't need any carbohydrates in my body at all. I could do it if I felt dizzy, so I cut out almost all food. This wasn't hard. I was keen to lose the weight to give me the edge on that first move and I was so excited about doing it that I could hardly eat anyway. I took two rest days to give my skin a chance to recover. On the first I sat around and did some stretching. Second day, I didn't eat anything except for a small salad. Late in the day, I went for a two-hour uphill hike to Yosemite Falls to burn off more calories. My stomach was a void. But I didn't care. I will eat after I do this, I thought. At night, because of my lack of food, I just lay awake thinking about the moves.

On the third day I woke up and knew the time had come. It had rained in the night and everything was wet. However, things were drying and I was hopeful. After rain, the air is less humid and the drying effect can actually give better friction, so I relaxed and warmed up a little. I felt super light, as strong as I'd ever felt and I was psyched. The rock was feeling better than it had for weeks. I made my way to the problem.

Every time I tried it, because it was obviously something special, a crowd of people would come and watch. They would ask if I minded. While I would rather be by myself, I said no, I didn't mind, as long as they remained totally quiet. Sometimes people shout encouragement when you're trying something and I find that off-putting. You can be so focused, the last thing you want is someone breaking your concentration. No one can say anything that will make me pull harder. They were cool about that.

I sat below the problem, visualised the moves and got myself into the correct state of mind. When I am about to try a problem, I have one thing in my mind – smooth focused aggression. I chalked up. The night before, to give me every possible advantage, I had microwaved my chalk for about five minutes, thinking that if there was any moisture in there at all, this would get rid of it. I sealed it in a Tupperware box and put it in the fridge all night. Even my chalk felt great.

I tried the first move, the crux, the move I had never yet done. I threw my body from the pinch towards the small edge. I hit this, but failed to hold it properly. I tried again two or three times, but each time I just wasn't getting my fingers on it perfectly. I sat on the ground, wondering why I kept missing the hold. The thought occurred to me that if it had been a pocket, then I would get it better. Something about the round shape seemed to allow more accuracy. With this being a long, flat hold, there was no single point to aim for.

Wondering about this, I had an idea. I got some white sticky tape and stuck a white circle of tape around the part of the edge I had to hold, making it look like a pocket. Then I returned to the ground. Visualise. Relax. Focus. Ready. Pull on. Throw.

My body went through the air. It was like slow motion. I stuck the hold. My feet came off the footholds and I put them on the higher ones. I threw the next move. Bam! And the next. Bam, bam! And that was it. A moment before I was on the ground, wondering if I would ever do this move and the next moment I was at the top of one of the hardest bits of climbing I have ever done.

That night I had been in Kauk's house playing on his computer. I had typed the word 'power' in and was looking at it on the screen. There was a thesaurus on the computer and I looked up some other words for power. Dominate, it suggested. It sounded good. And now there it was, The Dominator, smack in the middle of Camp 4. Ben Moon repeated it the following year. Ben was bouldering as well as anyone then and was travelling a lot. He said it was the hardest problem he had ever done. After that, despite being a very famous problem, in the middle of one of the world's best bouldering areas, The Dominator wasn't climbed again until 2002.

That left The Nose. Feeling guilty, Kurt and I decided we had better at least get up the thing. People usually take three or four days to climb the route, sleeping on ledges, but it was also climbed fast sometimes in under a day. It can't be that hard, we thought. We'll do it in a day too. We started climbing at 3am, hoping to be on the top around 6pm. I just hadn't realised how big it was. The thing is a mile high. By midday we were both snoozing at different ends of the rope about halfway up, each thinking the other was climbing. Further on, we got one of our ropes caught and had to cut it in half to free it. Higher still, night started to fall, and so too did my torch. I watched the beam tumble for thousands of feet before going dark as it smashed into the ground. In darkness, we arrived amid melting snow patches on the summit, dressed only in light shirts, where we were forced to sit out the night. I spent the hours of darkness doing star-jumps to try to keep the cold at bay. Kurt, who is a terrific sleeper, lay down on a rock and within moments was snoring. All night I wanted to kick him.

'How dare you sleep without me?'

At the first hint of light in the sky I gave him a boot.

'Morning Kurt; let's go.' And we scurried down the complicated descent. This was our last day. We had to hop straight into the hire car and drive to San Francisco airport to fly home. In 1993 Lynn Hill was the one to free The Nose. It was an outstanding achievement.

The Dominator was a new level for me in terms of difficulty, and it was one of the world's hardest and most beautiful boulder problems. Several years later I added a problem on my home crag of Stanage that was in every way an equal to it. It was to be one of my last really hard first ascents.

The Stanage Plantation area is the Peak District's most popular bouldering venue, and somewhere I had bouldered a lot over the years. There is a large boulder there, which didn't have any problems on it. In 1996 I noticed that on the steep, flat front face of this boulder, there are two small sloping fingerholds. I found that if I leaned in from an adjacent boulder, I could reach these, then drop onto them before making an explosive slap to the top of the boulder. I did it. It was a fantastic problem, and again, perfect in the sense that it was just one very hard move. And it was the sort of problem that once you did it, once you had learned the movement, then that was it, you had it. After I managed it for the first time, I was almost always able to repeat it. I called it The Joker. It was perhaps the hardest problem on grit at the time.

I was pleased with The Joker, but the way it started, leaning in from the other boulder, didn't feel quite right and I wondered if the problem could be improved. The rock at the base of the problem is scooped out into a small cave, and on the lip of this cave, at chest level, there is a good hold. At the time I was doing The Joker, I looked at the moves going from this into the sloping fingerholds that would maybe provide a better, harder start, but it looked far too desperate. After doing The Joker this hold nagged at me for a bit, and in 1999, I decided to see if it was possible to do the whole problem from the ground. The moves seemed like they might just be possible, but it was significantly harder than The Joker. I spent most of the winter of 1999 trying it.

Every opportunity I had, I made the trek out to Stanage. It turned out to be a terrible winter, and often I would walk up hoping it would dry, only to walk back down again as it started to snow. Getting up at 7am I'd head straight to the crag, hoping to beat the weather, only for the skies to open as soon as I got there. In between times, I was constantly training, working out on a campus board to keep my power up, dieting, trying to keep injuries at bay. As well as that, I was trying to keep it all quiet. The Peak has lots of superb climbers, and having discovered the problem and worked out the moves, I didn't want someone else to come along and do it. To be honest, it was only Ben Moon who would have stood a chance and he wouldn't have tried it knowing I was working on it. But still, the worry was always there at the back of my mind. Eventually the winter went by, a winter where I had sacrificed all other climbing trips in order to wait for good conditions on this problem. When the warm weather returned in spring, I still hadn't done it. I was so frustrated.

Next winter I was at it again. The moves out of the cave were the living end. When I took my feet off holds at the back, my body swung out. The crux was trying to control the swing. Go too far and I swung off the tiny finger holds. Still, I was getting closer. I was trying it one bleak midweek morning and there happened to be a couple of other climbers at the crag. One of them, a climber called Stuart Littlefair, suggested a different sequence of foot moves. As I had always tried it by myself, I had become a bit entrenched in the sequence I was using, but trying his method, I got through the crux first time. Wow! This was a lot easier. I knew there and then that given a rest day and the right conditions, I would do it.

I was right. Two days later, I pulled through the lower moves into the better sequence on the crux and through to the easier moves on The Joker. I had done it. I called it The Ace. Even today, several years on, it has only had a handful of ascents.

For me, it really was an ace – and my final card. With it, I knew I had gone as far as I was going to go with bouldering. It had taken a lot out of me, had stretched me almost to my limit. It had felt tough, but it was worth it and I was so happy to have done the problem.

In climbing, where there are no Olympics, no gold medals and no trophies for doing the hardest routes, doing the first ascent of a boulder problem is incredibly important. A new problem is like a monument. It's your performance, your ability and your vision set in stone forever. In Camp 4, everybody will have checked out Midnight Lightning and understood something about Ron Kauk in 1978. Now everyone can check out The Dominator. They can feel that first hold, look how far away and how small the next one is and imagine how hard it is to move on through. If anyone ever wants to know how well Jerry Moffatt was climbing in 1993, they can go to The Dominator and feel those holds. They can go to Stanage and hang on the holds on The Ace, and imagine what it would take to lock their body weight off on one of them and pull through. Those problems are there forever, and through them the world can understand.

That's something no one can ever take away.

SIXTEEN

The Next Move

I had done The Ace. There it was, in the middle of The Plantation, a classic problem and one of my hardest. It felt great to have done it at last, and I was more than happy. Yet I also felt a sense of relief. The Ace had taken a lot out of me. I had worked hard at it for some time, training all the time, dieting, always on the verge of injury from such a debilitating regime, always worrying that someone else might do it before me. I hadn't been able to go away or do anything else. Towards the end, just before I succeeded, the problem had started to feel like a shackle.

My next major climbing holiday was a bouldering trip to South Africa. I had been invited over by their mountaineering association and stayed on to visit a couple of areas I had always wanted to see. The Rocklands in particular were fantastic and I managed to repeat some good problems. Towards the end of my trip, I visited a superb area called Topside and found a project there, a really inspiring line that no one had managed yet. I got stuck in and spent a couple of days learning the moves. On the last day of the holiday we went back and I managed to battle my way up the problem, getting the first ascent.

That evening I made the hour-long walk down the hill to the car alone. It was late in the day and the light was fading from the flat land below. I was absent-mindedly rubbing a painful finger in my left hand, thinking about my life and I found that I was looking at it all with a sense of sadness. This was all about to end and I knew it.

I still loved climbing as much as ever, and the last three weeks I spent in South Africa were as good as any, not just in the quality of climbing but for the sheer fun of it all. But my life was changing and my lifestyle was changing with it. Back home in Sheffield, my wife Sharon was expecting our first child. Business demands were getting heavier. Things had changed.

Many of the great friends I had gone climbing with had dropped away. They started taking jobs. Some had families and others moved away. Without them, it wasn't the same. Even though I had travelled the world to climb, some of my favourite days were out in the Peak. Driving to Stoney Middleton with a bunch of mates and setting up a top-rope on Wee Doris, doing that a bunch of times, taking the mickey out of each other, going over to Minus Ten, trying to work out some eliminate that the others couldn't do, getting back in the car and stopping off at the shops for a pork pie and a cake.

I must also admit that things were becoming harder. The level of the top routes was rising all the time. People were now often spending a lot longer on their climbs, making it more of an issue to travel around and repeat the top climbs as I'd done in the mid 1980s. It was feeling like a young man's sport. For years, I had been living on 1500 calories a day. I was training nearly every day as hard as possible. My immune system was beaten down from all the work I had done over the years. Because of this I was often ill or injured.

I'd had a good innings. From the moment Dougie Hall and Kim Carrigan had seen me catch the finger hold on the crux of Little Plum in 1982, all the way up to doing The Ace, the hardest problem in the Peak District in 2002, I had been around the top. Solos, redpoints, trad routes, on-sight ascents, bouldering, competitions – I'd done them all at some point in my career.

I'd also enjoyed the great privilege of climbing with many of the best climbers in the world. Didier and Stefan were fantastic competitors, rivals and friends. They had been hard to beat, and beating them meant something. I admired Jacky Godoffe, Marc le Menestrel, Alain Ghersen and all those Fontainebleau boys for their power and bouldering ability, something I know is extremely rare. To be a great boulderer is to be a great climber. Antoine le Menestrel and John Bachar moved on rock like few others, before or since. But then there were my closest friends whose talent had inspired me: Ron Kauk, not just for his ability on all sorts of rock and styles of climbing, but for the attitude he brought to the crags; and Ben Moon and Wolfgang Güllich, two climbers that pushed the boundaries of their era.

Now a new breed of climbers was arriving. Climbers were getting good younger, training harder and becoming stronger. In competitions, climbers like François Legrand and Yuji Hirayama, who dominated in the late 1990s, had stamina far beyond anything I ever had. After I got out of competitions myself I did some route-setting for them. I have always known what makes a good competition route, a challenge that constantly drains a climber's energy. So I tweaked and tweaked the routes I made to make sure there were no hiding places, nowhere to rest and recover. Despite this, climbers like François and Yuji seemed to be able to shake out the whole way up the climbs. Then there were climbers like Malcolm Smith, and the Americans Dave Graham and Chris Sharma. These guys had incredible power and finger strength and amazing levels of ability and determination. I felt that as I began to move away from climbing, Chris Sharma was becoming the most impressive climber, having the ability to travel the world and create really hard climbs in various disciplines – bouldering, redpointing, on-sighting, competitions – all the disciplines that really mattered at that time. To watch him climb was inspiring and it's always obvious how hard he tries, something I think I understand.

As I walked back from the crag that evening in South Africa, I thought about all the other things I wanted to get out of life. I wanted to try other things. I wanted to go surfing. I wanted to get my business sorted out. And I was very much looking forward to having a family.

I had always wanted to have children. In the years when I was obsessed by climbing, I had had several girlfriends, but these were never the right person, and my climbing lifestyle wasn't conducive to something more stable and committed. It definitely was not the right time to consider having a family. I met Sharon Wallace through a friend, and found to my immense good fortune that she was the right person at the right time. Sharon was a bank manager from Sheffield, and we saw each other when we were out on the town sometimes. We hit it off immediately and later moved in together.

I'd been with Sharon for some time. We were very happy together, and now seemed like the perfect time to start a family. Not long before I went on my trip to South Africa, I was out playing golf with some friends. It was a classic encounter, and on the eighteenth green, I managed a fantastic, ten-foot putt to snatch the game. As we shook hands, I heard my phone ringing.

'Hello?'

It was Sharon. I told her about the putt. She told me she was pregnant. My jaw dropped. I was speechless.

'Are you okay Jerry?' she asked.

'Yes,' I managed to say.

'Okay, well, see you when you get back.'

'Okay.'

I went to hang up but heard her say:

'Oh, and Jerry, don't tell anyone, right.'

I hung up.

'What is it Jerry?' my friend asked.

'Nothing... it's...' I was still stunned. My friend's eyes lit up and he grinned.

'She's pregnant, isn't she?'

'Yes, she's pregnant,' I couldn't help but say. A massive grin came across my face.

Lily was born in 2002. Everything went smoothly.

Sharon had always wanted us to be married, but I was apprehensive. What was the point? I was already totally committed to being with her. Marriage wouldn't have made any difference to that. It wouldn't make us stay together, and I hated the thought of anything like a stag do, any of that backslapping, congratulatory stuff. It just wasn't me. But during Lily's birth, as Sharon was on gas and in great pain, I thought to myself, now *that's* commitment. The idea of marrying Sharon became something I very much wanted to do.

My brother Simon was living in Brazil at the time. He and his family had planned to visit England together the following month, so that seemed like the perfect opportunity. In my parents' parish church, on 27 June 2003, we were married. Only my immediate family were there and I got a bit choked up, which surprised me. Barnaby was born a year later. I realise now that not having children would have been a terrible gap in my life.

But at the time, it certainly wasn't like I had decided to give up climbing. After my South African trip, I was still keen to climb and work it in around my family life, but this coincided with my buying the pub in Sheffield. Suddenly I was at work seven days a week, hands on, morning till evening. This wasn't how I had expected it, but suddenly, climbing was out of the question and it would be six months before I felt I had any free time. When that free time came, the motivation to train was harder to find.

Climbing is often seen as a lifestyle thing, something that a lot of people dedicate their lives to. They do it obsessively when they are young, then fit it in around work and family commitments, and later carry on doing it for as long as they are physically able. It's one of the biggest things in their lives and some people build everything around it. There are climbers who never lose the drive, even when their ability dies off. After I stopped climbing and had to spend all my time setting up my businesses, renovating the pub and starting my family, climbers I knew often asked me whether I was going to get back into it again.

It was always hard to explain how I felt. Climbing means different things to different people. To some it's a way of getting fresh air. For others it's an adventure. Then again it's a social thing, a chance to catch up with mates. For me, above all, it was about putting one hundred percent of my energy into it, all the time. It was about travelling to the world's best places and doing the hardest and best routes. It was about training, and being constantly at my physical peak. That's what climbing was to me.

I saw myself as a professional and felt that I approached the sport in the same way that someone like David Beckham approaches football, or Kelly Holmes would athletics. David Beckham plays on the world stage against the greatest teams. When he retires from that, I don't imagine he's still going to spend five days a week down the local park playing kickabout. Even if he does, it won't be football as he knows it. Kelly Holmes might jog around the track at her local leisure centre with a bunch of her mates, but it won't be the same as training for gold.

When people asked me about getting back into it, I tried to explain what 'it' is to me. 'It' is working out on a campus board five days a week, twice a day. It's doing weighted pull-ups. It's starving myself seven days a week, watching everything I eat and letting everything else take second place. It's finding the hardest route in the world and going and doing it. At least it was. Like Beckham, I played on the world stage against the best. That took total dedication. I can't do that any more. My body couldn't take it and I haven't the time. So, in a way, I can't get back into it.

Without climbing, my life was completely changed. For the past twenty-five years, I had got up and trained or climbed, or done something for climbing, every day. That stopped, and it took me a few years to get over the guilt, the feeling that when you wake up you should get out and train or climb. The feeling that I shouldn't really have that slice of toast.

But I was never one to sit in the house and watch daytime television. I was always into other sports and activities. There had been the bikes, and I'd had great times racing those around racetracks or out in the Peak. Later, I bought a Group A Peugeot 205, a proper rally car, and got into rallying. That was fantastic fun and I think because I was used to ripping it up so much on the bike, I took to it quite well. I did mostly tarmac events and some forest. The first rally I did was in Lincolnshire, and at the midway point, I was seventh out of 135 drivers. Motorsport Magazine mentioned the 'sensation of the early stages, Jerry Moffatt' in its report on the event. Unfortunately, I whacked into a massive rock later on and ruined my front wheel, so the sensation didn't last. Rallying was fun, but it turned out to be very expensive.

Johnny Dawes had started kart racing and got me to try it. These were little 100cc two-stroke machines, low-slung frames with incredible acceleration. This was in the mid-1990s, around the time I was trying a new and very difficult route at Raven Tor which became Evolution. I had fallen off it really high on a redpoint, and knew I was really close to success. Next day, for a rest, I took my kart over to the Three Sisters track in Wigan for a blast. There is a superb section where you go over a crest, then drop down into a really fast chicane. Those karts felt incredibly quick. Not only are you doing a ton at twenty thousand revs, but you're right down at ground level, and there is no protection on top, so they are quite a psyche-out. Every time I took the crest, I lifted my foot off the accelerator, just a little bit. I tried to take it flat-out every lap, but was always just lifting off a little. I had to really wind myself up to do it and finally I gassed into the crest with my foot flat to the floor.

Suddenly, right in front of me, was a woman, all dressed in white.

'What's she doing there?' I wondered.

The front wheel clipped the outside kerb. I spun off to the other side of the tarmac, hit that kerb and flew into the air. The kart landed in the grass and the front wheel dug in so I spun upside down and landed on my head. My helmet smashed into my shoulder, injuring it quite badly. I didn't climb again for two months. Evolution had to be put on hold for another year. It was just like Liquid Ambar again. I had to pack karting in.

I still ask myself who that woman was.

These high-speed sports were proving too risky while I was still a professional climber. To relax properly, I needed something more sedate. With climbing, you can't do it all day, especially if you are training hard. There's a lot of free time. Golf was the perfect answer. No broken collar bones, no landing on your head, no losing control at 120 mph. Just a relaxing way to spend a day with some friends, a perfect complement to hard climbing. Golf was perfect and I have been playing it now for fifteen years. I really love it and my handicap varies between seven and eight. I joined the Hallamshire Golf Club, the best in the area, right on the edge of Sheffield, overlooking the moorland of the Peak District. When I was young and used to sleep on Noddy's floor in Broomhill, I would often get up and go for a jog from his house, always to and around the Hallamshire course. Behind the second tee is a little bouldering spot called Bell Hagg, and on my runs I would drop down there and traverse back and forth in my trainers, before running around the golf course again and heading back to Noddy's. I have a lot of happy memories there and even today, you still see people walking across the first fairway with bouldering mats over their shoulders, off to climb on Bell Hagg.

Nothing will replace climbing, or the place it holds in my life, but these days, since stopping climbing, the big passion in my life is surfing. In 1991 I was in America. I had done the first ascents of Stick It and The Force, before rupturing a tendon in my finger. Climbing was out for some time. I had a friend, Kevin Worrall, an American photographer living in La Jolla near San Diego. He was a keen climber, but was also into surfing, and suggested that I came down and hung out with him for a while. I had a choice. Go back to Britain with an injured finger and spend a wet summer watching television, or go surfing in California? A tough call.

San Diego was just perfect. Kevin lived in a beautiful house on the shore, above a famous beach break called Windansea. We would get up and sit on the step of his place looking at the sea while Kevin played guitar. Eventually we'd wander down to a coffee shop and sit around chatting, dragging that out until lunchtime. Then we would go somewhere for lunch, usually to a place belonging to a friend of Kevin's that sold beautiful fresh fish. Eventually, we would drive to a surf spot and check out the waves. Then we'd drive around to look at two or three others, before usually going back to surf the first one. We did the same thing, every day, for three weeks.

When I stopped climbing, I realised a lot of my old climbing friends had got into surfing. With climbing, to get to a good standard, you have to put a lot of work in. A lot of them found that with work or family commitments, they were no longer able to maintain that standard and found climbing less satisfying. Surfing was something new for them and offered the rewards and sensations they had first got from climbing: being outdoors, the thrills, the skill, being with a group of your friends in a beautiful place. It was perfect.

They would often go surfing on the east coast of Yorkshire and I started going along too. On the east coast, the weather can be gnarly. The sea is cold and there are big waves. It can feel a bit full on. The first day I went over, an old climbing friend, Gavin, took me to a reef near Scarborough. It was a wild, stormy day and raining heavily. On our way down to the sea, a man came walking away from the shore carrying his board. It was smashed in two. There was a big cut above his eye and blood was dripping onto his wetsuit.

'I can't believe you're going out here today, Jerry, on your first day on the east coast. Good effort.'

I thought, what's he on about? I got down to see great big black breakers peeling down the rocky point. I paddled out and spent the next hour trying to avoid the waves.

From that point on, I got really into surfing in the UK and started doing it all the time. I'm not great at it, but I'm okay and I'm still getting better. It can be scary, but that's something I love about it. I'll never forget my first barrel, being tucked right up inside the wave, looking out. It's a feeling like no other and anyone who has experienced it will understand. It's like time stands still.

I've travelled around the world to some great surfing destinations, but I think the reefs north of Whitby in Yorkshire remain my favourite place. I have some great friends up there and I hardly ever miss it when there's a good forecast. I can go there by myself and will nearly always meet people I know in the water. It can be gnarly, so there are not a whole lot of people doing it. You get out there with one or two friends, or by yourself, paddle out and try to catch some waves. There are no winners and no losers. Often my best days have been in really hideous conditions. Once I'm out there, having a great time, it's just like the old days at Stoney Middleton. I love it.

I do wish the water could be warmer though.

At least twice a week, I go to Whitby and surf. I play golf regularly. If it's a cold, crisp blue-sky winter day, I will still get out and go bouldering and soloing or do a few routes. I do some sport most days, but I try to be home when Lily and Barnaby get back from school.

Nearly all my friends now know nothing about climbing. But I know that it has given me everything. I had a fantastic life because of it. I am proud of what I have done, but I very seldom think about it. Today I look back at that young, nineteen-year-old with the curly hair, looking into the camera on that American climbing film, saying: 'Yeah! I love burning people off.' And I wonder. Was that really me?

Epilogue

Stay Hungry

Bloody weather. Why is it always freezing here?

The car is being rocked by gusts of wind. We watch the rain and sleet pelting the windscreen. There's a DJ playing pop tunes and Noel Craine is singing along.

'I can't believe you made us camp last night Noel. I didn't get a wink of sleep in that bloody wind.'

Noel is a lifer. After all these years he would still rather save a couple of quid and camp, even though we were awake all night as the wind and rain lashed against the tent, rather than spend extra on a cosy bed and breakfast. Last night he cooked vegetable slop on a camping stove rather than go for a curry. Just as he did back in his climbing days, as he's been doing now for thirty years.

'Now, Jerry, you're just going soft in your old age. Where's the old killer instinct? Stay hungry, isn't that what they say?'

'You can't be hungry after that breakfast, Noel. You must have had four sausages, you fat git.'

'Insulation, Jerry; it's going to be a tough day out there. Look at it.'

We peer through the hail at the grey and heaving Atlantic Ocean. We are in Bundoran, on the west coast of Ireland, desperate to get some surfing done. Yesterday the waves weren't very good, but we had gone out anyway. The wave forecast was better for today, with perfect light winds. Definitely worth an early start.

The alarm went off at six. We crawled out of the tent, cold and sleepy, and drove to the shore. For some reason we thought it got light at seven, but we had sat in the car staring out at nothing but blackness. To pass the time, we drove to a petrol station and drank coffee. Now we are back again, two hours after getting up and we can just about make out waves in the gloom. The sea looks angry and big breakers thump down on the black reef. The car park is deserted.

'I think it looks quite good,' Noel says.

'You are kidding. Look at it. It's death out there.'

'Nah, you just don't want to go out in this rain.'

He's right.

'Come on, we can't sit here all day.'

With that, he jumps out of the car and opens the back. A blast of cold wet air rushes in, chilling me. I suppose it's time to go.

Out in the rain, I pull an icy and sodden wetsuit from my bag and strip off. I have to force my feet into the legs. The fabric feels like a dead fish and the sleet is lashing my naked back. I keep struggling and get the suit on. Then we take our boards out of the back and rush down to the sea. Noel crashes into the water and I follow. We begin to paddle, waves slapping us in the face, the chilling, salty water like acid on my tired eyes. I spit and blink.

I keep paddling, trying to get further out to sea, but this morning everything feels difficult. A little further Noel waits for me. We have paddled around behind a reef and now the waves are breaking in front of us. A few smaller ones go past us, but we're looking out for bigger sets. On land, I see rows of seaside shops and houses: all dark, no lights on, curtains drawn. They look strange in the gloom. Suddenly a very heavy shower comes on. Hailstones the size of sweets, drum on the surface and sting my face. I have to shield my skin to stop the pain. I can't bear to look.

'Something's coming and it's got your name on it Jerry. Get ready.'

I risk a quick glance through the pelting hail. Below the horizon I can see a big black line rolling my way. It looks huge and it's getting closer. I feel my stomach tighten and my heart thumps under my wetsuit. This is the one. No pulling back now. God, I think. Why can't I be at home watching Saturday Kitchen, playing with my kids or in the pub watching football? Why do I have to be doing this? Why can't I be normal? Noel is laughing, his shrieks just audible over the noise of the sea and the waves and the hail.

'You have to stay hungry, Jerry,' I hear him shout.

I begin paddling as hard as I can to get the board up to the speed of the wave. Faster and faster, then I feel the force of the wave accelerate under me and it's time to go.

The wave is going to be perfect. I start grinning to myself.

God I love this.

Significant Ascents and Dates

This list is a collection of selected highlights from Jerry's climbing career, together with other key dates in his life. An extended list of all of his climbs, including first ascents, repeats, flashes and on-sights, would be enough to fill another book.

FA = First Ascent

1963 18 Mar Born Jeremy Charles Moffatt.

1978	Takes up climbing while at St David's College, Llandudno.
1978	First lead of a route (VDiff).
1979	First extreme route: Mojo (E1 5b, FA: Rowland Edwards, 1975), Craig-y-Forwyn, Wales.
1979	First extreme grade lead: Hydro (E1 5b, FA: Rowland Edwards, 1973), Little Orme, Wales.
1980	Leaves St David's College.
1980	Moves to Tremadog. Repeats many routes including Strawberries (E6 6b, FA: Ron Fawcett, 1980), with rests and Zukator (E4 6b, FA: Pete Livesey, 1976).
1980	Moves to Peak District/Stoney Middleton.
1981	FA: Helmut Schmitt (E6 6b), Stoney Middleton, UK.
1981	FA: Little Plum, Pitch 1 (E6 6c), Stoney Middleton, UK.
1981	FA: Psyche n Burn (E6 6b), Tremadog, Wales.
1982	FA: Little Plum, Pitch 2 (E6 6c), Stoney Middleton, UK.
1982	FA: Rooster Booster (E6 6c), Raven Tor, UK.
1982	Repeats: Fast, second ascents of three Ron Fawcett routes – The Prow (E7 6c, 1982), Indecent Exposure (E6 6b, 1982) at Raven Tor, and Tequila Mockingbird (E6 6b, 1982), Cheedale. All Peak District, UK.

1982	Flash: Supercrack (5.12c, FA: Steve Wunsch, 1974), Shawangunks, USA.
1982	Repeat: Psycho Roof (5.12d, FA: Jim Collins, 1975), Eldorado Canyon, USA.
1982	Repeat: Genesis (5.12d, FA: Jim Collins, 1979), Eldorado Canyon, USA.
	The second ascent of Jim Collins' route. Jerry subsequently climbed the route in his trainers.
1983	Flash: Equinox (5.12d, FA: Tony Yaniro, 1980), Joshua Tree, USA.
	The quartet is complete. Still only 20 years old, Jerry leaves the US with groundbreaking ascents of four of the country's hardest routes.
1983	FA: Together with Pete Kirton, establishes many boulder problems on The Bowderstone in the Lake District. Problems include, Picnic Sarcastic (V7), Impropa Opera (V7), Inaudible Vaudeville (V9) and Slapstick (V7).
1983	FA: Ulysses (E6 6b), Stanage, UK.
1983 14 Jul	FA: Master's Wall (E7 6b), Clogwyn Du'r Arddu, Wales.
	As if one hard route was not enough, Jerry also climbed The Purr-Spire (E5 6b) the same day.
1983 15 Jul	Jerry solos seven routes on Dinas Cromlech, Wales: Cemetery Gates (E1 5b, FA: Joe Brown and Don Whillans, 1951), down Ivy Sepulchre (E1 5b, FA: Peter Harding, 1947), up Left Wall (E2 5c, FA: R Moseley, 1956), Cenotaph Corner (E1 5c, FA: Joe Brown, 1952), Memory Lane (E3 5c, FA: Pete Livesey, 1976), Foil (E3 6a, FA: Pete Livesey, 1976), and Right Wall (E5 6a, FA: Pete Livesey, 1974).
	A huge day in British climbing history.
1983	Neil 'Noddy' Molnar dies, soloing on Carreg Wastad, Wales.
	His ashes were scattered at Stoney Middleton.
1983	FA: Parisella's Roof (Font 7a+), Llandudno, Wales.
	"Pretty cool, huh?"
1983	FA: Oyster (F7c), Pen Trwyn, Wales.
1983	FA: Masterclass (F8a), Pen Trwyn, Wales.
	The first route of its grade in the UK.
1983	Meets Wolfgang Güllich.
1983	On-sight: Solo of Linden (E6 6b, FA: Mick Fowler, 1976), Curbar, UK.
1983	On-sight: Sautanz (IX, F7b+, FA: Kurt Albert, 1982), Heisse Finger (IX+, F7c, FA: Wolfgang Güllich, 1982)

and Chasin' the Trane (IX+, F7c, FA: John Bachar, 1981), Frankenjura, Germany.

Stunning ascents of three of the Frankenjura's hardest routes.

1983   FA: Ekel (IX+, 7c+), Frankenjura, Germany.

The first route graded IX+ in Germany.

1983   FA: The Face (X-, F8a), Frankenjura, Germany.

The first route graded X- in Germany.

1984   Flashes Chimpanzodrome (F7c+, FA: Jean Pierre Bouvier, 1981) and a 7b and 7b+ on his 21st birthday and repeats Bidule (F8a+, FA: Marc le Menestrel, 1984), Saussois, France.

At the time, Bidule was France's hardest route.

1984   On-sight: Pol Pot (F7c+) Verdon Gorge, France.

1984   FA: Papy on Sight (F8a), Verdon Gorge, France.

1984   Repeat: Statement of Youth (F8a, FA: Ben Moon, 1984), Pen Trwyn, Wales.

A one-day ascent of Ben Moon's groundbreaking route.

1984   FA: Verbal Abuse (E7 6c), Raven Tor, UK.

1984   FA: Revelations (F8a+), Raven Tor, UK.

1984   FA: Messiah (E6 6c), Burbage South, UK.

Probably the hardest route on gritstone at the time.

1984   Flash: Super Imjin (5.12b/c, E6 6b, FA: Isao Ikeda, 1984) Ogawayama, Japan.

Japan's hardest route at the time, Super Imjin was flashed by Jerry one month after the first ascent.

"Many top climbers had been to Japan in the 1980s, such as Stefan Glowacz, Marc le Menestrel, Ron Fawcett and Patrick Edlinger, but the most impressive 'incident' was Jerry's [flash of] Super Imjin." Makoto Kitayama, Editor of Japanese climbing Magazine, Rock & Snow.

1984   Repeat: Midnight Lightning (V9, FA: Ron Kauk, 1978), Yosemite, USA.

The first one-day ascent of Ron Kauk's then cutting edge, and now legendary boulder problem.

1984   On-sight: The Phoenix (5.13a, FA: Ray Jardine, 1977), Yosemite, USA.

The first on-sight of this route and this grade.

1984/1985   Injury begins to worsen.

1984   Early visit to Hueco Tanks, Texas.

1985   Starred on ABC's Wide World of Sport with Ron Kauk, the pair making a first free ascent on the Lost Arrow Spire

	next to Yosemite Falls.

Attracted a TV audience of around 30 million.

1986   During March and April, undergoes a series of operations on his elbows in the Olympic Hospital, Munich.

1986   Given the all clear and starts training again in November.

1987 3 Apr   Jerry's brother Toby dies in the USA.

1987   Begins competition climbing. Comes 6th in Troubat and 8th at Arco.

1987   Repeat: Ghettoblaster (X+, F8b FA: Wolfgang Güllich, 1986), Frankenjura, Germany.

1987   Repeat: Le Rage de Vivre (F8b+, FA: Antoine le Menestrel, 1986), Buoux, France.
Second ascent.

1987   Repeat: Le Minimum (F8b+, FA: Marc le Menestrel, 1986), Buoux, France.
Jerry makes the third ascent, after years plagued by injury.

1988   Repeat: La Spectre des Surmutant (F8b+, FA: Jean Baptiste Tribout, 1988), Buoux, France.
Jerry becomes the only person to climb the three hardest routes in France.

1988   Repeat: Scarface (5.14a, FA: Scott Franklin 1988), Smith Rock, USA.

1988   Repeat: White Wedding (5.14a, FA: Jean Baptiste Tribout 1988), Smith Rock, USA.

1988   Repeat: To Bolt Or Not To Be (5.14a, FA: Jean Baptiste Tribout 1986), Smith Rock, USA.
Jerry becomes the first person to climb all three F8b+ (5.14a) routes in both France and the USA.

1988   FA: Stone Love (X+/XI-, F8b+), Frankenjura, Germany.

1988   Competition results: Seynes (1st place), Lyon (3rd) and Arco (4th).

1988   FA: Superman (Font 8a+), Cressbrook, UK.

1989   Crashes bike at Cadwell race track, breaking wrist, ankle and ribs.

1989   Competition results: Bercy (3rd place), Munich (4th place), Leeds (1st place), Lyon (2nd place), La Riba (Equal 1st place), Cologne (1st place), Bardonecchia (2nd place) and Madonna (1st place). Also came 3rd at Nürnburg, 2 months after crashing on bike.
Jerry emphatically wins at Leeds in front of a home crowd.

1990   Competition results: Bercy (1st place), London National (1st place), Vienna (2nd place), Maurienne Masters

ASCI WORLD COMPETITION RANKING   20/6/89

After contributing competitions in 1989; Bercy, Grenoble, Munich, Leeds,
                                         Marseille and La Riba:

Each climber's _five_ best results count in the ranking out of ten contributing
competitions in 1989. The ten competitions are made up of the six above plus
Bardonnecia, Snowbird, Arco and Lyon.

Men	Points		Women	Points	
1 Moffatt, J	-	84	1 Patissier, I	-	130
2 Raboutou, D	-	72	2 Raybaud, N	-	80
3 Tribout, J B	-	68.75	3 Jovane, L	-	60.5
4 Glowacz, S	-	61.833	4 Hill, L	-	60
5 Cortijo, R	-	55	5 Labrune, C	-	50.5
6· Edlinger, P	-	46	6 Erbesfield, R	-	44
7 Nadin, S	-	45	7 Destivelle, C	-	38
8 Ghersen, A	-	27	8 Richer, N	-	22.5
9 Godoffe, J	-	21.833	9 Pons, P	-	21.5
10 Steulet, P	-	18.5	10 Maurel, C	-	19.75
11= Brasco, C	-	11	11 Dorsimont, I	-	19
11= Ghesquiers, Y	-	11	12 Eisenhut, A	-	17.75
11= Legrand, F	-	11	13 Dalmasso, M	-	14
14 Masterson, B	-	10.5	14= Barthelemy, P	-	11
15= Cabanne, R	-	10	14= Duval, M A	-	11
15= Duboc, A	-	10	16 Noel, P	-	9.25
17 Kauk, R	-	9.166	17 Galland, P	-	9
18= Gallo, A	-	8.333	18 Brard, A	-	8
18= T'Kint, A	-	8.333	19 Planchin, V	-	7.75
20 Leach, M	-	8.25	20= Guerin, R	-	5
21 Furst, S	-	8	20= Luzzini, D	-	5
22 Vincent, I	-	7	22= Gloesner, C	-	4.75
23= Delsinne, S	-	6	22= Osius, A	-	4.75
23= Gomez, T	-	6	24 Ibanez, A	-	4.5
25 Kostermayer, G	-	5.25	25 Cole, J	-	4
26 Suter, T	-	5	26 Kosmacheva, N	-	3.5
27= Biechy, J P	-	4.5	27 Peschl, S	-	3
27= Dreyfus, F	-	4.5	28= Bertholon, N	-	2.5
27= Moon, B	-	4.5	28= Dykstra, I	-	2.5
30 Faudou, P	-	4.333	28= Helfert, S	-	2.5
31 Lamberti, A	-	4	31 Grouiller, C	-	2
32 Lombard, F	-	3.833	32= Laffont, I	-	1.75
33= Garcia, C	-	3.75	32= Michoulier, C	-	1.75
33= Goddard, D	-	3.75	34 Ohshima, M	-	1
33= Tchertov, A	-	3.75			
36 Robert, A	-	3.5	* * *		
37= Hirayama, Y	-	3			
37= Plantier, P	-	3			
39= Blein, S	-	2.5			
39= Dunne, J	-	2.5			
39= Lafaille, J C	-	2.5			

- 1 -   /contd

(1st place), Japan (2nd place), La Riba (3rd place), Berkeley
(5th place) and Arco (5th place).

1990	Jerry retires from competition climbing.
1990 May	FA: Liquid Ambar (F8c/+), Pen Trwyn, Wales.
	Named after the Liquid Ambar, a type of tree, in memory
	of Jerry's younger brother Toby.
1991	Opens Harrods sale for Swatch watches.
1991	The Foundry climbing wall opens in Sheffield.

1991	FA: Stick It (Font 8a+, V12) and The Force (Font 8a, V11), Yosemite, USA.
1992	Wolfgang Güllich dies in a car crash in Germany.
1992	Repeat: Punks in the Gym (32, F8b+, FA: Wolfgang Güllich, 1985), Grampians, Australia.
	Then the hardest route in Australia.
1992	FA: Zorlac the Destroyer (31, F8b), Grampians, Australia.
1992	On-sight: Serpentine (29, F8a, FA: Malcolm Mathesen 1988), Grampians, Australia.
	A world-class on-sight ascent in 35 degree heat.
1992	Visits Hampi, India with Kurt Albert and Johnny Dawes. Makes the first ascent of Hanuman (Font 8a+) plus many other problems.
1993	FA: The Dominator (Font 8b, V13), Yosemite, USA.
	The sit-start to The Dominator was added by Chris Sharma in 2002.
1993	Makes a one-day ascent of The Nose (5.9, C2, 2900 feet, FA: W. Harding, W. Merry, G. Whitmore, 1958), El Capitan, Yosemite with Kurt Albert.
1993	Visits Chad with Bruno Baumann and photographer Heinz Zak.
1994	FA: Big Kahuna (5.13c/d, F8b), Lions Head, Ontario, Canada.
	Then the hardest route in Canada.
1995	FA: Evolution (F8c), Raven Tor, UK.
	Extended by Steve McClure to give Mutation (F9a).
1995	FA: Renegade Master (E8 7a), Froggatt Edge, UK.
	Subsequent ascents have finished to the right, with Jerry's original finish (the crux) being repeated only once, by Rich Simpson.
1995	FA: Progress (F8c), Kilnsey, UK.
1995	FA: Sean's Roof (F8c), Blackwell Dale, UK.
1996	Nelson's Column (E6 6b/5a), London, UK.
	Climbed with Johnny Dawes and Simon Nadin on behalf of Survival to publicise the plight of Canada's Innu people.
1996	FA: The Joker (Font 8a), Stanage, UK.
1996	Conceived the idea for, produced and starred in *The Real Thing* climbing film with Ben Moon.
	Filmed by Simon Tucker, the film focused on the bouldering in Fontainebleau, France.
1997	FA: Samson (E8 7b), Burbage South, UK.
1998	Andrew Henry dies.

2000   FA: The Ace (Font 8b), Stanage, UK.
        Jerry's bouldering legacy. The most difficult boulder problem at
        the home of UK bouldering; the Stanage Plantation.

2002   Repeat: Nutsa (Font 8a+, FA: Fred Nicole, 2000),
        Rocklands, South Africa.
        Jerry also established many first ascents, including a new Font
        8a+ boulder problem (Ard eh?) on the same trip before drawing
        his professional climbing career to a close.

2002   First child born, Lily Rose Moffatt. Married Sharon Wallace
        in 2003. Barnaby James Moffatt born in 2004.

Acknowledgements

I have wanted to write down my story for years. On a couple of occasions I have made attempts, getting chapter titles written down with ideas of what I might put in them. Realistically though it was just too much work for me to do alone. I feel there are so many untold stories from this era – tales about hitching, dossing out, climbing loads of routes on gear – that seem to have been forgotten and may not be passed on to future generations. My hope is that this book inspires people to get out there and give it everything in whichever sport they do.

Hooking up with Niall has been just massive to help me put my story into words. We really have had fun and I have enjoyed his company immensely. I can't thank him enough.

Thanks also to John Coefield for pulling together such a diverse bunch of photos, it's a much tougher job than I could have ever imagined. Our editor Ed Douglas has also done a great job tightening up the story and giving some wise advice. All the guys behind the scenes at Vertebrate also deserve credit, thanks.

I would like to thank Sharon, my wife, for letting me take off and go surfing, golfing, climbing, drinking whenever I ask. I couldn't wish for a better wife and mother to our gorgeous children, whom I adore.

I must also mention my parents who have only ever been supportive, giving invaluable advice and direction; I know I am very lucky.

Finally, I would like to thank all my climbing buddies, particularly anyone who has had the unfortunate task of belaying me, my surfing mates for giving me the odd wave and my golfing partners for helping me find my ball.

Jerry Moffatt
Sheffield, December 2008

ACKNOWLEDGEMENTS

Jerry would like to extend great thanks to those companies that have sponsored him throughout his career: Boreal, Wild Country, DMM, VauDe, Edelweiss, Cousin, Beal, Stubai, Patagonia, Oakley, Arnette, No Fear, DR Climbing Walls, Pusher, Cordless, Snow and Rock, Moon Climbing.

The authors and Vertebrate Publishing wish to acknowledge gratefully the following works that are referenced in this book:

With Winning in Mind: The Mental Management System
by Lanny Bassham [Bookpartners, 1988]

John Gill: Master of Rock
by Pat Ament [Stackpole Books]

We would also like to extend our thanks to all of the photographers who have supplied images and who, in many cases, have had to dig incredibly deep into their archives to unearth *the* shot.

A Note from Niall

As someone who lived in Sheffield in the 1990s, I got to know most of the greats of British climbing, and through them, a few of the world's greats. Often these would be the same person – Ben Moon, Johnny Dawes, John Allen. Yet one climber, perhaps the greatest of the lot, remained unknown to me. Jerry Moffatt was pure legend, not only in Sheffield but around the world.

I first met Jerry while writing an article for *On The Edge* magazine. I had watched a movie called *The King of Comedy*. In it, Robert de Niro plays a character called Rupert Pupkin, an aspiring yet moribund US TV comic. Aided by Sandra Bernhard as Masha, Pupkin kidnaps big-time comedian, Jerry Lewis. His ransom is a slot on Lewis's prime-time TV show. Inspired, I wrote one of the first things I had ever written, *King of the Crag*.

In it I, as a disturbed Pupkin/Fearless Francie Brady-type character, kidnap Moffatt, my demand being a couple of day's climbing with big shot, Ben Moon. The mag liked the story, and suggested getting Ben and Jerry in on a photo-shoot. They agreed, and, star-struck, I spent a day setting up stupid shots with the two of them, including one of me asking a naked and tied-up Moffatt, imprisoned in a Stoney doss-house, whether he preferred Rocks or Wallnuts (opposing brands of climbing protection). At one point walking up to Stanage, Jerry, ever-aware of the value of any publicity, and the potential shock-value of the article, turned in mock glee to Ben, and said:

'This is great, Ben. When this is published, we won't have to do another route all year.'

In later years, I organised Ape Index. This was a series of, as they were at the time, slideshows, where I would compere an evening, and get a famous climber in to headline the main slot. They're called Multimedia

Presentations now, and you have to pay more to get in. Kicking off a second winter series of these shows, I managed a coup. Jerry said he would do one. He did. He rocked the house. Jerry, renowned as a brash brat, avoided the spotlight himself, and instead, set himself up amongst the crowd with a projector. With this, he let his achievements speak for him. Even today, years on, people remember it as the best slideshow that they have seen.

After that it was great honour, a few years later, to be asked to ghost write his autobiography. Sure I would, I'd love to. I love ghosts. We got together.

The legendary hip-hop producer, Rick Rubin, was a surprise choice of producer for Johnny Cash's fabulous farewell to the world, American Recordings. Rubin recalled of the first meeting:

'I said to Johnny, Johnny, we are not leaving here until you have made the best possible record you can make.'

That is the way I have always felt about this project. Seeking, as best I can, to work with Jerry to tell his story. And it's been great. Jerry's stories needed only to be written down, rich with his storytelling and humour, and I loved listening to them. Yet they were also inspiring and motivating, and listening to the passion, motivation, self-belief and fun that he seemed able to bring to so many aspects of his life was a great experience. Years ago I interviewed Fontainebleau boulderer, Marc le Menestrel. Afterwards, I went to Stanage, and inspired by his attitudes had the best evening of bouldering I'd had up to that point. Tonight I write this having been again to Stanage. Because of the time I've spent on this project, climbing has been out the window for many months now, but I'm finally free to climb again. Despite my long break, I still managed to do two of the hardest problems I've ever done, consciously inspired and motivated by what I have picked up, and giving these problems everything I had: what Andy Cave referred to as 'The Moffatt 100'. Standing below the problems, stripped off, I mutter to myself the most powerful mantra in climbing:

'I *am* Jerry Moffatt.'

Cheers Jerry, it's been a hoot.

There are many people I'd love to thank, people who made this project possible and special. Firstly, all the people who provided me with my 'writers retreats', bolt-holes where I could get away from it all, stroke my chin and blow bubbles out of a bubble-pipe while wearing a silk kimono. Alice and the Brockingtons, and their boat-on-the-land in Anglesey, the icy cold beach in the evening light; Hannah and the Skeldons, and the little pebble-dashed house on the bottom left of the Lake District, looking out at the lovely, anonymous rounded hill; Hannah and the Nixons, and that beautiful terrace in Shrewsbury, looking out through that mad window/door thing to the canal at the bottom of the garden; especially the Bushs, Anne and Brian, and their great, relaxed home in Bristol, and the furry and feathered visitors who looked through the windows to say hello.

Thanks to Vertebrate for everything, especially Teija for always being so nice on the phone, and John Coefield for sharing with me the childish enthusiasm – 'We're doing Jerry's book!' – as well as everything else he has done to bring it along. And Captain Q, Nathan, Jon and Simon. Thanks a million to Ed Douglas for his terrific work on editing the book. Ed spared no effort in this task and more than anything this has made it the book that it is.

The greatest thanks go to my wife Helen, for the support, the space, the belief, the expectation, the love, the cups of tea, and everything else.

Niall Grimes
Sheffield, December 2008.

Glossary

Abseil   A controlled slide down a rope.

Arête   The outside edge of a corner, often lacking in cracks, and therefore protection, which is usually climbed by leaning off to the side and running the hands and feet up the rock. Jerry's route, Ulysses, at Stanage, is a good example of an arête climb.

Belay   *Noun.* The stopping points that mark the top of a pitch, where a leader stops and secures himself to the rock, and either brings up the second, or abseils off.
Verb. The act of safeguarding a leader or second by paying out or taking in the rope as the other climbs.

Belayer   The person who belays. Someone who belays a lot, and seldom actually gets to climb, is called a belay bunny or belay slave.

Bolt   A protection method consisting of a drilled hole, into which a bolt is screwed, to attach a metal ring. This allows protection where no cracks or other natural methods are possible. Commonly used in Europe, although its use in the UK or America is limited to certain areas or rock types. Where it strays outside these defined areas, it can lead traditionalists into apoplexy.

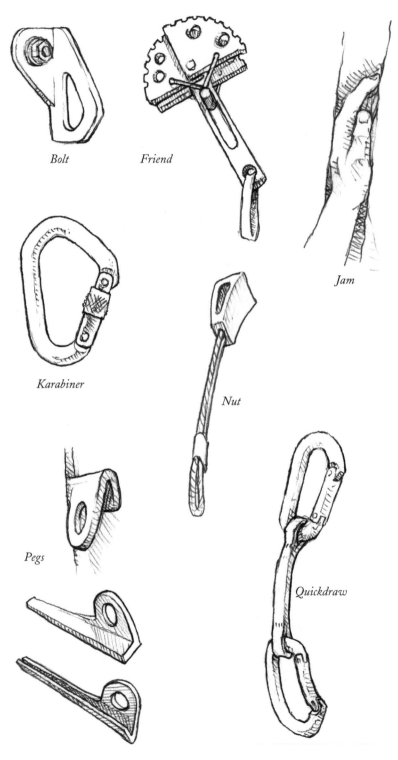

Bolt

Friend

Jam

Karabiner

Nut

Pegs

Quickdraw

Bouldering A type of climbing, not involving ropes, on short routes where falling is usually without physical consequence, often no more than twelve feet high. It is best suited to powerful, explosive movement rather than long endurance. The safety and lack of other paraphernalia allows for the very hardest of moves and sequences. A bouldery route is a roped climb where the hardest part is a short, very difficult section.

Dyno A dynamic move, where sometimes the whole body loses contact with the rock, flying upwards to catch holds that are otherwise out of reach. A double-dyno is where both hands leave lower holds simultaneously and catch higher holds together, a move often used on a campus board.

Edge A small, flat hold, usually big enough comfortably to fit the fingertips, and generally fairly positive.

Flash Climbing a route first try, with no falls, with some knowledge of the moves, or without *on-sight*.

Friend A protection device used in traditionally-protected climbs, consisting of a series of spring-loaded cams that expand inside a crack. Also called a cam.

Grades Lots of different grading systems are used throughout this book. The first one to appear is the traditional British system, running from V Diff and Severe, which are low grades, to Very Severe and Hard Very Severe, considered medium, then into the Extreme grades, E1, E2... E7. This system was used in Britain for many decades, and still is for the majority of climbs. It takes into account the physical difficulty of a climb, as well as its danger, and as such is perfect for bold British-style climbs. The French system (7b, 7b+, 7c etc) differs from the British system, as it only describes physical difficulty, as that country has less of a tradition of bold climbing. French grades began to be used for bolt-protected sport climbs in Britain during the 1980s. This change is reflected in the book. German and Australian systems are much like the French one, and can be directly translated (*see chart overleaf*).

GRADES

Admittedly quite difficult to understand, this grade table is intended to demonstrate how the various grading systems used in different areas around the world roughly equate to one another.

UK adjectival	UK technical	French	US	Aust	UIAA
Mod		F1/2	5.2	10	I
Diff		F1	5.3	11	II
VDiff	3c	F2	5.4	12	III
S	4a	F3	5.5	13	IV
HS	4b	F4	5.6	14	IV+
VS	4c	F4+	5.7	15	V- V
HVS	5a	F5	5.8	16	V+
		F5+	5.9	17	VI-
E1	5b	F6a	5.10	18	VI
		F6a+	5.10+	19	VI+
E2	5c	F6b	5.10++	20	VII-
		F6b+	5.11a	21	VII
E3		F6c	5.11b	22	VII+
E4	6a	F6c+	5.11c	23	VIII-
		F7a	5.11d		VIII
E5		F7a+	5.12a	24	VIII+
	6b	F7b	5.12b	25	IX-
E6		F7b+	5.12c	26	
		F7c	5.12d	27	IX
		F7c+	5.13a	28	IX+
E7	6c	F8a	5.13b	29	X-
		F8a+	5.13c	30	X
E8		F8b	5.13d	31	
		F8b+	5.14a	32	X+
E9		F8c	5.14b	33	XI-
	7a	F8c+	5.14c	34	XI
E10		F9a	5.14d	35	

For bouldering, there is another system, using V grades (originating in the US) or Font grades (originating in Fontainebleau). Again, both these systems are directly comparable, and better describe the short explosive climbing style found in boulder problems.

Competition climbing doesn't use grades, as it is about pitching climbers together on a similar climb.

Hex   A massive, six-sided fist-sized monster of a nut (see *nut* below) favoured by climbers operating in lower grades. Sometimes called a cow-bell.

Jam   A way of climbing cracks by inserting the fingers, hands or fists, and twisting them so that they lock in place. Ouch!

Karabiner   The oval-shaped metal ring with a sprung gate used to clip the rope into bolts, nuts and other protection.

Lead   To climb a route with a rope, clipping it into protection as you go, safeguarded by a belayer from below.

Nut   A protection method used in traditionally-protected climbing, consisting of a length of wire or nylon webbing with a blob of metal on the end. The metal is slotted into cracks and the rope clipped into them. These originated from the use of engineering nuts by climbers in the 1950s and '60s.

On-sight   Climbing a route with no knowledge of the route, such as where the holds are and what protection is required.

Peg   A spike of metal, usually five to ten inches long, that can be hammered into cracks and holes where other protection will not go. It is permanent and can damage rock. For this reason, it is often considered unethical, and at certain British venues, their use is frowned upon.

Protection The pieces of metal that the leader places (nuts, Friends, hexes) or that are already in place in the rock (bolts, pegs), into which a leader clips a rope for security.

Pump   A swelling, mainly in the forearms, caused by strenuous climbing. Blood collects in the exerted muscles causing a loss of strength, bulging Popeye-like members, and an exquisite pain level.

Quickdraw   A length of nylon webbing, 6 to 8 inches long, with a karabiner at each end. This is used as the link between protection and the rope, the assembly allowing more flexibility and less rope drag than just using a single karabiner.

Rack   A climber's collection of nuts, Friends, hexes and quickdraws.

Redpoint   In sport climbing, a successful ascent in which the climber climbs from the bottom to the top of a climb, clipping the rope into runners as he goes, and without falling or weighting any runners along the way. It is often preceded by rehearsal of the route, resting frequently on all the protection, or working the moves on top-rope.

Runner   A running belay, any of the points along the length of a climb where the rope is clipped into protection. Runner is often used as another word for protection.

Second   The person who comes up a route after the leader, climbing the route on top-rope, and removing the protection placed by the leader. It is an essential part of traditional climbing.

Slab   Rock at an angle that feels less than vertical, where technique and footwork matter more than upper body strength.

Sport climb   A climb protected mainly by bolts or other types of protection that are left in place, as opposed to the traditional British method of leader-placed protection. This generally makes for very physical, though safe, climbs.

Top-rope   To climb a route with a rope through the belay at the top of the climb. It removes any danger or need to clip protection. It is not considered a valid ascent.

Traverse   Climbing sideways as opposed to upwards.

Undercut   An upside-down hold that is used by turning the hand
around, palms upwards. These make for very strenuous
climbing as a lot of force must be used to keep the body
in place.

Yo-yo   A style of climbing, once considered to be a valid ascent in
Britain, Germany and America. When the leader falls off
a route, he is allowed to lower to the ground, rest and then
try again with the ropes still clipped through the highest
protection. This meant that he would not have to clip
the protection the next time, making the climbing easier.
However, it was often done by starting from the ground,
without any abseil inspection of the route or top-rope
practice. It would be replaced in the 1980s by the French
redpointing method of ascent.

Index